FORGING A FATEFUL ALLIANCE

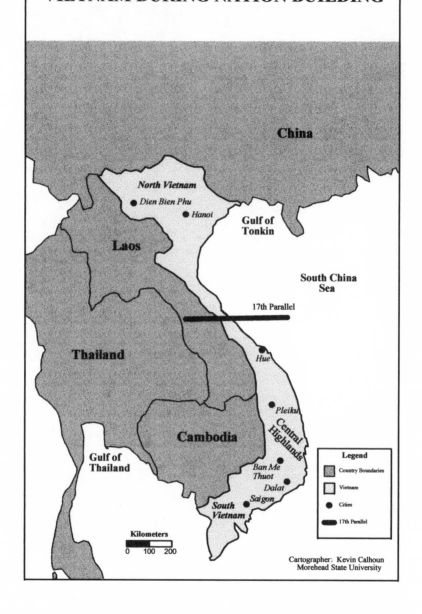

VIETNAM DURING NATION BUILDING

China

North Vietnam

● Dien Bien Phu

● Hanoi

Gulf of
Tonkin

Laos

South China
Sea

17th Parallel

Thailand

● Hue

● Pleiku

Central
Highlands

Cambodia

Gulf of
Thailand

Ban Me
Thuot

● Dalat

● Saigon

South
Vietnam

Legend

Country Boundaries

Vietnam

● Cities

17th Parallel

Kilometers

0   100   200

Cartographer: Kevin Calhoun
Morehead State University

FORGING A FATEFUL ALLIANCE
Michigan State University and the Vietnam War

John Ernst

Michigan State University Press
East Lansing

All Michigan State University Press books are produced on paper which meets the requirements of American National Standard of Information Sciences—Permanence of paper for printed materials ANSI Z39.48-1984.

Michigan State University Press
East Lansing, Michigan 48823-5202

03 02 01 00 99 98   1 2 3 4 5 6

Library of Congress Cataloging-in-Publication Data

Ernst, John, 1962-
    Forging a fateful alliance : Michigan State University and the Vietnam War / John Ernst.
        p.   cm.
    Includes bibliographical references (p.   ) and index.
    ISBN 0-87013-478-7 (alk. paper)
    1. Michigan State University—Faculty—Political activity. 2. Michigan State University. Vietnam Advisory Group. 3. Vietnamese Conflict, 1961-1975—United States 4. Technical assistance, American—Vietnam. 5. Vietnam—Politics and Government—1945-1975. I. Title.
LD3248.M5e76   1998
378.774'27—dc21   98-415952
                                                                                       CIP

All photographs are courtesy of the Michigan State University Archives and Historical Collections.

For Joanne and her gift to me,
Sonny Edward

CONTENTS

Acknowledgments ix

Preface xi

1. "The World Is Our Campus":
   The Creation of the Michigan State University Group 1

2. COMIGAL: Michigan State and Refugee Resettlement 21

3. The National Institute of Administration:
   A Civil Servant Training School 41

4. Michigan State University and Police Administration 63

5. Michigan State University and the Participant Program 91

6. "A Crumbling Bastion": The End of Consensus 115

   Conclusion 141

   Bibliography 149

   Index 159

ACKNOWLEDGMENTS

I am indebted to numerous people for their assistance in preparing this book. Terry Birdwhistell and Jeff Suchanek of the University of Kentucky Special Collections offered friendly advice and recording equipment to conduct oral history interviews. The staff of the Michigan State University Archives and Historical Collections was both efficient and kind. Fred Honhart, Dorothy Frye, and Lisa May made my work a joy. Moreover, they allowed me to examine the Wesley Fishel Papers while the collection was being processed. For this courtesy and their support, I am eternally grateful. I made many friends in East Lansing and think of them often. In particular, I miss the late Ralph Turner, who provided invaluable help.

The staff at the Michigan State University Press was a delight to work with. Julie Loehr and Annette Tanner were always supportive and patient. Victor Howard was a wonderful editor. He never lost his sense of humor and had a number of positive suggestions which greatly enhanced the manuscript.

Four scholars have had a significant impact on my development as a historian. Nancy Forderhase first stirred my interest in history and has been an unfailing friend and adviser. I am proud to have been a staff member of the *Kentucky Encyclopedia*. Its editor, John Kleber, taught me a great deal about the history profession and life. I cherish his friendship and consider him part of my family. I place Tom Appleton in this same category. During the summer of 1991, I served as his intern at the Kentucky Historical Society. Since that time, he has been a close confidant whose continued support and guidance have meant the world to me.

I am extremely proud to have worked with George C. Herring. He is both a gifted scholar and a good friend. I hope that he and his wife, Dottie, know how much they mean to me. I wish life afforded more chances to sip bourbon together.

Although I thoroughly enjoyed writing this book, there were many difficult times that friends and family saw me through. My colleagues at Morehead State University, Yvonne Baldwin, Kevin Calhoun, Andrew Curtis, Ron Mithchelson, Tim Pitts, and Ed Reeves willingly listened to my grumbling and offered advice. Jeff and Erin Jacobs and Chris and Jana Apel provided a shoulder to lean on. Kenny, Bernie, Bob, Scott, Chris, James, Joey, and Cassie helped me keep life in perspective. My parents, Sonny and Roseann Sundberg and Don and Flossie Ernst, provided constant emotional support. My brother Don Ernst and my sister and her husband, Karen and Dan Kaylor, never stopped believing in me. Uncle Danny and Aunt Janie always let me know that they understood, while Uncle Donald and Aunt Jenny made sure that occasionally I had a slab of ribs or a good steak from "Buffalo & Dads." Grandma Yates always knew and I miss her a great deal.

My wife Joanne remained patient and loyal. She is my best friend and I could not have completed this project without her encouragement and love. This book is as much hers as mine.

PREFACE

"[I]n the lands of the blind," Dwight D. Eisenhower observed in October 1954, "one-eyed men are kings."[1] Reflecting on the American decision to intervene in South Vietnam, the president acknowledged that significant obstacles existed in building an anticommunist, democratic nation there. Yet there were none that good old Yankee ingenuity could not overcome. Vietnam became the flash point of America's fight against communism. When insurgents defeated French colonizers there, fear of continued communist expansion in Southeast Asia resulted in the United States' supplanting France in Vietnam. Though U.S. intelligence officials warned that Vietnam was a poor choice in which to take such a stand, Eisenhower and Secretary of State John Foster Dulles could not be dissuaded. Recent success at suppressing other communist-led movements, including one in the Philippines during 1953–54, emboldened the administration. Freed from the taint of colonialism that plagued the French, American policy makers hoped for similar results in Vietnam.[2]

By 1957, thanks to large amounts of U.S. aid, Vietnamese nationalist Ngo Dinh Diem had solidified his position as South Vietnam's leader. That spring he triumphantly journeyed to America and received a hero's welcome as the savior of Vietnam and the brightest hope for Southeast Asia. During his visit, Diem took care to thank the many friends who had facilitated his rise to power. The Michigan State University campus in East Lansing was an important stop on the trip.

Wednesday, 15 May—"Ngo Dinh Diem Day" by order of Michigan's Governor G. Mennen Williams—was a joyful celebration for Diem as he returned to Michigan State University. Addressing approximately four thousand faculty and students, the South Vietnamese president remarked that the occasion was "in a sense a home-coming for me—a very pleasant and warming home-coming." Dressed in formal academic robes, Diem was on campus to receive an honorary

xi

degree. He observed that his stay at Michigan State earlier that decade had "blossomed into a relationship of great scope and tremendous importance to my government and people."[3]

Diem was referring to the Michigan State University Group (MSUG), a technical-assistance program established under Eisenhower's Third World "nation-building" effort during the 1950s. The goal was to bolster underdeveloped countries threatened by communism and was consistent with the belief of postwar policy makers that communism could be—and must be—stopped.

The MSUG existed from May 1955 to June 1962, closely paralleling the life of the Diem regime. Michigan State entered nation building at the ground level and remained close to Diem until the early 1960s. As MSUG anthropologist Gerald Hickey observed, Diem initially "was really impressed by American efficiency. There was a magic involved, it was as if we had this amulet around our neck." The Vietnamese president "believed that the Michigan State group was going to work wonders, so all doors were open for us."[4] Diem's personal relationship with Wesley R. Fishel, a Michigan State political scientist, led to the project's creation. Fishel, along with various other American anticommunists, many of whom were influential Catholics, formed a loosely organized coalition called the Vietnam Lobby, which promoted Diem in the United States. For much of the 1950s and early 1960s, Fishel was a close friend and adviser to the Vietnamese leader. In a 1972 interview, Fishel recalled that Diem once visited his Saigon home, on which occasion "[m]y son chased him around the front yard with a switch—much to his amusement."[5]

Under contract to the U.S. government and South Vietnam through the International Cooperation Administration (ICA), the MSUG provided technical assistance, such as training and consulting, in both police and public administration. The police administration staff worked with South Vietnamese law enforcement agencies assigned to internal security: the civil guard, municipal police, and sureté. The MSUG's public administration division was less well defined and far more diverse. Projects ranged from a school for civil servants, the National Institute of Administration, to overseas participant training and cultural studies of the South Vietnamese highlanders, the Montagnards.

Members of the MSUG served as advisers to the South Vietnamese government, but with mixed results. In some instances, Michigan State pressured Diem to implement programs that improved his country. In others, however, the university either failed to persuade him to act or initiated poorly conceived plans that did not take into account American and Vietnamese cultural differences.

Diem's 1957 visit foreshadowed trouble. To ensure that the convocation honoring the Vietnamese dignitary was well attended, Michigan State President John Hannah canceled afternoon classes. Not everyone, however, appreciated the decision. A university economist, Walter Adams, recalled a colleague from the English department, Herbert Weisinger, complaining bitterly as the two men put on their academic regalia in the auditorium's basement: "I don't know why we are here to pay tribute to that fascist."[6] Wesley Fishel, whose duties as MSUG project head prevented his being in East Lansing, was aware of Diem's reluctance to implement reform in South Vietnam and sent directions from Saigon about which topics to avoid discussing with him. A topic "one might well avoid in talking with the President," Fishel wrote, "is his family, and his sister-in-law, Madam Nhu, in particular." According to Fishel, Diem was "extremely sensitive to remarks in this connection." Fishel and Weisinger identified a serious problem, and their concerns were well founded. In years to come, Diem increasingly placed more power into his family's hands and refused to grant democratic reforms. His intransigence threatened the survival of South Vietnam's government and strained relations with U.S. officials and Michigan State.[7]

During the early 1960s, the university was embroiled in two controversies that had national implications. The first emerged in 1962 when Diem terminated the university's technical-assistance contract because of two articles written by Michigan State professors in the *New Republic*, accusing him of destroying South Vietnam with dictatorial rule. The second occurred four years later, when *Ramparts* magazine published a scathing critique of the MSUG Vietnam project. Among other charges, *Ramparts* claimed that Michigan State had housed a Central Intelligence Agency (CIA) unit in Vietnam

A self-described muckraking journal, *Ramparts* often sensationalized the truth to sell copies, and at times the accuracy of its reporting was questionable. Using "color, gloss and flamboyance," Warren Hinckle, the magazine's young editor, set out to "make *Ramparts* pay."[8] He considered the Michigan State story their "biggest exposé," and stood by it before a hearing of the Michigan House of Representatives. As journalist Angus Mackenzie recently odserved in *Secrets: The CIA's War at Home*, the agency began actively investigating *Ramparts* because of the Michigan State piece. Hinckle welcomed the notoriety. In 1973, he facetiously noted that critics, desperately searching for "'factual errors'. . . to ding the article," charged that the edition's cover, featuring a "busty" Madame Nhu as an MSU cheerleader, was incorrect because she "did not, in fact, have tits *that* big."[9]

The backlash from the *New Republic* and *Ramparts* articles contributed to a reexamination of the propriety of university participation in foreign affairs. The

Ramparts piece added fuel to a growing antiwar movement on American campuses. Students and faculty alike increasingly denounced United States intervention in Vietnam and argued that institutions of higher education should not serve as adjuncts to the federal government in other countries.

MSU President John Hannah strongly disagreed. A proponent of the land-grant philosophy, Hannah believed that universities should serve the community. Moreover, as a pragmatic administrator with vision, he recognized that U.S. technical-assistance contracts would financially benefit the campus. Hannah used the revenue from such programs to expand the school's physical plant and improve academics. According to Walter Adams, a provost once suggested to Hannah that the administration had "built the university in size" and "should build it in terms of quality." Hannah then asked "How do you do that?" Adams recalled. "The provost, with tongue in cheek, said, "You do it the same way you build a football team. You buy it!" Hannah said, "Okay, go ahead." To attract talent, Michigan State began offering young professors some of the highest starting salaries in the Midwest. Although a number of faculty, including Adams, disagreed with the university's involvement in Vietnam, they still "appreciated" and "admired" Hannah. "In my view, we haven't had a president since John Hannah—of his stature," Adams later observed. "But the Vietnam project, I think, was a sad mistake."[10]

A contingent of professors on campus, including Adams, viewed the MSUG as having "a totally corrupting influence" on scholars. "You could tell who the people were who participated in the Vietnam project," Adams observed. "They all came back with tailor-made suits from Hong Kong."[11] Wesley Fishel, in particular, the individual who secured the Vietnam contract, was susceptible to this type of criticism. Asserting that his role in the venture was less than altruistic, *Ramparts* focused much of its attack on Fishel. "To make it, in the new world of Big University politics," the magazine asserted, one "had to get a government contract. You had to be an operator. And some people viewed Professor Fishel. . . as the Biggest Operator of them all."[12]

Fishel clearly enjoyed his status as an adviser to the South Vietnamese president. One of Fishel's colleagues, Ralph Smuckler, later characterized him as "a kind of flamboyant person who attracted what might be called groupies." After the *Ramparts* exposé, Fishel also had numerous detractors on campus who blamed him, in part, for the U.S. entrance into Vietnam. "The students treated him very harshly," Smuckler recalled, and were "egged on by faculty people, I think, in some cases."[13]

MSUG problems in Vietnam were the same ones that caused nation building as a whole to fail. Fueled by U.S. aid and counseled by American advisers, the

South Vietnamese government failed to produce broadly based or long-term economic and democratic reforms. Instead, Diem created a dictatorship and nation building bred economic and military dependence on the United States. By 1959, communist insurgents threatened the existence of South Vietnam's government; within six years U.S. combat forces would be committed to buttress a house of cards.

The "trauma of Vietnam," in part, destroyed American nation-building zeal. Other international factors also contributed to its demise. The widening gulf in the late 1960s and early 1970s between the two principal communist powers, China and the Soviet Union, eased concerns over communist expansion, diminishing the urgency for foreign assistance to countries such as Vietnam. Moreover, other concurrent nation-building experiments in Iran, South Korea, and Brazil had not adhered as closely to the American model of democracy and development as some U.S. policy makers would have liked.[14]

Contemporary scholarship places a large measure of blame for American involvement in Vietnam and for the failure of nation building at Eisenhower's door. As one historian recently noted, the Eisenhower administration "declined to ask hard questions about whether Diem was an authentic representative of the Vietnamese people or whether Vietnam's village-based culture was receptive to American wealth and good intentions."[15] Analysis of Hannah's and Fishel's activities during the 1950s and of the MSUG sheds light on academia's involvement in the cold war. In particular, it provides valuable insight into Diem's rise to power in South Vietnam and the miscalculations of both the American and South Vietnamese governments afterward. Moreover, Michigan State's Vietnam experience foreshadowed the tragedy that followed. Like other U.S. policy makers, Fishel conceded that Diem had faults, but supported him because he was considered the best—and possibly only—choice to represent American interests during the postwar period. Diem fit America's criteria. Irreproachable nationalist credentials reportedly provided him with Vietnamese political support, and his firm anticommunist views served American geopolitical goals.[16]

NOTES

1. Quoted in George C. Herring, *America's Longest War: The United States and Vietnam, 1950–1975*, 2d ed. (New York: Knopf, 1986), 47.
2. Ibid., 47–48; George McT. Kahin, *Intervention: How America Became Involved in Vietnam* (New York: Knopf, 1986), 69–70.

3. "Ngo Dinh Diem Address at Michigan State University," 15 May 1957, box 672, folder 67; *Ann Arbor News*, 15 May 1957, box 657, folder 51, Michigan State University Vietnam Project Papers, Michigan State University Archives and Historical Collections, East Lansing, Michigan (hereafter cited as Vietnam Project Papers).

4. Gloria Emerson, *Winners and Losers: Battles, Retreats, Gains, Losses and Ruins from a Long War* (New York: Random House, 1976), 283.

5. *Detroit Free Press Magazine*, 11 June 1972; Robert Scheer and Warren Hinckle, "The Vietnam Lobby," *Ramparts* 4 (July 1965): 18–20; David Anderson, *Trapped by Success: The Eisenhower Administration and Vietnam, 1953–1961* (New York: Columbia University Press, 1991), 92.

6. Walter Adams, interview by the author, 10 August 1993.

7. *Ann Arbor News*, 15 May 1957, box 657, folder 51, "Schedule of Diem's Visit to MSU, May 15–16, 1957," box 672, folder 66, Vietnam Project Papers; Wesley Fishel to Stanley Sheinbaum, 9 May 1957, box 672, folder 62, Vietnam Project Papers.

8. Carlene Marie Bagnall Blanchard, "*Ramparts* Magazine: Social Change in the Sixties" (Ph.D. diss., University of Michigan, 1969), 27, 18.

9. Warren Hinckle, *If You Have a Lemon, Make Lemonade: An Essential Memoir of a Lunatic Decade* (New York: G.P. Putnam's Sons, 1973), 166; Susan Cecilia Stasiowski, "A History and Evaluation of *Ramparts* Magazine, 1962–1969" (master's thesis, San Jose State College, 1972), 107; *Michigan State News*, 17 May 1966; *Detroit News*, 16 May 1966.

10. Walter Adams, interview by the author; *Time*, "University Presidents," 21 March 1969, 42.

11. Ibid.

12. Warren Hinckle, Robert Scheer, and Sol Stern, "MSU: The University on the Make," *Ramparts* 4 (April 1966): 13.

13. Ralph Smuckler, interview by the author, 13 May 1993.

14. Lucian W. Pye, "Foreign Aid and America's Involvement in the Developing World," in *The Vietnam Legacy: The War, American Society and the Future of American Foreign Policy*, ed. Anthony Lake (New York: New York University Press, 1976), 378–80.

15. Stephen G. Rabe, "Eisenhower Revisionism: A Decade of Scholarship," *Diplomatic History* 17 (winter 1993): 106.

16. Herring, *America's Longest War*, 48.

CHAPTER 1

"THE WORLD IS OUR CAMPUS": THE CREATION OF THE MICHIGAN STATE UNIVERSITY GROUP

On 8 May 1957, President Dwight D. Eisenhower stood in the humid noon heat, awaiting the arrival of his private plane, the *Columbine III*, at Washington National Airport. Aboard the jet was the president of South Vietnam, Ngo Dinh Diem. In his welcoming remarks, Eisenhower declared that Diem epitomized "patriotism of the highest order" in Southeast Asia. Diem replied that the combination of the Vietnamese people's bravery and "your faith in my country" had produced the "miracle of Vietnam." After posing for pictures, Diem was presented with the key to the city. The two leaders then sped toward the capital in an open-air limousine.[1]

Diem joined a succession of leaders so honored, including Jawaharlal Nehru of India and King Ibn Saud of Saudi Arabia. During his term of office Eisenhower had made a concerted effort to improve relations with Third World nations deemed vital to American security. South Vietnam was the flash point of America's fight against communism, and U.S. officials hailed Diem as the "tough little miracle man" of Southeast Asia.[2] By 1957, thanks to U.S. nation-building efforts, Diem had secured his position as South Vietnam's leader. While in the United States, he stopped at Michigan State University to thank personally the professors for their assistance.[3]

During the 1950s, Michigan State actively aided U.S. policy makers in containing communism. University president John Hannah believed in the land-grant philosophy of public service and offered to share the know-how of his institution whenever the need arose. As one faculty member observed, "it could be said, the world was its campus, and seldom did the university regard any clientele—domestic or foreign—beyond the range of its responsibility or the pale of respectability."[4] The Michigan State University Group (MSUG), a technical-assistance program in Vietnam, was the most significant project the school undertook in conjunction

1

with the federal government. Hannah's commitment to the project and Diem's friendship with Wesley Fishel, a Michigan State political scientist, were the basis of the MSUG.

Global concerns and misperceptions about communist expansion directed post-war American foreign policy. Indochina, including Vietnam, was a French colony until the Second World War, when Japan replaced France as colonizer. France intended to reassert its control with Japan's defeat in 1945, but was opposed by American President Franklin D. Roosevelt. France had "milked" the region "for one hundred years," he averred. "The people of Indo-China are entitled to some-thing better than that."[5] Moreover, Roosevelt believed France incapable of gov-erning this mineral-rich region, especially since Japan had humbled the white colonialists. To prepare it for eventual independence, he wished to make Indochina a United Nations trust under Chinese and American auspices. Just before his death in April 1945, however, the president reconsidered the matter because of the deficiencies of Chinese nationalist leader Chiang Kai-shek and pressure to retain overseas possessions by British Prime Minister Winston Churchill and his French counterpart, Charles de Gaulle.[6]

Roosevelt's successor, Harry S. Truman, facing perceived Soviet (communist) aggression in Eastern Europe, acquiesced to French demands to regain control of Vietnam. By 1947, the new president had decided that a more vigilant approach was necessary. In March, he requested funding from Congress to assist Greece and Turkey, two countries threatened by communist takeovers. Moreover, he outlined the broad parameters of the Truman Doctrine, which pledged to assist any nation threatened by communist takeover.

Truman's initiative reflected the thinking of George Kennan, America's spe-cialist on Soviet affairs. In two influential documents, Kennan argued that the Russians were expansionist and would not stop unless an outside force purposefully contained them.[7] Soviet policy, he contended, was based on the premise that "there can be no compromise with rival power and that constructive work can start only when Communist power is dominant."[8] Kennan's solution was an "adroit and vigilant application of counter force at a series of constantly shifting geographical and political points."[9] In his memoirs, Kennan later indicated that he had not intended for containment to become an all-encompassing commitment to stop-ping the spread of communism everywhere. Only areas with strong military-indus-trial capabilities, such as the United Kingdom, needed to remain noncommunist.[10]

Subsequent events seemingly confirmed the suspicions of American policy makers that a Soviet-directed communist conspiracy threatened Asia. As a result,

U.S. involvement in Vietnam deepened. In the wake of China's "fall" to communism in 1949 and communist North Korea's 1950 invasion of South Korea, America soft-pedaled its anticolonial stance. U.S. officials feared the further spread of communism in Southeast Asia. France's defeat by communist-led forces in Vietnam in 1954 resulted in America's supplanting the French there.

Going hand in hand with a policy of containing communism was the emergence in the 1950s of the modernization school of thought among American social scientists. Following the Second World War, the United States was financially and technologically able to assist Asian leaders, who appeared to want help in modernizing their countries. American missionary zeal overflowed, and advocates believed that exported U.S. technology and training would improve underdeveloped nations. Motives for providing assistance "ranged from anxiety over the spread of communism to exhilaration" over the "presumed ability" of the United States to help impoverished nations by manipulating their economic and social systems.[11]

Various theorists and American policy makers believed that U.S. security depended on the successful use of modernization techniques, with Third World countries emulating Western economic and political systems. Academicians, such as historian and economist Walt Whitman Rostow, later an adviser to John Kennedy and Lyndon Johnson, contended that "economic assistance promote[d] economic development" and "economic development promote[d] political stability."[12] Heavily influenced by Charles Darwin's theory of evolution and biased toward Western institutions, proponents of modernization pushed for the industrialization and democratization of former colonial nations.[13]

Rostow, among others, identified "the threat of communism in the Third World as a modernization problem."[14] U.S. officials concurred, asserting that communism stemmed from poverty and that a country's political stability depended on economic development. This "dogma" became "ingrained in the thinking" of U.S. foreign aid officials.[15] Arguing that the costs would be small, "compared with the costs of waging limited wars," Rostow called for America to provide the Third World with extensive financial and material assistance.[16] The United States needed to promote the development of "democratic societies abroad," he concluded, so that they could be "relied upon not to generate conflict because their own national interests parallel ours and because they are politically healthy and mature."[17]

To address this situation in Vietnam, the Eisenhower administration turned to nation building. Although modernization theorists advocated various nation-building methods, most of them "looked upon modernity as incompatible with tradition," and established mores, practices, and institutions were often destroyed in the process. The problem for U.S. policy makers was to restructure South Vietnam according to American economic, military, and political models while minimizing its cultural disruption.[18]

Academia actively participated in nation building during the 1950s and 1960s as an adjunct to the U.S. government. The MSUG, in particular, played a significant role in South Vietnam, where the group wanted to create a "Good Society." Patterned after the West, the embryonic nation would become "wealthy, just, democratic, orderly," and capable of controlling its own affairs.[19]

Michigan State's optimistic faith in the benefits of the Western system clashed with the realities of modernizing a Southeast Asian culture emerging from colonial rule. The MSUG and U.S. officials both acknowledged that difficulties existed and mistakes would be made in establishing an anticommunist state, but felt that none would arise that Uncle Sam could not overcome. Nation building "tapped the well-springs of American idealism," and assumed the "trappings of a crusade," historian George C. Herring has noted. "Only at the end of the decade, when South Vietnam was swept by revolution, did Americans begin to perceive the magnitude and complexity of the problem they had taken on."[20]

Higher education became increasingly involved in federally sponsored programs during the Second World War as the Allies tried to stay ahead of the Axis powers technologically. With the onset of the cold war and heightened concern over communist expansion, this relationship solidified. The federal government offered grants to the universities for defense and weapons research and to educate individuals to serve as "foreign-area specialists" and technical-assistance engineers in the Third World. In the mid-1950s, universities received about $300 million a year from the Pentagon. Schools such as the Massachusetts Institute of Technology (MIT) and Stanford University became weapons laboratories. Among others, Michigan State and the University of Kentucky sent advisers to assist politically troubled developing countries threatened by communism.[21]

For financial and patriotic reasons, university presidents eagerly helped in this effort. Many of them, such as Harvard's James B. Conant and MIT's Karl T. Compton, had worked for the federal government in some manner during and after the Second World War. Distinguished scholars, both had advised the White House on the development and postwar regulation of the atomic bomb. Most university presidents, including Conant and Michigan State's John Hannah, were also virulently anticommunist. During the early 1950s, Hannah decided that members of the Communist Party would be dismissed from the school's faculty; only those who renounced the organization would remain.[22]

John Hannah did not possess Conant's and Compton's intellect. The Michigan native, however, was a persuasive, charismatic figure who, it was said, "could charm the birds out of the trees."[23] He proved to be an ambitious, effective administrator in both East Lansing and Washington.

Hannah had graduated in 1923 with a degree in poultry science from Michigan State, then the Michigan Agricultural College, one of the first land-grant institutions. In 1938 he married Sarah Shaw, the daughter of the school's president, Robert Sydney Shaw. Three years later he succeeded his father-in-law as president, and he went on to lead Michigan State for nearly three decades.[24]

A visionary and pragmatist, Hannah was an "institution builder" both at home and abroad.[25] Accessing both private and public funds, he greatly expanded Michigan State's physical plant and enrollment. A journalist once noted that Hannah "will get for 'State' whatsoever it may need and make even the poor taxpayer and his agent, the legislator, like it."[26] He foresaw the growth potential afforded by the GI Bill, which provided returning servicemen with financial assistance to attend college. To accommodate the influx of veterans, Hannah initiated various construction projects and purchased surplus U.S. Army barracks. Eleven apartment buildings, several dormitories, numerous Quonset huts and other military-style structures were erected during the Fall 1946 term. Eight years later, Michigan State was the ninth-largest university in America, with approximately 15,000 students and two thousand professors. By 1969, the last year of Hannah's tenure, enrollment reached 42,541 and the campus covered five thousand acres. His successor, interim president Walter Adams, later recalled that he came to Michigan State in 1947, in part, because it offered faculty housing during the postwar population explosion on American campuses. Coming from Yale University, "I did not know where the hell East Lansing was," he said, but available housing held great allure.[27] Adams contended that Hannah had "converted a sleepy cow college. . . into a megaversity of national stature and international note—an empire on which the sun never set and where the concrete never hardened."[28]

Academia, California University President Clark Kerr observed in 1963, had become "an instrument of national purpose," a "multiversity" serving both the private and public sector.[29] Hannah, the "master pragmatist," had led the way. *Fortune* magazine noted in 1969 that Hannah was "the model for a president of megaversity: no scholar, but an astute politician and a skillful manager."[30] When the National Association of Food Chains and its counterpart in the mobile-home industry approached him about shortages of college-trained employees, Michigan State created study programs for both. In each case, they served the community and were self-liquidating and funded by their respective sponsors, and that was what mattered to Hannah. According to Adams, however, the mobile-home program became an embarrassment, and, "being a good pragmatist," Hannah realized his mistake and terminated the venture. "He was an experimenter in the best sense of the term," Adams concluded, and numerous Michigan State faculty, even those who sometimes disapproved of his policies, "appreciated him" and "admired him."[31]

Stanley Sheinbaum, a Michigan State economist who later broke with Hannah over the MSUG project, once characterized him as a "good solid citizen, the quintessential public servant."[32] Hannah actively assisted the federal government and came to know every president from Herbert Hoover to Gerald Ford. Therefore, Michigan State's decision to aid South Vietnam was not an unusual step for the school to take, especially since Hannah had pioneered the use of university assistance abroad. Realizing the expanded role America would play in the postwar world, he created an Institute of Foreign Studies in 1943 at Michigan State. Eighteen years later, during the height of the cold war, Hannah asserted that "our colleges and universities must be regarded as bastions of our defense, as essential to the preservation of our country and our way of life as supersonic bombers, nuclear-powered submarines and intercontinental ballistic missiles."[33] Hannah advocated the university land-grant philosophy of public service; he was fond of saying that "[t]he State is our Campus," and easily took it one step further to "the World is our Campus."[34] Using lands from the "vast public domain," the Morrill Land-Grant College Act of 1862 created in each state at least one school to "teach such branches of learning as are related to agriculture and the mechanic arts."[35] In the words of one educator, the legislation was intended to open "the doors of universities to the children of farmers and workers," and provide horticultural assistance to communities through school outreach programs.[36] Like the early land-grant leaders, Hannah embraced the role and sought closer ties to the federal government.[37]

As president of the Association of Land-Grant Colleges and Universities, Hannah offered President Truman "full cooperation" to assist underdeveloped countries under the Point Four program. He served as a member of the International Development Advisory Board of Point Four from 1950 to 1952, and Michigan State sent staff to train counterparts in agricultural colleges in Colombia, India, Taiwan, and Nationalist China. Hannah took a nineteen-month leave of absence from the college during 1953–54 to serve as Eisenhower's assistant secretary of defense for manpower and personnel. The Michigan State president oversaw racial integration of the armed services and the conclusion of the Korean War. Hannah returned to campus with the Medal of Freedom, the highest American award for civilian service. In 1957, he agreed to chair the newly established Civil Rights Commission, a position he continued to hold during the Kennedy and Johnson administrations. When he retired as Michigan State president in 1969, he became head of the Agency for International Development (AID) under President Richard Nixon.[38]

Contracted through a U.S. government agency such as AID, many universities sent representatives to foreign countries to provide technical assistance. Although begun under the Truman administration's Point Four program in 1950 with $35 million, government-sponsored technical assistance expanded dramatically under Eisenhower. These universities offered aid in programs that promoted a country's economic development. Agriculture, engineering, general and public education, public administration, and business management were among the primary fields of interest. The MSUG, the largest of the technical-assistance projects abroad, aided South Vietnam, increasing the number of U.S. government-sponsored university programs to forty-three by the mid-1950s. During the 1957–58 academic year, Turkey alone had three schools providing assistance: Georgetown University, New York University, and the University of Nebraska.[39]

When Michigan State agreed to aid South Vietnam, the institution was already involved in three other technical-assistance projects. Colombia was the first, in 1951, followed by the Ryukyuan Islands and Brazil. The Colombian government asked the U.S. Technical Cooperation Administration (TCA) to help strengthen academically that country's two agricultural colleges, in the cities of Medellin and Palmira. Michigan State signed a contract with the TCA and Colombia, sending four faculty members to Medellin and three to Palmira. They assisted in curriculum development and field training, including the creation of research farm demonstrations and "extension work for farmers." Michigan State considered the project a success that had improved the U.S. image in Latin American eyes.[40]

Also in 1951, Michigan State agreed to help establish the University of Ryukyus in the Ryukyuan Islands. Controlled by the Japanese during the Second World War, the strategically important islands had fallen into American hands following Japan's defeat. Okinawa, the chain's largest island, had never had a university and was chosen as the site for the new school. Previously, Ryukyuans who sought university training had had to attend schools in Japan. Founded by the U.S. Army and the American Council on Education, Ryukyus was patterned after the

Michigan State land-grant model. Because ownership of the islands eventually was to revert to Japan, Japanese educational philosophies were incorporated into the institution. Michigan State advisers were involved in almost every facet of the school's creation, including designing buildings, developing curricula, establishing a library, and training staff.[41]

In addition to Colombia and the Ryukyuan Islands, Brazil also received technical assistance from Michigan State in the early 1950s, when the Michigan State School of Business and Public Service helped establish Sao Paulo's School of Business Administration. The university provided local assistance and also advanced degree training to Brazilian faculty who came to East Lansing. Michigan State considered the project successful, and similar programs were introduced at the University of Rio Grande Do Sul and the University of Bahia.[42]

The Vietnam project was more ambitious than Michigan State's previous assistance programs because of the university's association with Ngo Dinh Diem and the U.S. government's commitment to containing communism. Michigan State remained closely connected to Diem for most of the program's tenure because of Professor Wesley Fishel's relationship with the Vietnamese president. Fishel exercised great power in South Vietnam during the mid-1950s because of his friendship with Diem and because of American concern over communist expansion in Southeast Asia.

An examination of Fishel's and Diem's relationship reflects America's apprehension over communism and reveals the emphasis put on modernization, placing the creation of the MSUG in context. Fishel supported Diem at a pivotal point, allowing the future South Vietnamese premier to court American policy makers by portraying himself as an ardent anticommunist with Western sympathies. Diem was persuasive and fit American policy makers' criteria. Irreproachable nationalist "credentials" reportedly provided him with Vietnamese political support, and his firm anticommunist views served American geopolitical goals. Until the early 1960s, policy makers continued to support Diem and viewed his role as that of a local modernization manager. An examination of Fishel's and Michigan State's roles in Vietnam shows why America intervened there, what it hoped to do, and why it failed to establish an effective South Vietnamese government and military.

Fishel first met Diem in Japan in July 1950. The men enjoyed each other's company and exhibited several similarities. Both were well educated, firmly anticommunist in their political views, and short in stature (5 feet 4 inches). Born in Cleveland in 1919, Fishel graduated from Northwestern University in 1941 and served in the Pacific during the Second World War as a military language specialist.[43] "I was on

Iwo Jima, attached to the 3d Marine Division," Fishel later recalled in an interview. "I was an Army officer, commanding a detachment of interrogators . . . It was 1945 and we had the job of trying to persuade Japanese soldiers to surrender."[44] After obtaining a doctorate in international relations in 1948 from the University of Chicago, he joined the staff of the University of California at Los Angeles and began teaching American servicemen in Japan.[45] In 1952, the University of California Press published his dissertation, *The End of Extraterritoriality in China*. At about this same time, Fishel became involved in a classified research project for the U.S. Army in Korea, examining the impact that cultural and language differences had on the United Nations war effort there. For his work, he received a United Nations medal in 1953.[46]

Diem, an imperial official's son, studied at French Catholic academies and Hanoi's public school of administration. Because of his education, he was recruited by both the French, Vietnam's colonial ruler, and their communist-led opponent, the Vietminh. The murder of his brother, Ngo Dinh Khoi, by the Vietminh in 1945, combined with his Catholic beliefs, dissuaded Diem from turning to communism. At the same time, Vietnamese patriotism precluded his cooperation with France. His political options limited, Diem went into self-imposed exile abroad. While touring Japan, he visited an old friend, journalist Koyashi Komatsu, who had saved him from being shot when Japan invaded Vietnam during the Second World War. Komatsu introduced Diem to Fishel.[47]

Diem's anticommunist and sociopolitical reform views impressed Fishel, and the two men later corresponded frequently. Diem appreciated Fishel's counsel and on a number of occasions thanked him for his "suggestions" and "comments" on "the situation in VN [Vietnam]."[48] "I received your most welcome letter," Diem wrote in one note, "and am grateful for the interest you are taking in the affairs of my country."[49] They discussed the history of Vietnam and the current struggle between the French and the communist-led Vietminh. Diem's disdain for both groups shone clearly in his writing. He informed Fishel that in Vietnam, "[t]he general attitude is resolutely hostile to communism. The discontent lies in the fact that the communist propaganda benefits from the French attitude which is resolved not to consent to true independence."[50]

When Fishel went to Michigan State in 1951, Diem followed. Fishel's office mate, political scientist Ralph Smuckler, recalled that "Wes. . . always had the impression that Diem was. . . a very prominent . . . powerful person in Saigon," and would discuss his "family connections and everything else about him."[51] At the time, Smuckler teased his colleague about "delusions of grandeur." Later, *Ramparts* magazine would assert that Fishel "was taken lightly" because he had "neither the swagger nor the stripes of a kingmaker."[52] Fishel, however, flew Diem in at university expense and, as assistant director of the university's Governmental Research Bureau, appointed him the bureau's Southeast Asian consultant in 1953.[53]

While working in that position, Diem prepared a five-page outline specifying Vietnam's future needs. Divided into three major parts—public administration, public finance, and police administration—the plan became the basis for Michigan State's Vietnam project. Diem targeted these three areas because of Vietnam's shortage of trained government personnel. During ·colonialist rule, French administrators had trained only a minimal number of Vietnamese to assist in running the government. In addition, French administrators refused to prepare the Vietnamese for upper-level management.[54]

During Diem's stay in the United States, he cultivated enough U.S. political support to become South Vietnam's prime minister in July 1954. Diem's American backers, the so-called Vietnam Lobby, were a loosely organized, diverse group of influential anticommunists who became the American Friends of Vietnam, of which Fishel was chairman between 1964 and 1966. Included in the lobby were such prominent figures as Francis Cardinal Spellman of New York, millionaire Joseph P. Kennedy, his son, U.S. Senator John F. Kennedy of Massachusetts, fellow Senator Mike Mansfield of Montana, Supreme Court Justice William O. Douglas, Air Force Colonel and CIA operative Edward Lansdale, and, of course, Wesley Fishel.[55] Circumstances surrounding Vietnamese Emperor Bao Dai's appointment of Diem to the prime ministership remain vague, and although the lobby's unfailing support of him doubtless had an impact, it is impossible to calculate fully the significance of their efforts.[56]

Diem's Catholicism and friendship with Fishel, however, served him well. For Spellman, Mansfield, and the Kennedys, all prominent Catholics, Diem possessed the perfect leadership qualities: "ardent Catholicism and rabid anti-Communism."[57] The Church pumped money into South Vietnam to help Catholic refugees, and in early 1955, the sixty-seven-year-old Spellman, clad in army khaki, demonstrated both his and the Pope's support by visiting Diem in Saigon. Some lobby members, such as the Cardinal and the Kennedys, were friends prior to their association with Diem, and many worked together later to assist him. At least one source credits Fishel with having "started the chain" leading to the Vietnam Lobby's creation.[58] Reportedly, Fishel introduced Diem to Spellman, who in turn introduced him to Justice Douglas, who hosted a luncheon where the Vietnamese leader met Senators Mansfield and Kennedy.[59] During the first, fragile moments of Diem's regime, in 1954–55, Fishel, Lansdale, and Mansfield cooperated to help shore up Diem's position.[60]

Following the end of the First Indochina War with France in 1954, Vietnam was in turmoil. The Geneva Accords divided the country at the seventeenth parallel, with the promise of unification elections in 1956. Hoping to maintain a modicum of influence over its former colony, France was not very enthusiastic about accepting Diem, a nationalist, as the South's new leader. Eisenhower evidently persuaded France, however, and in October 1954 assured Diem that America would help South Vietnam "in its present hour of trial."[61] Soon after Diem's appointment, Fishel unofficially assumed the role of presidential adviser. In his memoirs, John Hannah contends that Secretary of State John Foster Dulles personally telephoned him to request that Fishel accompany Diem to the Geneva Conference, where Vietnam's future was being decided by a delegation of nations.[62] Although in the end Diem did not attend the conference, representatives of his government did, including several relatives, and Fishel met with French, Vietnamese, and other officials in Paris afterward in July to discuss Vietnam's problems further.[63]

Fishel's formal title changed periodically during the Diem regime's chaotic early years, but his role remained that of presidential consultant and promoter. The South Vietnamese president trusted him as an adviser, while the U.S. State Department used him as an informant. In 1954 and 1955, he was a staff member for General J. Lawton Collins, Eisenhower's special representative in South Vietnam, serving as liaison between Collins and Diem. The general noted that "Dr. Fishel did a splendid job while he was here and enjoyed both Ngo Dinh Diem's and my confidence and respect."[64] Unsure whether his government would last, and not knowing in whom to confide, Diem turned to Fishel. Diem valued the American's advice and for a time moved him into the presidential palace along with Wolf Ladejinsky, an American land reform expert. The three often shared breakfast and discussed government policies. In September 1954, Fishel wrote Edward Weidner, the chairman of Michigan State's political science department, "I go in and out of the palace so often these days I'm treated as one of his staff by the guards. Yesterday I was there for fifteen hours, and on Saturday for nineteen hours."[65]

The reform program Diem had drafted while serving as a university consultant was initiated in the fall of 1954 when he requested aid and technical assistance from the United States and Michigan State. On 26 September, Weidner and three other Michigan State personnel—James H. Denison, Hannah's administrative assistant and head of public relations; Arthur F. Brandstatter, chairman of the police administration department; and Charles C. Killingsworth, chairman of the economics department—departed East Lansing to evaluate whether a technical-assistance program would benefit both the university and South Vietnam.[66] The "special mission" visited Washington, D.C., the Philippines, and Vietnam, returned two weeks later, and filed its report with the United States Foreign Operations Administration (FOA), predecessor to the AID, under whose authority both Fishel and the mission had gone to Saigon.[67]

Submitted in October 1954, the report recommended that Michigan State College, in "joint agreement" with South Vietnam and the FOA, provide technical assistance to the South Vietnamese government in four major disciplines: public administration, police administration, public information, and public finance and economics. The report was based on interviews conducted with numerous American, Philippine, and Vietnamese officials, including Diem, and President of the Philippines Ramón Magsaysay. Approximately seventy to eighty Vietnamese officials were interviewed, generally in one-hour meetings, though in some cases "follow-up visits" were held. The mission explained its strikingly brief two-week time frame by saying that a crisis existed, making a six-month or one-year in-depth study impossible. Mistakes would be made in "any emergency program," they contended, "but the important thing is to get a program under way that has at least a reasonable chance of success."[68]

Having been invited by Diem himself, Michigan State's team was generally welcomed by the Vietnamese government. There were exceptions, however. Brandstatter, the mission's police administration representative, had difficulty obtaining information about South Vietnam's internal security. Initially, Diem controlled only the provincial police departments. Saigon's police were controlled by the Binh Xuyen, a corrupt gang of bandits and river pirates. To understand the status of Vietnam's police, Brandstatter had to deal with a Binh Xuyen representative, from whom he received no cooperation. Although Diem was feuding with the Binh Xuyen, he spoke with its leadership and secured Brandstatter a special appointment. Brandstatter made it clear to the Binh Xuyen that he was authorized to recommend that the U.S. spend "millions to reestablish police service" in Vietnam, but he needed assistance in obtaining data. He received the information. Addressing such bureaucratic resistance would be a perplexing problem that the MSUG would continually face and one in which Diem would later become a hindrance.[69]

Although all of the mission's major recommendations were adopted in some form and contracted through three periods, 1955–57, 1957–59, and 1959–62, significant modifications were made. The U.S. State Department had reservations about allowing Michigan State too much independence. Theoretically, the university would be under the "close control" of the U.S. ambassador and the FOA mission chief. Consultative assistance to the Vietnamese government would occur only when necessary and would require the approval of both the U.S. embassy and its aid division, the United States Operations Mission (USOM).[70] Under the terms of the contract, the university was limited to "in-service training, development of the public administration institute (NIA) and civil police training."[71] Since the U.S. government already had both an information service and economists in Vietnam, the public information section was completely discarded and the public finance and economics section was severely curtailed.[72] The American government reluctantly accepted Michigan State's assistance in public and police administration because the USOM's public administration division was insufficient and because no public safety division existed in either USOM or the FOA's Washington, D.C., department.[73] In addition, Washington's hands were tied because of Diem's great confidence in Michigan State, based on the prime minister's friendship with Fishel. Diem wrote Hannah in October 1954 praising the university's mission to Saigon and thanking him for permitting Fishel to remain in Saigon for so long.[74]

Fishel's relationship with Diem was a double-edged sword for the U.S. government. Although Fishel had served the U.S. government before, working in military intelligence during the Second World War and directing a "top-secret" U.S. Army study in Korea in 1953, his position in Vietnam was less well defined.[75] He was more a friend and confidant to Diem than a U.S. government employee. Although Fishel provided information to the State Department, American officials in Vietnam became irritated because they often had to consult him as an intermediary rather than speaking with Diem personally.[76]

Initially, Fishel was to brief the Saigon mission, return to East Lansing, and resume teaching political science at Michigan State.[77] However, mission chief and political science chairman Ed Weidner requested that he stay in Saigon. Writing Hannah in October 1954, Weidner insisted that the Vietnam situation was critical and that Fishel's presence was "essential to American policy as long as Diem stays in power."[78] In addition, he advised Hannah that Fishel should be Michigan State's first Vietnam project head. Hannah approved, and Fishel moved his family to Saigon, where he remained project head until 1958.

Although Fishel was an Asian studies specialist, most MSUG personnel were unfamiliar with Vietnam; they had acquired only scant knowledge of the emerging country from the Vietminh's defeat of France at Dien Bien Phu. Both individual-ized and group orientation programs were necessary to introduce elements of Vietnam's language and culture to the team. Conducted on Michigan State's cam-pus, the intensive orientation lasted only three weeks. The MSUG's lack of prepa-ration thus made project members dependent on local interpreters. Although half of the orientation was language instruction, MSUG participants never mastered Vietnamese. Training sessions in Vietnamese and in the government's second lan-guage, French, were continuous until departure. Later, reflecting on the hurried training period, one early group member commented that Michigan State did not really have an orientation program.

To avoid depleting the home campus, MSUG personnel were actively recruited from outside Michigan State's staff. Representatives from the university attended academic and criminal justice conferences to recruit members, and numerous pub-lic administration advisers came from state and federal government agencies. One hundred and four American personnel, excluding twenty-two "short-term consul-tants and inspectors," were employed through Michigan State during the three contract periods.[79]

The majority of the MSUG staff were not from the university, and not all of the participants served as advisers. Just eighteen of the seventy-two MSUG members acted as advisers; only thirteen of the thirty-two service personnel, secretaries, and administrative assistants were from the university's faculty. The public administra-tion division was moderately balanced, with eleven of the thirty-four advisers com-ing from the university, while the campus was significantly unrepresented on the police staff, with only four of the thirty-three advisers being part of the Michigan State family. The project's upper echelon, however, was essentially composed of Michigan State professors. Only one of the MSUG's five Saigon mission chiefs was not a Michigan State faculty member when selected, and even his acceptance of the position was contingent upon the promise of a faculty appointment after his Saigon service ended. The project's remaining support positions, such as drivers and interpreters, were filled by Vietnamese.[80]

Vietnam was in turmoil when the first MSUG members arrived in Saigon on 20 May 1955. Diem had just gained control of the army, defeated the dissident Cao Dai and Hoa Hao sects of the western and southern Vietnamese lowlands, and sub-dued the Binh Xuyen. Just a few months earlier, U.S. officials had speculated on whether he could even remain in power. Eisenhower's agent in South Vietnam, General Collins, did not think the Vietnamese leader capable of doing so. In late April, he returned to Washington to inform the president and Secretary of State

Dulles that "Diem must be replaced . . . immediately."[81] During the next few days, however, circumstances changed quickly. First-hand accounts from Saigon indicated that Binh Xuyen forces, a group Fishel referred to as "a kind of super Murder, Incorporated," had bombarded the presidential palace with mortar fire, causing Diem to deploy the Vietnamese National Army.[82] After "[h]eavy fighting," Diem's troops overcame the opposition, and American support swung firmly behind him.[83]

Although Diem had solidified his position, he still faced numerous difficulties. In accordance with the Geneva agreements, many of the Vietminh left the South, while the North's anticommunist refugees fled southward. About three thousand individuals per day entered the South and needed to be fed and sheltered. In addition, the countryside had to be secured if resettlement was to succeed. After visiting Vietnam, the chairman of the Joint Chiefs of Staff, Admiral Arthur Radford, noted that one of Diem's "biggest problem[s] is the refugee problem—the caring for and relocating of refugees from North Vietnam in such a way that they will be able to care for themselves over the long pull and feel themselves identified with the country."[84] At this critical juncture, the MSUG would be called on to help.[85]

Several Michigan State faculty vividly remember the first tumultuous days in Saigon. Project member and later MSUG chief Guy Fox recalled that during the night the city "was rocked by dynamite explosions" and terrorist bombs while "mortar fire could be heard" as the Vietnamese army engaged the last of the Binh Xuyen's forces.[86] One MSUG member was even kidnapped by the Cao Dai, but later freed uninjured. Ralph Smuckler noted that before his family departed for South Vietnam, American newspapers headlined stories about street fighting in Saigon. As a result, his insurance policy was canceled.[87]

Smuckler, Fox, and numerous other MSUG personnel witnessed an anticommunist riot at the Hotel Majestic on 20 July 1955. A protest marking the first anniversary of the Geneva Conference was taking place at the time. Demonstrators gathered at the hotel because delegates of the International Control Commission (ICC), the body charged with enforcing the Geneva agreements, were staying there. The demonstrators believed that the commission was partial to the North Vietnamese communists. Having been "tipped" to get out of the hotel by a friendly waiter at breakfast, Smuckler, unlike some other MSUG members, was able to move his family to safety. Rocks were thrown, windows were broken, ICC automobiles were burned, and the hotel was ransacked. Although the MSUG was not affiliated with the ICC, its members sustained property damage and loss. MSUG psychologist Fred Wickert recalled that members of his family

15

had to barricade themselves in their room. Hiding across the hall was Pulitzer Prize-winning writer James A. Michener and a traveling companion. Michener later informed Wickert that he and his friend "were personally never so scared in their lives." Also in the hotel was Perle Mesta, the Washington "hostess with the mostest," who from 1949 to 1952 served as ambassador to Luxembourg. Marines from the U.S. Embassy in Saigon rescued Mesta, two secretaries, and seventeen pieces of luggage, but let the other Americans "figure out how to survive the best they could."[88] Fox was left with only "the clothes on his back and four shirts."[89]

The MSUG's initial assignments reflected Vietnam's crisis-laden atmosphere. MSUG personnel could not immediately implement their academic program because Diem and the USOM requested they first address urgent problems dealing with regional and provincial government administration and police services.[90] Most important, Diem wanted to bring the refugee problem under control.[91]

NOTES

1. *New York Times*, 9 May 1957.

2. Quoted in George C. Herring, *America's Longest War: The United States and Vietnam, 1950–1975*, 3d ed. (New York: McGraw-Hill, 1996), 72.

3. James Aronson, *The Press and the Cold War* (Indianapolis and New York: Bobbs-Merrill Company, 1970), 186; David Anderson, *Trapped by Success: The Eisenhower Administration and Vietnam, 1953–1961* (New York: Columbia University Press, 1991), 160–61.

4. Walter Adams, *The Test* (New York: Macmillan, 1971), 18.

5. Quoted in David W. Levy, *The Debate Over Vietnam* (Baltimore: Johns Hopkins University Press, 1991), 29.

6. Ibid.; Daniel Yergin, *Shattered Peace: The Origins of the Cold War* (New York: Penguin Books, 1990), 88; John Lewis Gaddis, *The Long Peace: Inquiries into the History of the Cold War* (New York: Oxford University Press, 1987), 161. Southeast Asia possessed a number of natural resources in large quantity, including oil, rice, rubber, and tin. Walter LaFeber, *America, Russia, and the Cold War, 1945–1992*, 7th ed. (New York: McGraw-Hill, 1993), 107.

7. U.S. Department of State, *Foreign Relations of the United States, 1946, vol. 6, Eastern Europe; The Soviet Union* (Washington, D.C.: U.S. Government Printing Office, 1969), 696–709; George F. Kennan, "The Sources of Soviet Conduct," *Foreign Affairs* 25 (July 1947): 566–82.

8. *Foreign Relations*, 706.

9. Quoted in LaFeber, *America, Russia, and the Cold War*, 64.

10. George Kennan, *Memoirs, 1925–1950* (Boston: Little, Brown and Co., 1967), 359.

11. Lucian W. Pye, "Foreign Aid and America's Involvement in the Developing World," *The Vietnam Legacy: The War, American Society and the Future of American Foreign Policy*, ed. Anthony Lake (New York: New York University Press, 1976), 374–76.

12. Samuel P. Huntington, *Political Order in Changing Societies* (New Haven and London: Yale University Press, 1968), 6.

13. Alvin Y. So, *Social Change and Development: Modernization, Dependency, and World-System Theories* (Newbury Park: Sage Publications, 1990), 261–62, 30, 34; Max F. Millikan and W. W. Rostow, *A Proposal: Key to an Effective Foreign Policy* (New York: Harper & Brothers, 1957), 1–4.

14. So, *Social Change and Development*, 36.

15. Huntington, *Political Order*, 6.

16. Millikan and Rostow, *A Proposal*, 2.

17. Ibid., 4.

18. So, *Social Change and Development*, 262.

19. Samuel P. Huntington, "The Goals of Development," in *Understanding Political Development*, ed. Myron Weiner and Samuel P. Huntington (Boston: Little, Brown and Co., 1987), 6.

20. Herring, *America's Longest War*, 47–48, 51; George Kahin, *Intervention: How America Became Involved in Vietnam* (New York: Knopf, 1986), 69–70; Anderson, *Trapped by Success*, 142–43; Arthur F. Brandstatter, James H. Denison, Charles C. Killingsworth, and Edward W. Weidner, *Chief of Mission, Report of the Special FOA Mission from Michigan State College for Public Administration, Public Information, Police Administration, and Public Finance and Economics* (Saigon, 16 October 1954), i-3, Michigan State University Vietnam Project Papers, Michigan State University Archives and Historical Collections, East Lansing, Michigan (hereafter cited as Vietnam Project Papers).

21. Kenneth J. Heineman, *Campus Wars: The Peace Movement at American State Universities in the Vietnam Era* (New York and London: New York University Press, 1993), 13–19; Howard W. Beers, *An American Experience in Indonesia: The University of Kentucky Affiliation with the Agricultural University at Bogor* (Lexington: University Press of Kentucky, 1971), 1, 5; *National Review*, January 1970, 18; Michael T. Klare, *War Without End: American Planning for the Next Vietnams* (New York: Alfred A. Knopf, 1972), 79.

22. *Saturday Evening Post*, 15 September 1956; Walter Adams and John A. Garraty, *Is the World Our Campus?* (East Lansing: Michigan State University Press, 1960), 2; Heineman, *Campus Wars*, 13–19; Paul L. Dressel, *College to University: The Hannah Years at Michigan State, 1935–1969* (East Lansing: Michigan State University Publications, 1987), 11–12; Vannevar Bush, *Pieces of the Action* (New York: William Morrow and Company, 1970), 33–37, 316; James B. Conant, *My Several Lives: Memoirs of A Social Inventor* (New York: Harper & Row, Publishers, 1970), 286–304, 357, 520, 561. See also Sigmund Diamond, *Compromised Campus: The Collaboration of Universities with the Intelligence Community, 1945–1955* (New York and Oxford: Oxford University Press, 1992).

23. Adams, interview.

24. Dressel, *College to University*, 3, 5; Heineman, *Campus Wars*, 20–21; Richard Niehoff, *John A. Hannah: Versatile Administrator and Distinguished Public Servant* (Lanham, Md.: University Press of America, 1989), xvi.

25. Adams, *The Test*, 18.

26. *Fortune*, May 1967, 160.

27. Adams, interview.

28. Ibid.; Dressel, *College to University*, 394–95; *New York Times*, 29 September 1946, 30 May 1954; *Time*, 21 March 1969, 42.

29. Quoted in Sidney Lens, *The Military-Industrial Complex* (Philadelphia and Kansas City: Pilgrim Press and The National Catholic Reporter, 1970), 126.

30. *Fortune*, May 1967, 161.

31. Adams, interview; *New York Times*, 13 October 1949.

32. Stanley Sheinbaum, interview by author, 18 March 1993.

33. Quoted in Lens, *Military-Industrial Complex*, 127.

34. Stanley K. Sheinbaum, "Vietnam—A Study in Freedom," *Michigan State University Magazine* (February 1956), Vietnam Project Papers; Adams, interview.

35. Quoted in Roger L. Williams, *The Origins of Federal Support for Higher Education: George W. Atherton and the Land-Grant College Movement* (University Park: Pennsylvania State University Press, 1991), 12.

36. Clark Kerr, *The Uses of the University, With "Postscript-1972"* (Cambridge: Harvard University Press, 1972), 15.

37. Williams, *Origins of Federal Support*, 12; *New York Times*, 21 November 1943.

38. Dressel, *College to University*, 3, 5, 7–11, 14, 276–300; *Michigan State University State News*, 25 February 1991; *John A. Hannah, A Memoir* (East Lansing: Michigan State University Press, 1980), 138; Niehoff, *John A. Hannah*, 133, 214–16; Heineman, *Campus Wars*, 21; *U.S. News & World Report*, 16 October 1953; *New York Times*, 17 September, 13 October and 26 November 1953, 27 and 30 July 1954.

39. Beers, *American Experience in Indonesia*, 1; *Saturday Evening Post*, 15 September 1956; George Brown Tindall, *America: A Narrative History* (New York and London: W.W. Norton and Co., 1984), 2:1261; Adams and Garraty, *Is the World Our Campus?*, 2, 8.

40. Dressel, *College to University*, 276–77, 394–95.

41. Ibid., 277. In 1972, Japan resumed administration of Okinawa and Ryukyus became a Japanese national university.

42. Ibid.

43. Bio-Data File 1974 and *New York Times* Bio-Service, Wesley R. Fishel Papers, Michigan State University Archives and Historical Collections, East Lansing, Michigan (hereafter cited as Fishel Papers).

44. Quoted in Gloria Emerson, *Winners and Losers: Battles, Retreats, Gains, Losses and Ruins from a Long War* (New York: Random House, 1976), 304.

45. Bio-Data File 1974, Fishel Papers; *Detroit Free Press Magazine*, 11 June 1972, Vietnam Project Papers; Fred Wickert, interview by author, 20 July 1992.

46. *Saturday Evening Post*, 15 September 1956; Bio-Data File 1974, Fishel Papers; *Detroit Free Press Magazine*, 11 June 1972; Wesley Fishel, *The End of Extraterritoriality in China* (Berkeley: University of California Press, 1952); Wesley R. Fishel and Alfred H. Hausrath, *Language Problems of the US Army during Hostilities in Korea* (Chevy Chase, Md.: Johns Hopkins University Operations Research Office, 1958); American Friends of Vietnam Biographical File, box 3, folder

18

18, Gilbert Jonas Collection 166, Gilbert Jonas Papers, Michigan State University Archives and Historical Collections, East Lansing, Michigan; Herbert Garfinkel to Wesley Fishel, 8 July 1952, box 1184, Fishel Papers; John Davis to Wesley Fishel, 16 November 1954, box 1184, Fishel Papers; Wesley Fishel to John Davis, 19 November 1954, box 1184, Fishel Papers.

47. *Saturday Evening Post*, 15 September 1956; George C. Herring, *America's Longest War: The United States and Vietnam, 1950–1975*, 2d ed. (New York: Alfred A. Knopf, 1986), 47–48; David L. Anderson, *Trapped by Success*, 8; *Detroit Free Press Magazine*, 11 June 1972; Wickert, interview.

48. Ngo Dinh Diem to Wesley Fishel, 19 October 1951, box 1184, Fishel Papers.

49. Ngo Dinh Diem to Wesley Fishel, 3 June 1951, Fishel Papers, box 1184.

50. Ibid.; Warren Hinckle, Robert Scheer, and Sol Stern, "The University on the Make," *Ramparts* 4 (April 1966): 16. Very little correspondence between Diem and Fishel remains from this period. Fishel's family destroyed the bulk of the letters before donating his papers to the Michigan State University Archives and Historical Collections. Author's conversation with Michigan State University Archivist Dorothy T. Frye, 16 March 1994.

51. Ralph Smuckler, interview by author, 13 May 1993.

52. Ibid.; Hinckle et al., Michigan State University: "The University on the Make," 16.

53. *Detroit Free Press Magazine*, 11 June 1972.

54. *Saturday Evening Post*, 15 September 1956; Sheinbaum, "Vietnam—A Study in Freedom."

55. *Ramparts* 4 (July 1965): 16–20.

56. Anderson, *Trapped by Success*, 52; Herring, *America's Longest War*, 48–49.

57. John Cooney, *The American Pope: The Life and Times of Francis Cardinal Spellman* (New York: Times Books, 1984), 240.

58. Gregory A. Olson, *Mansfield and Vietnam: A Study in Rhetorical Adaptation* (East Lansing: Michigan State University Press, 1995), 268n.18.

59. In Joseph Buttinger, *Vietnam: A Dragon Embattled* (New York: Praeger, 1967), 2:847, he contends that Bishop Ngo Dinh Thuc, Ngo Dinh Diem's brother, introduced him to Francis Cardinal Spellman.

60. Cooney, *American Pope*, 242–44; Olson, *Mansfield and Vietnam*, 38, 58, 61, 64, 65.

61. Quoted in Herring, *America's Longest War*, 47 [1979 edition].

62. Hannah, *A Memoir*, 130.

63. Ibid.; Anderson, *Trapped by Success*, 59; Michigan State University *State News*, 27 September 1954.

64. J. Lawton Collins to John A. Hannah, 11 March 1955, box 42, folder 50, John A. Hannah Papers, Michigan State University Archives and Historical Collections, East Lansing, Michigan (hereafter cited as Hannah Papers).

65. Wesley Fishel to Edward Weidner, 20 September 1954, box 628, folder 101, Vietnam Project Papers; J. Lawton Collins to John A. Hannah, 11 March 1955, box 42, folder 50, Hannah Papers; Wickert, interview; "The Vietnam Lobby," *Ramparts* 4 (July 1965): 20; Anderson, *Trapped by Success*, 75.

66. Michigan State University *State News*, 27 September 1954.

67. Robert Scigliano and Guy H. Fox, *Technical Assistance in Vietnam: The Michigan State University Experience* (New York: Praeger, 1965), 2.

68. Brandstatter et al., *Report of the Special FOA*, I–3, Vietnam Project Papers.

69. Arthur Brandstatter, interview by the author, 17 July 1992.

70. U.S. Department of State Indochina Files, Reel 1, 19 January 1955, memorandum, (Washington, D.C.: U.S. Government Printing Office).

71. Ibid.

72. Scigliano and Fox, *Technical Assistance in Vietnam*, 3–4.

73. Ibid.; Contract between the Government of Vietnam and Michigan State University, 14 April 1955, box 628, folder 28, Vietnam Project Papers; Ralph Turner, interview by author, 9 July 1992.

74. Ngo Dinh Diem to John A. Hannah, 19 October 1954, box 42, folder 49, Hannah Papers.

75. Anderson, *Trapped by Success*, 75.

76. U.S. Department of State Indochina Files, Reel 1 and Turner, interview.

77. Michigan State University *State News*, 27 September 1954.

78. Edward Weidner to John A. Hannah, 6 October 1954, box 628, folder 101, Vietnam Project Papers.

79. Scigliano and Fox, *Technical Assistance in Vietnam*, 40.

80. Ibid., 40–41.

81. Memorandum from the Director of the Office of Philippine and Southeast Asian Affairs (Young) to the Assistant Secretary of State for Far Eastern Affairs (Robertson), 30 April 1955, reprinted in John P. Glennon, ed., *Foreign Relations of the United States, 1955–1957, vol. 1, Vietnam* (Washington, D.C.: U.S. Government Printing Office, 1985), 337.

82. Wesley Fishel, ed., *Vietnam: Anatomy of a Conflict* (Itasca, Ill.: F. E. Peacock Publishers, 1968), 84.

83. Editorial Note, Glennon, *Foreign Relations*, 299–300; Herring, *America's Longest War*, 54 [1979 edition]; Anderson, *Trapped by Success*, 115; Scigliano and Fox, *Technical Assistance in Vietnam*, 2–6.

84. Admiral Arthur Radford, Memorandum Prepared in the Department of Defense, 22 August 1956, reprinted in Glennon, *Foreign Relations*, 733.

85. Scigliano and Fox, *Technical Assistance in Vietnam*, 2–6; Fishel, *Vietnam*, 84.

86. *MSU Magazine*, 1 June 1960, 2.

87. Smuckler, interview; *Final Report of the Michigan State University Advisory Group*, 1962, 2, box 658, folder 6, Vietnam Project Papers.

88. Wickert, interview.

89. *The MSU Reporter*, November 1957, box 657, folder 29, Vietnam Project Papers; Press Release Saigon, Vietnam, 17 March 1956, box 657, folder 67, Vietnam Project Papers; *MSU Magazine*, 1 June 1960, box 657, folder 27, 2; Wickert, interview; *New York Times*, 21 July 1955; *Who's Who in America, 1954–1955* (Chicago: Marquis Who's Who, 1954), 28; Smuckler, interview.

90. Scigliano and Fox, *Technical Assistance in Vietnam*, 6.

91. *Final Report*, 6; Fishel, *Vietnam*, 84.

CHAPTER 2

COMIGAL: MICHIGAN STATE AND REFUGEE RESETTLEMENT

About 900,000 Catholic, Buddhist, and Protestant refugees fled North Vietnam following the 1954 Geneva Accords.[1] Signed by France and the communist-led Vietminh, the Accords concluded the First Indochina War but in many respects laid the foundation for the Second with America. The terms were vague in many sections and the principal reasons for which the war was fought remained unsettled. Moreover, neither Dwight Eisenhower nor Ngo Dinh Diem signed the agreement and, as a result, they did not feel constrained by it. The Accords outlined the procedure by which Vietnam was to become an independent country, providing for a cease fire, temporary division of the country at the seventeenth parallel, reunification elections to be held in 1956, and a 300-day period during which Vietnamese from the two regions were permitted to relocate. About 140,000 refugees, primarily Vietminh guerrillas, went North; the majority—some 900,000—came South. Most of these were Catholics fearing religious persecution in the communist-controlled North. In truth, U.S. policy makers viewed the collapse of French colonialism in Vietnam, as signified by the Accords, with "equanimity, if not outright enthusiasm."[2] Freed from colonialism's drawbacks, Eisenhower and Secretary of State John Foster Dulles believed they could help Diem build a non-communist South Vietnam. Catholics would play an important role.[3]

Numerous countries and organizations helped the refugees. The rescue operation was divided into two separate phases, relocation and resettlement. Dubbed "Passage to Freedom," relocation principally involved transporting refugees south aboard American, British, and French air and naval crafts.[4]

The Michigan State University Group (MSUG) and several private relief agencies, including the Catholic Church, assisted with resettlement. The university postponed implementation of long-range academic reforms in South Vietnam in order to aid the refugees. A northern Catholic himself, Diem provided emergency aid to those in flight and created the Commissariat for Refugees, more commonly known by its French acronym, COMIGAL. Michigan State acted as a consultant to COMIGAL. A number of MSUG personnel clashed with the Catholic Church and Diem over the bias shown toward northern Catholic refugees, however, as the Vietnamese president and the church favored Catholics to the detriment of both the South's Buddhist population and Vietnam's mountain people, the Montagnards. Refugee assistance initially monopolized most of the university's time and resources. Some twelve to fifteen advisers were in the first MSUG contingent, nearly one-third of whom worked with COMIGAL.[5]

Although the southern migration of refugees has often been labeled "voting with their feet," the so-called exodus was actively encouraged by Diem's regime. The South Vietnamese president planned to use Catholic refugees to create a loyal political following. He informed U.S. officials that if he could be publicly guaranteed American "aid and support" in moving the refugees, approximately one to two million northerners could be persuaded to go south. What followed Diem's entreaty was an intensive propaganda campaign supported by the Catholic Church, France, and the United States. Former American advertising executive Edward Lansdale, now a CIA operative, played an active part in what Vietnamese specialist Bernard Fall termed a "psychological warfare operation." Catholics were told that their religious rights were threatened in the North but would be protected in the South. Further, they would be governed in the South by one of their own: Diem. A frequently used slogan was "Christ has gone to the South . . . the Virgin Mary has departed from the North."[6] The tactics worked.[7]

The successful propaganda campaign produced the enormous logistical problem of how to integrate a massive influx of refugees, including about 794,876 Catholics.[8] Lacking a mechanism for assimilating the refugees, Vietnam's government was quickly overwhelmed. A steady stream of some five thousand refugees entered the South daily, but permanent resettlement locations had not been chosen. To handle the problem, temporary "reception camps" were created, typically near Saigon. The arrival of monsoon rains, "macerating the earth as well as men's spirits," made camp conditions harsh. "There was no real shelter," except for some large tents, but they provided little privacy and "no sanitation or civilized amenities."[9]

Although South Vietnam had plenty of cultivable land, several obstacles hampered resettlement. Jungles and swamps covering much of the unoccupied land had to be cleared and drained. Abandoned property claims had to be resolved. Security in the countryside was questionable. When the Vietminh went north, a power vacuum emerged. Diem's Saigon-based government had not yet consolidated its power and could not protect individuals living outside the city. In July 1955, the Binh Xuyen, a gang of outlaws, attacked Phuoc-Ly, one of the first resettlement communities. The bandits robbed the refugees and burned their homes. As scholar Louis Wiesner notes, Diem's control of South Vietnam at this juncture was "tenuous at best."[10]

During July, the Vietnamese government and the United States Operations Mission (USOM), the agency that administered nonmilitary American aid, asked the MSUG to develop an emergency "field administration" program to provide the refugees with "essential government services."[11] A newly created Field Administration Division soon advised Diem's government on how best to establish self-sufficient refugee villages. Prior to this, COMIGAL had dispatched teams of specialists and commission employees to search the countryside for appropriate settlement sites and to consult with province chiefs and local leaders. Project plans were then devised by COMIGAL's Planning Office, sent to its director, Bui Van Luong, for approval, and given to the USOM. Michigan State's initial contact with the chief of USOM's Refugee Resettlement Division, Alfred L. Cardinaux, and Luong was encouraging. Luong, a Catholic, was extremely religious and a "good friend of Diem."[12] Not long before the Field Administration Division arrived in Vietnam, COMIGAL had decided to terminate direct "subsistence payments" and allocate funding on a "project basis." It wished to provide aid only for specific undertakings such as home, school, and road construction. Since COMIGAL wished to modify its operations, Luong asked that Michigan State submit suggestions on how to restructure the agency.[13]

New to Vietnam, the personnel of the Field Administration Division needed to gather both general and specific information about COMIGAL's refugee problem. The division's staff of four consisted of a civil servant and three academics: Walter Mode, group chief; Ralph Smuckler, research coordinator; Frederic R. Wickert, in-service training coordinator; and Wayne W. Snyder, a statistician. A respected public administrator from the U.S. Social Security Administration, Mode had been recruited by Ed Weidner, a personal friend and the MSUG's first chief adviser. Smuckler, a U.S. Army veteran, had obtained a political science doctorate after the Second World War and in 1951 had joined the Michigan State faculty. His areas of concentration were economics and international relations. In addition, he was a close friend of Wesley Fishel, with whom he shared an office in the political science department. Wickert, also a Michigan State faculty member, was a psychologist who taught management. A young man, Snyder was a doctoral student in economics when he joined the MSUG. He was experienced in technical assistance and economic development and later finished his degree at Harvard University, joining its "international development group" that worked in Indonesia. In addition, the staff included several Vietnamese who served as interpreters and consultants.[14]

From July through September 1955, Michigan State's Field Administration Division conducted research and interviewed a number of Saigon-based COMIGAL employees, province chiefs, and refugees on how to improve resettlement. Their work yielded four significant reports. The MSUG proposed that COMIGAL streamline its resettlement methods, utilizing decentralization, a public administration "device" that was supposed to stimulate economic development by encouraging regional and village-level input and experimentation. Theoretically, the refugees knew better than the Saigon bureaucrat what types of construction projects (schools, wells, clinics, and mills) would benefit their lives socially and economically. The MSUG also suggested that COMIGAL reduce its Saigon-based operations, principally by placing more of its personnel in the field to help the refugees develop new projects. Finally, to give the agency more authority and reduce red tape, Michigan State recommended that COMIGAL's Planning Office be promoted to directorate level within South Vietnam's government. Luong generally welcomed the suggestions and implemented them over time. As a result, refugees had a voice in policy conception and implementation. Resettlement became a joint venture coordinated between Saigon and the emerging communities.[15]

On 1 September, MSUG members began researching the provinces to determine how to improve COMIGAL's field operations. Once again, they relied on interviews. The members spoke with officials and village leaders from fourteen provinces in the Highlands and South and Central Vietnam where the refugees were concentrated. Refugee representatives from forty-three villages answered questions, and COMIGAL and the USOM provided additional information.[16]

The results of the Field Administration Division's research, contained in a 20 September report, reiterated the concept of decentralization. To reduce the amount of time required to develop, approve, and implement a village-level project, the MSUG recommended that COMIGAL field offices be created in provinces heavily populated by refugees. In these areas, COMIGAL field representatives would act for Director Luong and serve as members of the province chief's staff. Field representatives would maintain contact with Luong and local leaders, involving both COMIGAL and the individual villages in project planning and implementation. The Field Administration Division believed that decentralization would move the refugees quickly toward self-sufficiency.[17]

24

By mid-1956, COMIGAL had implemented decentralization and sent representatives to a number of provinces, including Cho-Lon, Gia-Dinh, Bien-Hoa, Dinh-Tuong, Tay-Ninh, and Binh-Tuan, where "two-thirds of the refugees" had been relocated. Recognizing that decentralization's success depended on local cooperation, COMIGAL, the MSUG, and the USOM created a team of "troubleshooters" who visited the provincial representatives, listened to their problems, and assured the province chiefs that their participation was important. The chiefs typically responded to the gesture and promoted decentralization, permitting "direct communication" between local representatives and COMIGAL. To evaluate decentralization's effectiveness, the MSUG conducted a six-month follow-up using a "random sampling." They happily discovered that COMIGAL had decreased the number of Saigon-based employees and had placed more "into the field" to work directly with the refugees. On the average, only a seven- to twelve-day lag existed between the proposal of refugee projects and their processing in Saigon.[18]

To enhance decentralization, Michigan State recommended that COMIGAL increase its technical assistance to the refugees, since the established government ministries and their field divisions rarely provided this service. Numerous specialists in various fields, including experts in agriculture and public works, were needed to make surveys and guide construction. Of the six provinces most heavily populated by refugees, only Gia-Dinh did not complain of a shortage of trained technicians; their leaders felt they could call upon Saigon personnel if necessary.[19]

Further, the MSUG aided COMIGAL in a two-week training course in January 1956 for fifty-six of its field representatives. Michigan State's recommendations and assistance to COMIGAL established a precedent that allowed "successive Refugee Ministries" and their "American advisory counterparts" to finance and hire experts when normal government channels failed to—or were not asked to—deal with problems.[20]

Although the MSUG's principal role in resettlement was training and advisory, its direct contributions to refugee relief were also notable. In January 1956, Father Bui Ngoc Tre, pastor of the Quang Nam refugees in central Vietnam, wrote the MSUG requesting aid in building a school. While thanking the university for its previous efforts, he expressed an interest in developing closer ties. "In this way we can create a close, strong relationship with your students," he noted. "Last November, we had the honor to receive the gifts that your students sent to us. We maintain a good, warm impression of this occasion." Two years later, under similar circumstances, Michigan State again assisted the refugees. The University's

Vietnam contingent and the East Lansing campus combined to raise 12,352 piasters (approximately $350) to build a school for Gia Kiem, a village seventy-five miles north of Saigon that was destroyed by fire.[21]

Most scholars agree that refugee relocation was a significant achievement, possible only through the combined efforts of foreign volunteers and the Vietnamese themselves. There is some debate, however, over how successful resettlement really was. According to Director Luong, all of the refugee communities became self-sufficient and integrated into South Vietnamese society by mid-1957. Geographically, the villages were dispersed in three areas: 207 in the Mekong Delta, 50 in the central coastal lowlands, and 62 in the Highlands. Of the 319 refugee resettlements established, 288 were agrarian-based, 26 were for fishermen, and 5 for craftsmen. Using public works as an indicator, Luong argued that living conditions in these villages, in most instances, surpassed those in North Vietnam. Approximately 92,443 houses, 6,029 wells, 317 elementary schools, 18 secondary schools, 2 hospitals, and 143 infirmaries were constructed for the refugees in the South.[22]

Luong's findings are suspect for a number of reasons. His failure to present data on North Vietnamese living conditions precluded any serious comparison, leaving the impression that he was spreading propaganda. Furthermore, although public works can be used as one gauge, other information is also needed to have a balanced picture. Citing Saigon government statistics on land distribution and farming as evidence, Vietnamese specialist Bernard Fall asserted that by July 1957 resettlement had not provided "gainful employment for [many of] those refugees involved in agriculture," causing them to live off "hand-outs." Since the vast majority of new arrivals were farmers, Luong's contention that all refugee villages were self-sufficient by mid-1957 must be viewed with skepticism.[23]

Michigan State was not the only organization in Vietnam that aided the refugees. The International Rescue Committee (IRC) and the Catholic Church, both politically influential within South Vietnam, also assisted in resettlement. Established in 1933 to support victims of Nazi Germany, the IRC had a significant impact in Vietnam. Directed by Monsignor Joseph J. Harnett, the U.S. National Catholic Welfare Conference (NCWC), one of the first "private voluntary" organizations to help the refugees, also made substantial contributions to refugee relief. Like the IRC, the NCWC had been active during the Second World War, aiding the Catholic churches and victims in war-torn countries.[24] Harnett had worked in France and Italy prior to serving in Vietnam.[25] By the end of 1957 the NCWC and its successor, Catholic Relief Services (CRS), had donated $35,000,000 in aid to the Vietnamese refugees. The money went for such items as medicine, food, clothing, tractors, chain saws, and water pumps.[26]

These three groups were connected on several levels. The leaders of all three knew each other, were personally close to Diem, and were active in the American Friends of Vietnam (AFVN), an organization created to promote a democratic South Vietnam. In reality, this frequently meant providing unwavering support for Diem.

The IRC's leadership typified the network between the refugee resettlement program and the AFVN. Leo Cherne, head of the IRC, went to Saigon for several weeks in August 1954 to consult with Diem on how to assist the refugees. After his trip the IRC decided to send Joseph Buttinger, the organization's vice president, to head a relief project. Buttinger went to Saigon in October 1954, met Diem, and the two men became friends.[27]

Buttinger, like Fishel, was an active supporter of Diem and a prominent member of the AFVN, serving as its vice chairman and chairman of the Executive Committee. Aided by Cherne, Buttinger had been one of the AFVN's original organizers. Buttinger, Cherne, Fishel, and others wrote articles, made speeches, and lobbied Washington officials on behalf of the Vietnamese president.[28]

Like Michigan State and the IRC, the Catholic Church strongly supported President Diem. Francis Cardinal Spellman of New York had permitted the self-exiled Diem to stay at the Maryknoll Seminaries in Lakewood, New Jersey, and Ossining, New York, during the early 1950s. He also cultivated U.S. support for Diem through the influence of such powerful Catholic politicians as Joseph P. and John F. Kennedy. In addition, as a member of the informal "Vietnam Lobby" that had preceded formation of the AFVN, Spellman had either worked with or became acquainted with Fishel, Cherne, and Buttinger.[29]

Although Catholics were a minority in South Vietnam, they had a disproportionate influence in the country's government. Diem's brother, Ngo Dinh Thuc, the bishop of Vinh Long, introduced the Vietnamese president to Cardinal Spellman and was a principal Catholic figure in the country.[30] Like the French colonials before him, Diem was openly biased toward Catholics. Vietnamese Catholics had enjoyed a "privileged position" under the French, and by 1954 were entrenched in the country's civil service. The French believed that Catholics were "politically more reliable" than other religious groups in Vietnam. Diem generally agreed and cultivated them as part of his political power base.[31]

Diem's favoritism toward Catholics colored his judgments and adversely affected refugee resettlement, producing political consequences that jeopardized

27

America's nation-building effort in South Vietnam. Diem encouraged northern Catholics to migrate to the South and gave them preferential treatment over other refugees. Catholics received more financial and material assistance than either Buddhists or Protestants. The Vietnamese mountain people, the Montagnards, were often displaced to make room for the Catholic refugees. Moreover, Diem granted Catholics an unproportionately high number of civil and military appointments in the government. He sought to consolidate and expand his political power base with the Catholic refugees and was willing to alter South Vietnam's sociopolitical structure to achieve this. Further, he appointed Bui Van Luong, a fervent Catholic, to head COMIGAL and accepted large amounts of financial aid from American Catholics, allowing the church to have significant influence on the resettlement process. In a number of instances, CRS assumed the role of policy maker, devising and initiating "area development program[s]."[32]

Members of the MSUG's Field Administration Division clashed with the NCWC and CRS over the administration of resettlement. Certain Michigan State personnel were angered over the Catholic Church's desire to control resettlement and COMIGAL's failure to provide Buddhist refugees the amount of assistance given the Catholics. Typically, Spellman's representative in Vietnam, Monsignor Joseph Harnett, quarreled with the Field Administration Division's in-service coordinator, Frederic Wickert, over which organization was better qualified to direct resettlement.[33] According to Wickert, Spellman hoped to control resettlement in order to assist the Catholics at the expense of the Buddhists. Aware that the Catholic refugees already received most of the aid, the Buddhists welcomed MSUG's Field Administration staff into their camps as "potential rescuers." Wickert recalled that the Buddhist camps lacked refrigeration, with the result that Field Administration members were always greeted with a beverage made of "warm beer and lemon pop."[34]

Regardless of Spellman's motives, Buddhist refugees certainly received less aid than their Catholic counterparts, and the church sought more influence over resettlement. During the summer and fall of 1955, Harnett tried to assume control of resettlement. He argued that the system set up by the USOM and COMIGAL was inefficient. "[I]t envisioned," he said, "the construction of a large bureaucracy, made few provisions to eliminate bottlenecks that would obstruct actual operations, and was less firmly based on the efforts of the people themselves for the development of their villages" than on COMIGAL's technical-assistance staff. Harnett visualized a simpler system that placed resettlement in the hands of the village priests, who, he believed, could expedite the process because they were familiar with refugee needs. Although other resettlement experts did not openly accuse the church of having ulterior motives, some asserted that it was ill-prepared to handle such a situation. Jean Le Pichon, a technical expert for COMIGAL from 1955 to 1957, commented that "For many priests the task was too demanding, and Monsignor Harnett, in my opinion had overestimated their capabilities in this respect. It would have been dangerous to have given the parish priests the full responsibility for the resettling program, including the drawing of the budgets."[35]

The MSUG's plan for resettlement—decentralization—incorporated many of the ideas that Harnett was advocating, including placing a greater amount of responsibility into the hands of the refugees themselves. However, some Michigan State personnel differed with Harnett over the treatment of the Buddhists and preferred the use of technical and financial experts to parish priests. The latter point was conceded by some refugees and by the church itself. The Vietnamese "parishioners quickly realized the doubtful performance of their priests as administrators," Le Pichon commented, and the church preferred that the clerics concentrate on religious matters. As a result, the refugees increasingly assumed more responsibility for their own affairs.[36]

As much as possible, COMIGAL kept together northern refugees from the same villages and of the same religions. However, conditions caused by the massive exodus necessitated that Catholics and Buddhists from different villages and provinces often be relocated together. In a 1959 publication, Director Luong argued that Catholics and Buddhists cohabited "peacefully . . . and understandably so, considering that freedom of religion has long existed in Viet-Nam." He added that "the Communist danger served to unite people of different faiths and backgrounds." This may have been true in 1959, but Buddhists increasingly became politicized over the issues of religious persecution and Diem's discriminatory policies favoring Catholics. By 1963, the Buddhists were extremely vocal and represented a major threat to Diem.[37]

Despite the efforts of certain Michigan State personnel, the powerful Catholic presence, comprised of Diem and the Catholic relief agencies, prevented the Buddhist refugees from being treated fairly. Though Wickert acknowledged that Luong was a "reasonable guy," he contended that the 1963 demonstrations against Diem's regime, in which monks immolated themselves, reflected frustrations that had begun with the Buddhists' bad treatment during resettlement. The refugees were 90 percent Catholic, but the Buddhists comprised a significant majority of South Vietnam's population and resented being discriminated against and ruled by a religious minority. Diem's village- and provincial-level political appointments included a disproportionately high number of northern Catholic refugees, who spoke a foreign dialect and practiced a foreign religion. Diem's decision to appoint northern Catholics alienated the Buddhists by producing a "carpetbagger" effect reminiscent of what the American South experienced during Reconstruction. The Catholic Church also managed South Vietnam's school for senior civil servants. As political scientist George McT. Kahin noted, if Buddhists "were not already convinced that 'at least nominal conversion to Catholicism' helped ensure [civil and military] advancement, they presumably were when, in 1959, Diem formally dedicated" the country to the Virgin Mary.[38]

In 1957, the focus of Diem's political goals for resettlement switched from the lowlands to the highlands. About fifteen thousand Highland refugees from the North, Nung, Muong, Yao, and Tai-speaking tribes were immediately placed in South Vietnam's Central Highlands, thus paving the way for other Vietnamese to follow. For economic and security reasons, Diem wanted to incorporate this region into his new government, but it was largely populated by mountain tribesmen, collectively known as the Montagnards. Saigon officials classified these people as "ethnic minorities," considering them inferior and a hindrance to progress. Perceived to be "nomadic or seminomadic," the Montagnards relied on agricultural methods that were considered wasteful. Diem decided that "civilizing" them was the best way to achieve integration and promote economic growth. To facilitate the process, he resettled "anti-Communist Catholic refugees" and other Vietnamese into the highlands, thereby easing lowland overcrowding and providing additional security in the "sparsely populated" region.[39]

The Vietnamese people knew little about the highlands before the 1954 Geneva Accords. The French had generally kept the Vietnamese out, with settlement being "carefully controlled almost to the point of non-existence." The region was categorized as a Crown Domain, theoretically under Emperor Bao Dai's control. This classification separated the highlands administratively from the rest of Vietnam and preserved it for France. The French used the region for economic and recreational purposes. Plantations were established there for producing coffee, rubber, and tea. The highlands' moderate climate, ideal for escaping Saigon's heat, made it a popular French retreat where Bao Dai maintained a hunting lodge.[40]

To learn more about the region for purposes of resettlement, Diem sent Michigan State personnel into the highlands in 1956 and 1957 to conduct research and interview mountain tribesmen. The MSUG compared the situation of the highland peoples to that of the American Indians during the nineteenth century. The Saigon government, wishing to settle refugees and other Vietnamese in the region, argued that there would be plenty of land for everyone if the Montagnards ended their wasteful nomadic ways. In contrast, the tribesmen viewed the settlers as invaders illegally colonizing their land. In April 1956, Fishel wrote the United States Bureau of Indian Affairs requesting literature on agency policies. He noted that "From the Western and Vietnamese points of view, the Montagnards are primitive in respect to their social and economic way of life, and religious beliefs . . . On the more practical side, question of land alienation is coming to the fore. The Montagnards claim ownership of all of the land, and the intrusion of the Vietnamese settlers is raising the question of a land policy that would protect the Montagnards against the possible wholesale alienation of their land."[41]

Although the work was of a "preliminary nature," and tangential to the university's primary role as public and police administration advisers, the MSUG's highland research broke new ground, provoking a controversy with Diem.[42] Contrary to Saigon's perceptions, Michigan State discovered that the highlanders were neither nomadic nor wasteful in agriculture. In reality, many of the tribes used a "shifting field method" of planting that allowed previously farmed fields to lie fallow for a period of time and replenish. In addition, although tribesmen refused to sell land, they would lease it if properly compensated.[43]

Gerald C. Hickey, an anthropologist and MSUG member, conducted the bulk of the highland research. His interest in the region dated to 1953, when he had studied Indochina's ethnology during a fellowship in Paris.[44] As a Michigan State employee in 1956, he made an exploratory trip into the highlands. He met many youthful Montagnard leaders and became aware of a "rising spirit of ethnonationalism, a response to Saigon's attempt to integrate them into the Vietnamese cultural sphere." Hickey returned to the highlands several times during the mid-1950s. Twice in the spring of 1957 he visited there, examining "indigenous land tenure systems" and exploring the possibilities of Diem's land resettlement plans. In April he was accompanied by fellow MSUG member Fred Wickert, in May by Price Gittinger, a USOM agricultural representative.[45]

Hickey's first trip occurred when Saigon's land program, aimed at integrating the Montagnards, was just starting. The prevailing belief among American and South Vietnamese officials was that the highlanders had no land tenure systems. Consequently, Diem saw little need to worry about Montagnard land claims when resettling refugees in the region. To learn more about the tribesmen, Diem's government and Wesley Fishel authorized an expedition to the highlands. Hickey and Wickert, the only MSUG members with "anthropological backgrounds," explored the area and spoke with Montagnard leaders. Contrary to the official

Saigon position, they concluded that a Montagnard land tenure system existed and that any land redistribution policies must take their claims into consideration.[46]

Traveling through rugged territory in a Jeep station wagon, Hickey and Wickert visited numerous highland communities near Ban Me Thuot, Pleiku, Kontum, and Cheo Reo.[47] The trip was rewarding but difficult—and at times dangerous. Wickert recalled that an eight-foot cobra showed its fangs, chased them down the road, and attacked their Jeep. The heat of the recently run vehicle fooled the snake into believing that one of the tires was a person. He remembered the Montagnards as "accepting" and courteous hosts. Initiated into one of the tribes, he and several highlanders used straw to drink "fermented wild rice wine" together out of a large clay pot. Then a chicken was killed and the blood was dripped over Wickert. Hickey and Wickert often ate rice with the tribesmen and stayed in their homes. The houses were elevated off the ground to keep wild animals out. Wickert noted that while this effectively stopped tigers, it did not dissuade jungle rats. They "run all over you all night," he recalled, "are sexually very active, and squeal with joy right on top of you. It is awful!"[48]

In general, Hickey and Wickert found that the highlanders disliked Diem's government. Tribesmen typically complained about government-imposed rules, confiscation of their lands by Vietnamese settlers, and cultural discrimination. Rhadé tribesmen living near Ban Me Thuot told Hickey and Wickert of instances where Vietnamese "squatters" claimed lands already cleared by highlanders for planting. Further, the Rhadé asserted that communist guerrillas were active in remote areas of the province. To induce the tribesmen into joining their side, the communists promised them autonomy and were even reported to have assumed Rhadé ways of wearing "loincloths and breaking their teeth." Propaganda broadcasts on "Radio Hanoi" denouncing Diem's government were also made in several highlander dialects.[49]

Wickert's and Hickey's findings were reconfirmed in May 1957 when Gittinger joined Hickey on another highland expedition. Their assessment of the situation, presented in two separate reports, disturbed Diem and his land reform expert, Wolf Ladejinsky. Hickey asserted that the highlanders perceived the South Vietnamese as colonialists. Highlander interviews conducted during the 1957 trips reflected this. One Montagnard commented that "in their hearts, they [the Vietnamese] want to dominate us. They are colonialists. The French were bad at the mouth, but in their hearts they were good. Things were better." Another tribesman complained of racism, stating that "[t]he Vietnamese look down on us. They don't mean it when they call us brothers. Even little Vietnamese call Mountaineer functionaries *moi* and *moi* means savage. The Vietnamese think they are all mandarins." Supported by Gittinger, Hickey reiterated that highlander land claims should be recognized and negotiations should be conducted with the Montagnards before any government programs were implemented.[50]

According to Hickey, Ladejinsky was the "harshest" critic of the highland reports. He was closely connected to the MSUG staff and had an office at the university's Saigon headquarters. Ralph Smuckler recalled that "at one point Michigan State was going to hire him." Instead, Smuckler said, "we introduced him to Diem and Fishel saw to it that he was respected by Diem." Hickey contended that during one bitter exchange at the MSUG offices Ladejinsky called Hickey's report the worst ever produced by Michigan State. In addition, the land reform expert supposedly ranted that the Montagnards were "children," impossible to work with because they believed all the land was theirs. Hickey remarked that Ladejinsky's logic would produce few results and that such comments "only demonstrated that he had not read the report."[51]

Concerned, Diem personally undertook to investigate the situation by attending a meeting with highlander "notables." Forewarned of the president's visit and wishing to remain in his favor, Vietnamese provincial officials concocted a sham reception during which highlanders dressed in Vietnamese clothing greeted him at the landing strip. Diem returned to Saigon and happily informed Fishel that the reports were wrong. In reality, he said, the Montagnards "loved the Vietnamese and desired to emulate them." Satisfied that Hickey's and Gittinger's reports were incorrect, Diem implemented his land resettlement and development plans.[52]

According to Hickey, future problems were foreshadowed at a February 1957 government celebration of Diem's land polices at Ban Me Thuot. Designed to improve Saigon-Montagnard relations, the event initially had a carnival atmosphere, with elephant races, bands, and floats. This ended, however, when someone came out of the crowd and shot a pistol at Diem. The Vietnamese president was unharmed but a Saigon official near him was wounded. Although the government identified the would-be assassin as a communist, Hickey had his doubts. He later commented that he knew then that Diem's highland settlement policies "would have problems."[53]

In support of Diem, the USOM withdrew Gittinger's report and "locked [it] in a safe," but Fishel allowed Hickey's report to "circulate" unaltered. However, Hickey later commented that "both Gittinger and I were in disfavor," and, "[w]orst of all, it was quietly agreed in the American mission that the Land Development Program would move ahead without regard for highlander land claims." Prohibited by Diem's government from returning to the highlands, Hickey did not resume work on the Montagnards until 1964, by which time Michigan State's Vietnam project had ended and Diem was dead.[54]

In response to Saigon's land reforms, the Montagnards became militant; efforts to smash the phenomenon were ineffectual. The differing tribes organized and protested government attempts at assimilation. A feeling of antagonism developed toward Diem that "ultimately erupted in many localized armed rebellions."[55] His policies alienated many Montagnards, thereby facilitating communist infiltration of the highlands and the creation of a Montagnard nationalist movement, "Bajaraka."[56] Integration of the highlands into South Vietnam's government essentially began in 1955 with a "highlander resettlement program," which established six new communities.[57] Highlander resettlement "regrouped the Montagnards into defensible communities, to decrease their vulnerability [against communism] and ease the application of cultural uplift projects."[58] The tribesmen were relocated near major roads and away from their forest homes. As Louis Wiesner noted, this made "more Montagnard land available to the Vietnamese. Indeed, that seems to have been a principal reason for moving the highlanders." Saigon officials considered the highlander resettlement program part of the larger 1957 Land Development Project, which hastened the resettlement process. By 1958 there were thirty-eight new highlander villages.[59]

The Bajaraka movement began in May 1958 at a meeting of highland leaders in Pleiku. The term is an acronym representing the names of the major highland tribes. In direct contrast to Diem's goals, the leaders primarily demanded "autonomy and equality with the Vietnamese." Initially, they did so by petitioning Diem and several foreign dignitaries posted in Saigon, including American Ambassador Elbridge Durbrow. This accomplished little and Saigon officials, including some of the MSUG political scientists, were surprised at the Montagnards' attitudes. At the time, nation-building theorists believed that "ethnic identity" was a minor stumbling block, to be overcome and supplanted with loyalty to the state.[60]

Hickey's evaluation of the situation, as stated in his 1957 report on the highlands, argued that "forced assimilation would only generate resentment." He reiterated this position in his 1982 study on the tribesmen, *Free in the Forest*, asserting that early in 1957 it was already evident that Diem's highland policies were problematic. At that time the refugee problem was less urgent, and Diem began pressing the Montagnards harder for economic and cultural integration into South Vietnamese society. The Commissariat for Refugees became the Commissariat for Land Development, and Bui Van Luong was appointed its director. Diem went against Hickey's and Wickert's advice and actually created the scenario he had

34

been trying to avoid. He "facilitated rather than hindered the subsequent subversion of the tribes by the Viet Cong."[61]

Michigan State's role in the refugee resettlement program is complex. The MSUG tried to act as a positive force, and most of the Field Administration Division's recommendations were utilized with solid results, but because numerous organizations and factors were involved in the resettlement program, the university's overall impact is difficult to measure. Robert J. MacAlister, former director of the International Rescue Committee in Saigon, supported this conclusion. He commented that although Michigan State "was not contracted specifically to advise on refugee problem[s], administrative experts from MSU teams made many valuable suggestions to COMIGAL. Their contribution was not always visible but it was not less valuable."[62]

Political realities prevented Michigan State from securing more rights for the Buddhists and the Montagnards. Members of a multipronged assistance team that zealously supported Diem, the MSUG served the regime as advisers, not policy makers. In addition, the university's project leaders, including Chief Advisor Wesley Fishel and Michigan State President John Hannah, wholeheartedly supported Diem's government as the last chance for a democratic Vietnam. MSUG personnel were in the precarious position of having to decide how much pressure to apply when Diem opposed reforms they deemed necessary to South Vietnam's long-term survival. There at the president's request, the advisers wanted neither to alienate him nor to hinder the nation-building process.

At this time, U.S. policy makers considered the welfare of Diem and South Vietnam to be synonymous. They valued Michigan State's ability to assist COMIGAL without offending their Vietnamese counterparts. USOM's Alfred Cardinaux complimented Fishel on the MSUG's careful handling of Vietnamese sensibilities and acknowledged the university's accomplishments. Specifically, Cardinaux appreciated Michigan State's tempered use of criticism when advising COMIGAL. "I want to commend the members of your team especially for having understood the problem so well, and further more for having interpreted the spirit of good will which they have encountered in COMIGAL," he said. "I think that this attitude of theirs is primarily responsible for the constructive achievements."[63]

Michigan State's *Final Report* concluded that "the [u]niversity had a significant role in one of the most successful cases in history of mass population resettlement and rehabilitation." Essentially, this statement is correct. Michigan State worked well with COMIGAL's Vietnamese staff and made a sizable contribution to resettlement by introducing a decentralization plan and providing some technical assistance. Although Diem ignored Michigan State's advice concerning the

Buddhists and Montagnards and his actions later had negative consequences, the mass of northern refugees were transported south and resettled in the relatively brief span of two years, from 1955–57.[64]

The nature of the refugee problem and COMIGAL's leadership created a different set of circumstances from those surrounding later MSUG programs and facilitated cooperation from the Vietnamese bureaucracy. Unlike South Vietnam's other government agencies, COMIGAL welcomed outside assistance. Director Luong, confronted by such an enormous problem, was receptive to Michigan State's help. Ralph Smuckler contended that Luong's receptivity made him "an unusual person . . . he did accept advice and he read the reports that we prepared." Smuckler commented that he knew of no "other counterpart situation which was more effectively pursued. It was, of course, due to him that the resettlement actually occurred effectively."[65] As a new organization, COMIGAL was not bound by the bureaucratic restraints that the MSUG found in the established government agencies. Diem's actions during the refugee crisis impressed American policy makers, and the MSUG considered its role a success. Still, as would increasingly happen with Diem, long-range reform did not occur. Instead, COMIGAL was discontinued in December 1957 and Diem pushed ahead with land reform policies that increasingly caused turmoil in the countryside.

NOTES

1. Precise figures on the refugees are unobtainable because COMIGAL's files burned in May 1955 during a battle between Diem's troops and the Binh Xuyen, a group of Saigon criminals. The best estimates on the number of refugees who migrated south appear in a 1959 article by COMIGAL's commissioner, Bui Van Luong, and are debatable. Bui Van Luong, "The Role of Friendly Nations," in *Viet-Nam: The First Five Years, An International Symposium,* ed. Richard Lindholm (East Lansing: Michigan State University Press, 1959), 49.

2. George C. Herring, *America's Longest War: The United States and Vietnam, 1950–1975,* 3d ed. (New York: McGraw-Hill, 1996), 44.

3. Ibid., 41–45; Louis A. Wiesner, *Victims and Survivors: Displaced Persons and Other War Victims in Viet-Nam, 1954–1975* (Westport, Conn.: Greenwood Press, 1988), 3.

4. Wiesner, *Victims and Survivors,* 6.

5. Robert Scigliano and Guy H. Fox, *Technical Assistance in Vietnam: The Michigan State University Experience* (New York: Praeger, 1965), 6; *Final Report of the Michigan State University Advisory Group,* 1962, box 658, folder 6, Michigan State University Vietnam Project Papers, Michigan State University Archives and Historical Collections, East Lansing, Michigan (hereafter cited as Vietnam Project Papers); Ralph Smuckler, interview by author, 13 May 1993; Luong, "Friendly Nations," 50; Herring, *America's Longest War,* 51.

6. Quoted in George McT. Kahin, *Intervention: How America Became Involved in Vietnam* (New York: Knopf, 1986), 76.

7. Ibid., 75–76; Joseph G. Morgan, "The Vietnam Lobby: The American Friends of Vietnam, 1955–1975" (Ph.D. diss., Georgetown University, 1992), 53; Luong, "Friendly Nations," 49; Wiesner, *Victims and Survivors*, 7–8; Herring, *America's Longest War*, 51.

8. Wiesner, *Victims and Survivors*, 8.

9. Gertrude Samuels, "Passage to Freedom in Viet Nam," *National Geographic Magazine*, 167 (June 1955): 866–67; Wiesner, *Victims and Survivors*, 6.

10. Luong, "Friendly Nations," 50; Herring, *America's Longest War*, 51; Wiesner, *Victims and Survivors*, 12–13; Samuels, "Passage to Freedom," 867.

11. *Final Report*, 6.

12. Smuckler, interview.

13. *Final Report*, 6; Wiesner, *Victims and Survivors*, 13–14; Luong, "Friendly Nations," 52; Alfred L. Cardinaux, "Commentary on Father Harnett," in *Viet-Nam: The First Five Years, An International Symposium*, ed. Richard Lindholm (East Lansing: Michigan State University Press, 1959), 88.

14. Smuckler, interview.

15. *Research Report: Field Study of Refugee Commission*, September 1955, box 675, folder 49, Vietnam Project Papers, pp. 1–4; Roland F. Haney memorandum to Albert A. Rosenfeld, 27 May 1957, box 675, folder 61, Vietnam Project Papers, p. 1; Smuckler, interview; Edward Weidner, "Development and Innovational Roles," in *Development Administration in Asia*, ed. Edward W. Weidner (Durham, N.C.: Duke University Press, 1970), 416; Wiesner, *Victims and Survivors*, 13.

16. *Field Study of Refugee Commission*, 2–4.

17. Haney memorandum, Vietnam Project Papers, 1; Wiesner, *Victims and Survivors*, 13; Walter Mode to Commissioner for Refugees, 13 March 1956, "*Review of August 6, 1955, Report Concerning Proposed Reorganization of the Commissariat for Refugees,*" First Draft, 13 March 1956, 4, Michigan State University Archives and Historical Collections, East Lansing, Michigan (hereafter cited as "Review of August 6, Report").

18. Wiesner, *Victims and Survivors*, 13; *Outline of September 20, 1955 MSUG Report for COMIGAL*, 2; *Final Report*, 6; Haney memorandum, Vietnam Project Papers, 1; Mode to Commissioner for Refugees, "Review of August 6, 1955, Report," 6–7.

19. Wiesner, *Victims and Survivors*, 13; *Field Study of Refugee Commission*, Vietnam Project Papers, 13; *Final Report*, 6.

20. Wiesner, *Victims and Survivors*, 13; *Field Study of Refugee Commission*, 13; *Final Report*, 6.

21. Wiesner, *Victims and Survivors*, 14–17; Luong, "Friendly Nations," 52–53; Father Bui Ngoc Tre to the Director of Michigan State University, 18 January 1956, box 675, folder 21, Vietnam Project Papers; *Escanaba Daily Press*, 3 May 1958, box 657, folder 49, Vietnam Project Papers.

22. Luong, "Friendly Nations," 52–53.

23. Bernard Fall, "Commentary: Bernard B. Fall on Father Harnett," in *Viet-Nam: The First Five Years, An International Symposium*, ed. Richard Lindholm (East Lansing: Michigan State University Press, 1959), 94–95.

24. Morgan, "Vietnam Lobby," 55.

25. Ibid.

26. Wiesner, *Victims and Survivors*, 9–10.

27. Ibid., 9; Morgan, "Vietnam Lobby," 62, 76.

28. Wiesner, *Victims and Survivors*, 10–12; David Anderson, *Trapped by Success: The Eisenhower Administration and Vietnam, 1953–1961* (New York: Columbia University Press, 1991), 158; Morgan, "Vietnam Lobby," 84.

29. Robert Scheer and Warren Hinckle, "The Viet-Nam Lobby," *Ramparts* 4 (July 1965): 16–19; Herring, *America's Longest War*, 48; Kahin, *Intervention*, 79; Morgan, "Vietnam Lobby," 24. It will be difficult to discern the extent of Spellman's role in Diem's early affairs until the Cardinal's personal papers are opened to researchers.

30. Anderson, *Trapped by Success*, 48; Joseph Buttinger, *Vietnam: A Dragon Embattled* (New York: Praeger, 1967), 2:847.

31. Kahin, *Intervention*, 77.

32. Joseph J. Harnett, "The Work of the Roman Catholic Groups," in *Viet-Nam: The First Five Years, An International Symposium*, ed. Richard Lindholm (East Lansing: Michigan State University Press, 1959), 81; Fred Wickert, interview by author, 20 July 1992.

33. Wickert, interview.

34. Ibid.; Smuckler, interview. It is important to note that not all MSUG members were critical of Harnett. Although Ralph Smuckler admitted that he did not know Harnett "closely," he remembered the Monsignor as being "a positive force" in resettlement.

35. Joseph J. Harnett, "A Critique of the Program for the Economic Integration of the Refugees," in *Viet-Nam: The First Five Years, An International Symposium*, ed. Richard Lindholm (East Lansing: Michigan State University Press, 1959), 83–87; Jean Le Pichon, "Commentary: Jean Le Pichon on Father Harnett," in ibid., 96–97; Wiesner, *Victims and Survivors*, 9–10.

36. Wiesner, *Victims and Survivors*, 10; Le Pichon, "Commentary," 97.

37. Kahin, *Intervention*, 149; Luong, "Friendly Nations," 51.

38. Kahin, *Intervention*, 101, 77, 98, 148; Wickert, interview.

39. Wiesner, *Victims and Survivors*, 15–16; Gerald Hickey, *Free in the Forest: Ethnohistory of the Vietnamese Central Highlands, 1954–1976* (New Haven, Conn.: Yale University Press, 1982), xviii, 17.

40. Gerald C. Hickey, *Preliminary Research Report on the High Plateau* (Saigon: M.S.U.G., 1957), 8; Fred Wickert, "The Tribesmen," in *Viet-Nam: The First Five Years, An International Symposium*, ed. Richard Lindholm (East Lansing: Michigan State University Press, 1959), 128; Wickert, interview.

41. Wesley Fishel to U.S. Bureau of Indian Affairs, 10 April 1956; Hickey, Preliminary Research Report, box 676, folder 60, Vietnam Project Papers, p. 5.

42. Gerald Hickey, letter to author, 28 January 1993.

43. Wickert, "The Tribesmen," 130.

44. Gerald C. Hickey, *Kingdom in the Morning Mist: Mayréna in the Highlands of Vietnam* (Philadelphia: University of Pennsylvania Press, 1988), xxvii.

45. Hickey, *Free in the Forest*, ix, 32–42.

46. Ibid., 30–32; Wickert, interview.

47. Hickey, *Free in the Forest*, 32–41.

48. Wickert, interview.

49. Hickey, *Free in the Forest*, 36–37.

50. Ibid., 43–44; Hickey, *Preliminary Research Report*, 29.

51. Hickey, *Free in the Forest*, 44; Smuckler, interview.

52. Hickey, *Free in the Forest*, 44.

53. Ibid., 20.

54. Ibid., 44; Hickey, letter to author, 28 January 1993.

55. Kahin, *Intervention*, 99.

56. Wiesner, *Victims and Survivors*, 16, 22–24; Hickey, *Free in the Forest*, ix, xviii, 32, 42–44; Fall, "Commentary," 94.

57. It is not certain whether the new communities were populated by refugees.

58. Wiesner, *Victims and Survivors*, 23.

59. Hickey, *Free in the Forest*, 45–46; Wiesner, *Victims and Survivors*, 23.

60. Walker Connor, "Nation-Building or Nation Destroying?" *World Politics* 24 (April 1972): 319; Hickey, *Free in the Forest*, 6, 47–48, 54–57; Wiesner, *Victims and Survivors*, 24.

61. Quoted in Kahin, *Intervention*, 99; Wiesner, *Victims and Survivors*, 20, 361; Hickey, *Free in the Forest*, 47–54.

62. Robert J. MacAlister, "The Refugee in Retrospect" (paper presented 23 October 1959), Fishel Papers UA 1269, box 19, MSU Archives and Historical Collections, East Lansing, Michigan.

63. Alfred L. Cardinaux to Wesley Fishel, 10 September 1956, box 675, folder 21, Vietnam Project Papers.

64. *Final Report*, 6.

65. Smuckler, interview.

CHAPTER 3

THE NATIONAL INSTITUTE OF ADMINISTRATION: A CIVIL SERVANT TRAINING SCHOOL

"The NIA was an ongoing training institution which we fit into rather naturally," Ralph Smuckler, former Michigan State University Group (MSUG) chief adviser, recalled in a recent interview. "I think we were able to have some impact on the quality of the product that came out of the NIA . . . You could tell that they [NIA graduates] were quite successful and in positions of authority because a number of them were assassinated after they went out to their posts in the countryside."[1]

A principal problem of nation building in Vietnam, one the MSUG and other American agencies like the MAAG (Military Assistance Advisory Group) continually faced, was an inability to work with the bureaucracy. South Vietnam's government was a patriarchal, tradition-bound mechanism that valued age, formal education, and political loyalty. Ngo Dinh Diem and his officials relinquished power begrudgingly, at best, and both often viewed innovation as a threat to their positions. Introducing new training methods and procedures was difficult. Diem's regime accepted assistance from the MSUG only when necessary.[2]

Michigan State's association with the National Institute of Administration (NIA), a civil servant training school, reflected this quite clearly. The university's efforts yielded mixed results. Members of the MSUG acted primarily as advisers while the Vietnamese, under Diem's direction, guided NIA policy. Still, the university's influence was felt quite widely at the school. Michigan State dispensed vital U.S. aid to the school, helped establish a research library, and constructed a new Saigon campus. In addition, decisions concerning curriculum, teaching, and in-service training all reflected the university's influence.[3]

Michigan State's arrival in Vietnam in 1955 coincided with France's departure. When the French left, Vietnam confronted the vestiges of colonial administration, including a dearth of top-level bureaucrats. In 1914, France had ended Vietnamese civil service examinations, a merit-based system that dated to 1075. The French created their own school in 1917, the Ecole de Droit d'Administration. Located in Hanoi, it was renamed the Ecole des Hautes Etudes Indochinois in 1924 and closed in 1940. In January 1953, France established the National School of Administration at Dalat to train Vietnamese civil servants for "field positions," such as those of provincial and local administrators.[4] Situated northeast of Saigon, the Dalat school implemented a two-year program emphasizing juridical instruction rather than public administration. Courses included the administrative and juridical organization of Vietnam, administrative accounting, civil and penal law, civics, social legislation, and social and political economy. In 1954, upper-level Vietnamese officials replaced the school's French educators.[5]

Michigan State's South Vietnam contract stipulated that it would help establish an institute "for the purposes of improving the training and competence of government officials and employees."[6] In August 1955, "acting on MSUG advice," Diem officially established the National Institute of Administration in Saigon.[7]

Chosen through competitive testing, NIA students received scholarships and were obligated to work for the government after finishing their courses. To take the entrance exam, one had to be either a lower-level civil servant or a Vietnamese citizen (male or female) between the ages of eighteen and twenty-five, possessing a secondary school certificate.[8] The Dalat school's resources—one faculty member, two administrators, approximately fifty students, and numerous books—were transferred to an old Catholic mission near Diem's presidential palace and served as the basis for the NIA.[9]

It was soon apparent to Michigan State that the mission's three classrooms and small library located in the chapel were inadequate for the NIA's purposes. In just over one year the institute experienced numerous changes. The library was substantially improved, and plans were drafted for a new, larger campus. In addition, the NIA got a new rector, an expanded curriculum, night classes, and an enlarged student body and faculty (both American and Vietnamese).

During the 1950s, U.S. technical-assistance advisers assigned great importance to public administration in nation building. Implementing economic and social development programs required competent civil servants. France's withdrawal from Vietnam in 1955 had created a leadership vacuum, placing the Diem government in a precarious position. Michigan State psychologist Fred Wickert, who served as MSUG's in-service training specialist, noted that "very few Vietnamese were involved in civil administration of their own country. The reason for this was that the French wanted to maintain control over their colonies."[10] Under France, only select Vietnamese were prepared for government employment, and those few offered education were rarely exposed to public administration concepts because French doctrine treated the subject as a "branch of law."[11]

Michigan State considered a public administration library essential for training new civil servants to fill the void left by colonialism. American methods of teaching public administration, including the use of term papers and local case studies, necessitated collection of data and the development of a research library. Future progress depended on student and faculty ability to use and contribute to the library's resources.[12]

Michigan State political scientist Ralph Smuckler, a specialist in economics and international relations, supervised the establishment of a modern library. He was assisted by an American and Vietnamese staff. The MSUG furnished four advisers between 1955 and 1961 to provide library management training. Two of the consultants, Henriette Allubowicz and Richard Chapin, were from Michigan State. Moreover, the university sponsored two institute librarians who were sent outside Vietnam for instruction. The NIA's head librarian, Tang Thi Ty, went to Manila and obtained a bachelor's degree in library science from the University of the Philippines. Tran Thi Kim Sa graduated from Indiana University in the United States with a master's degree in library science.[13]

Funded by U.S. aid, the library put into operation America's Dewey decimal cataloging system, provided reference assistance, and employed open shelving. By 1962, the new facility had acquired a collection of some twenty-two thousand books, documents, and periodicals. Although some of the books were in French and Vietnamese, the majority were in English, which required students to take a foreign language. The library also housed some one thousand United Nations documents and over six thousand government records and periodicals, including thirteen daily and weekly newspapers, three on microfilm.[14]

Although the library made substantial progress, Michigan State received little assistance from either Diem's regime or the NIA. According to MSUG political scientists Guy Fox and Robert Scigliano, "[s]ervices and even basic maintenance of physical facilities were neglected after the Institute took over the library's operations."[15] The NIA could only pay library assistants a clerk's wages. Vietnam's Civil Service, based on the French educational system, set staff salaries according to the highest academic degree the employee held. Failing to persuade the NIA and Vietnamese Civil Service to reconsider, the MSUG supplemented library workers' wages. After Michigan State departed in 1962, quality people could not afford to work at the library. Only two librarians remained. Consequently, only

NIA personnel were allowed to use the facility. Although the institute asked the government for additional funding and a salary reclassification for librarians, its pleas went unheeded.[16]

NIA faculty deemed the library a low priority. Trained in the French tradition, Vietnamese instructors emphasized classroom lectures and discouraged students from using library sources. Few teachers checked out materials and those who did rarely returned them. The institute failed to provide librarians with course reading lists, and, to compound the problem, dropped English as a required language. As a result, library use declined further because most materials were in English.[17]

The entire institute suffered from a paucity of materials written in Vietnamese and applying directly to Vietnam. Of particular importance to Michigan State was the lack of Vietnamese textbooks and local case studies. Students obviously benefited from having textbooks in their native language. Furthermore, U.S. public administration theorists, including MSUG members, also argued that case studies enabled pupils to examine situations they would face as civil servants.[18]

Michigan State sought to address this deficiency by initiating a cooperative research program to examine various aspects of Vietnamese culture, economy, and government. In addition, the MSUG sought to "obtain all available publications in governmental administration written in the Vietnamese language."[19] Diem and many of the NIA's staff were reluctant to help. Despite Michigan State's appeals, Diem refused to designate the library an official government depository, thus precluding the use of current data in the research being conducted there. Obsessed with security and with maintaining complete bureaucratic control, Diem refused to permit open circulation of government documents. Many NIA instructors, afraid of offending the president and antagonistic toward administrative change, were disinclined to collaborate with MSUG members.[20]

Working with some NIA faculty, the MSUG published approximately twenty studies on numerous aspects of local administration, including the role of district chiefs, village finance, marketing, and kinship structures.[21] Most of the research, based on field investigations, was done in the Mekong delta and the Central Vietnamese coastal region. Although this was supposed to be a joint MSUG-NIA undertaking, Michigan State personnel did the majority of the work. For example, Michigan State anthropologist Gerald Hickey's *The Study of a Vietnamese Rural Community: Sociology* was produced with the help of a local MSUG employee, Bui-Quang-Da, not an NIA faculty member.[22]

One university project member, John D. Montgomery, a professor of public administration, had students conduct interviews in both the private and public sector. He wished to produce case studies examining how business and government operated. Worried that the Vietnamese bureaucrats would not discuss administrative matters with strangers, Montgomery used subtle tactics. The students' first interviews were with the Standard Vacuum Corporation, an international oil company that utilized Vietnamese management. After some of the companies' success stories had been detailed, Montgomery approached the South Vietnamese government. He found the Vietnamese "unexpectedly open to the idea."[23] The student interviewers, Montgomery commented, were "knocking on doors—and being admitted—in village, district, provincial, and national offices to ask detailed questions."[24] In 1959, the results were published in a 480-page volume, *Cases in Vietnamese Administration.*[25]

A number of NIA faculty published on their own for instructional purposes.[26] By 1962, approximately two hundred articles and twelve textbooks were either in production or already completed. The most notable was a three-volume examination of Vietnamese public finances, published in 1960 by Nghiem Dang, the NIA's vice rector. Also noteworthy was the institute's establishment in 1956 of a local public administration society, the Association for Administrative Studies, and its involvement with an international one, the Eastern Regional Organization for Public Administration (EROPA). By 1957, the Association for Administrative Studies had 160 members and a monthly journal, *Review of the Association for Administrative Studies,* to which both NIA faculty and Vietnamese government employees contributed. EROPA originated in 1960 to facilitate regional cooperation in public administration. Within a year, six Asian countries (India, Japan, the Philippines, South Korea, South Vietnam, and Taiwan) were sponsoring activities. According to MSUG members Fox and Scigliano, through "some strenuous politicking" by the NIA's rector, Vu Quoc Thong, EROPA located its Research, Documentation and Diffusion Center at the institute. Some NIA faculty members capitalized on this opportunity and published articles in the organization's journal, *EROPA Review.*[27]

Although the NIA faculty produced a significant amount of work, some Michigan State personnel questioned its quality and value. Fox and Scigliano complained that cooperative efforts were "largely the product of American, not Vietnamese, energies, and the numerous articles that NIA faculty members themselves wrote were for the most part neither empirical nor based on systematic research of any other kind."[28] Essentially, NIA instructors published their classroom lectures and other course materials in textbook and essay form.[29] Fox tempered his criticism, blaming institute staff shortages for the research's poor quality.

Primarily because of financial constraints, he observed, the NIA could not "free staff members from teaching and administrative responsibilities sufficiently to permit them to do much research."[30]

In contrast to Fox and Scigliano, Nguyen-Duy Xuan, an NIA instructor and South Vietnamese official, blamed Michigan State for the scarcity of Vietnamese resources. His main concern was not library research materials but instructional material for Vietnamese students, especially textbooks. Although Xuan acknowledged MSUG assistance in translating American lectures and other works into Vietnamese, he asserted that incentives should have been created to encourage low-paid NIA faculty to publish more. Xuan concluded that "[i]f one of the functions of a technical assistance mission is to help the host agency to identify its needs and to try to satisfy them, then MSUG partially failed in its task of providing teaching materials to NIA."[31]

By the time Michigan State left Vietnam in 1962, the NIA had a new library and campus. Three main buildings had been erected on approximately nine acres of land: a 114-student dormitory with dining hall, twelve classrooms, staff offices, a 500-seat auditorium, and a library capable of storing 100,000 publications. The United States financed the bulk of the project, some $995,000. Diem's government donated the land and $370,000, the sum that the United States had spent on the first Saigon campus.[32]

An ad hoc commission consisting of the NIA, the Vietnamese Directorate General of Reconstruction, the Vietnamese Directorate of Budget and Foreign Aid, the United States Operations Mission, and the Michigan State University Group, supervised construction of the institute. Proposed in 1956, the facility was expected to be completed the following year, but several problems—most notably bureaucratic inefficiency—delayed its dedication until August 1962.[33]

The institute's building plans, prepared by South Vietnam's Department of Reconstruction, were considered inadequate by the commission. Michigan State searched for an architect to either revise or produce new sketches. In September 1957, the acting MSUG chief adviser, political scientist John T. Dorsey, visited Hong Kong to hire someone. Gordon Brown, the architect Dorsey contacted, delivered preliminary drawings one month later. Officials from the South Vietnamese government, the NIA, and the MSUG agreed that Brown could make the appropriate changes.[34]

Indecision over who would employ Brown postponed the start of construction. Officially, Michigan State had to defer to the U.S. government's principal representatives in Vietnam, the United States Operations Mission (USOM) and the

International Cooperation Administration (ICA), the agency through which the university held its Vietnam contract. Seven months passed before the organizations determined that the USOM, not the ICA, should pay Brown. In April 1958, Dorsey wrote the architect about the problem. Apologetic in tone, he stated that "in view of our present unhappy experience in getting your payment, and of ICA's refusal to let us [MSUG] employ you as a consultant, we cannot propose it to you ourselves. We shall strongly urge USOM to make you such an offer to come as their consultant. . . ." In closing, Dorsey remarked: "Once more, please accept my most sincere apologies that our procedures have been so excruciatingly slow."[35]

Once the architectural problems were solved, government inaction slowed work. Obsessed with maintaining complete control of South Vietnam, Diem expected to be consulted about the most trivial bureaucratic matters, including those concerning the NIA.[36] Beginning in 1957, he increasingly concentrated on developing the nation's police and security forces to combat the mounting insurgency, and the institute suffered from inattention.[37] NIA officials, fearing the president's disapproval, did nothing. Fox noted that numerous "decisions on relatively minor and even ministerial matters regarding the Institute must be referred to President Diem. Moreover, even in instances where presidential decision is not legally required, Institute officials have sometimes been reluctant to act before receiving presidential approval."[38] This bureaucratic inertia allowed trivial matters to halt progress. Writing NIA rector Vu Quoc Thong in April 1958, Smuckler commented: "I understand that a major cause for future delay will be, not the lack of plans, but the problem of clearing the site for the Institute construction."[39] This situation, for example, persisted until January 1960, by which time structural work still had not started.[40]

At the NIA's dedication in August 1962, several dignitaries spoke, including President Diem, U.S. ambassador Frederick Nolting, and Rector Thong. Although Michigan State played a significant role in erecting the campus, it was not represented at the ceremony. Angered at the MSUG for allowing its former members to write articles critical of him, Diem terminated the university's contract two months prior to the celebration. Of the three speakers, only Thong acknowledged the university's contribution.[41]

His decision to do so was interesting. Smuckler recalled that Thong was "far from willing to accept advice and guidance . . . and he was a strongly committed political figure within the Diem entourage." At the time of his appointment as NIA rector, he was secretary of state for health and social action, vice president of the National Assembly, and president of the Council of State. Furthermore, he was a law professor at the University of Saigon. In 1957, he shed many of his adminis-trative duties to concentrate on institute concerns.[42]

The NIA's curriculum indicated that, like Thong, most of its instructors were lawyers. With mixed success, Michigan State had lobbied to supplant the juridical French method of instruction with an "Americanized model" based on public administration and the social sciences. Fox concluded that the result was "essen-tially a compromise between old and new ideas, as influenced by the expressed desire of President Diem that the courses be made 'practical.'"[43] Initially, techni-cal courses were stressed so that NIA graduates would understand current laws and regulations and be able to resolve administrative problems.[44]

Although revised several times as a result of Michigan State's efforts, the NIA's curriculum did not mirror the one used in American universities. In particular, some MSUG members complained of too much French influence, emphasizing the legal dimension of administration. In 1957, Diem followed Michigan State's advice and officially extended the degree program from two to three years. The use of MSUG personnel allowed for extra classes, including some at night. Part of the instructional focus switched from juridical studies to public administration.[45] First-year students received a general grounding in such courses as introductory public administration, economics, accounting, constitutional law, and statistics. The fol-lowing year more specialization occurred. Students were divided into two sections: general public administration and economics and finance. Those in general public administration took classes in administrative sciences, including administrative problems, civil service, labor, and law. Those in economics and finance studied capital formation, economic planning, and Vietnamese agricultural and economic problems.[46]

The final two years of instruction consisted of both classroom study and field-work. Second-year students made brief trips to government field projects and took such courses as budget practices, human relations, organizational methods, and office management. Third-year students were separated into small groups and served as "administrative interns" for seven and one-half months both in the gov-ernment's provincial offices and in the central ministries in Saigon.[47] While in Saigon, fieldwork was augmented by seminars at the NIA, where the final semes-ter was spent studying public administration, economics, and finance.[48]

In 1958, the institute created a short-lived graduate program for advanced study in public administration. The MSUG's involvement in the venture began one year earlier when Thong requested advice on curriculum. Skeptical of such an ambi-tious undertaking, Michigan State argued that the NIA itself was still evolving and cautiously proposed further reforms to the current system. Acting Chief Adviser Howard Hoyt, head of the MSUG's police program, told Thong that Michigan State could not "comment on the advanced program without reference to the newly adopted, regular three-year program to which the higher studies must be supplementary and complementary, and with which they must be co-ordinated."[49] Although the university viewed it as an improvement, the new three-year curriculum failed to provide students with a liberal arts background. Michigan State firmly believed that an understanding of history, political science, psychology, and sociology in relation to Vietnam was critical to developing management-level civil servants.[50]

The NIA partly addressed this problem by offering social science courses at the graduate level.[51] Hoyt and MSUG chief adviser Wesley Fishel considered this a mistake, however, asserting that the institute's leadership had the curriculum arranged backward. In a May 1957 letter to Thong, Fishel argued that "[i]f students received a broad, general background in the regular program, the advanced courses could be of a truly graduate nature, reserved for intensive studies within relatively limited areas."[52] In addition, more "students would be able to take the general courses if they were offered in the regular three year program. Thus the greater number of students leaving the Institute would not have what Mr. Hoyt called 'serious blind' spots which might distort their perspective and lessen their comprehension of important factors directly related to their work."[53]

Although it opposed starting a graduate program so early in the NIA's existence, the university provided advice and teaching assistance. In November 1958, those MSUG members teaching graduate courses compiled a list of recommendations for Thong. Complaints included low student attendance, English-language problems, and the inability of busy civil servants to devote enough time to class work. The next month, Smuckler suggested to Thong that a joint NIA-MSUG committee be formed to examine the institute's difficulties, especially those related to curriculum.[54]

In December 1958, the committee conducted its first meeting. Chaired by Vice Rector Nghiem Dang, it was composed primarily of four members: two from the NIA, Truong-Ngoc-Giau and Tran-Van-Kien, and two from the MSUG, political scientist Dorsey and professor of public administration Montgomery. They met six times and prepared a report for the spring. The same problem that Fishel and Hoyt had documented—the lack of social science classes within the institute's three-year program—again received attention. The group concluded that while there was no longer an immediate need to produce technicians for specific jobs, the institute "must think of a more distant future, and train administrative cadres in basic theory solidly grounded in the experience of both Viet Nam and foreign countries, so that these administrators can subsequently apply theoretical knowledge in performing their duties in all situations."[55]

Diem agreed with the committee, and steps were taken to offer a well-rounded education at the NIA. Although Michigan State believed that a graduate program should eventually be created, they advised the Vietnamese president first to make the institute a four-year school. This would permit students capable of civil service management to integrate more liberal arts courses into their technical studies. In June 1960, Diem authorized a revision of the curriculum. Submitted by the joint NIA-MSUG committee, it retained a "practical emphasis," while enhancing the "social science approach." Changes included the addition of two sociology classes, one of which was taught by Michigan State faculty, and courses in research techniques and case-study methods. By the time Michigan State departed Vietnam in 1962, the NIA had adopted the American custom of semester-end written examinations and was contemplating offering course work in business administration, foreign policy, and journalism. One year later, the institute followed the university's advice and added a fourth year to the degree program.[56]

Increased enrollment and the introduction of public administration classes forced the NIA to make compromises when establishing a faculty. During its first two years of operation, from 1955–57, the number of students in its regular degree program more than doubled. Only one staff member held a Ph.D.; most were trained only in law and unqualified to teach the new courses. Forced to seek assistance, the institute drew upon personnel from Michigan State, the University of Saigon, and the South Vietnamese government. In some instances, the MSUG successfully adapted to the situation. For example, Michigan State adviser Wickert taught public personnel administration at the NIA from the "point of view of the Vietnamese."[57] His experience as an in-service training specialist provided him with unique insight. Interviewing Vietnamese supervisors at every level, he examined in depth a number of the government's ministries. In a recent discussion, Wickert commented that "I understood what the personnel problems really were. It isn't as though I was just talking about general personnel administration out of an American public administration textbook."[58]

Although the MSUG was the most qualified in public administration, its members often could not communicate with students. Most of the Michigan State contingent, even those who knew French and Vietnamese, found it necessary to use interpreters. MSUG economist John Hunter, who spoke French, recalled that it "was a big culture shock" for both instructor and student. Hunter observed that he had an interpreter "whose English was only moderately good" and "whose economics was practically nonexistent."[59] Until 1957, the MSUG carried the brunt of the load, teaching five or six courses a semester. By then, the NIA had enough part-time instructors to permit most Michigan State personnel to reduce their course load to one or two classes.[60]

Philosophical differences between the Americans and Vietnamese prevented Michigan State from having an immediate impact upon pedagogy. Vietnamese students and instructors were accustomed to the more formal French system, which emphasized uninterrupted lectures and did not permit questions. MSUG members lectured and, in stark contrast to the Vietnamese, utilized variations of the Socratic method, stressing classroom discussions and seminars. In addition, Michigan State professors assigned readings from the library, something the Institute's staff deemed unnecessary and thus discouraged. According to Hunter, testing also reflected some interesting variations. He remarked that during his first accounting exam the Vietnamese students were "peering around to see what everyone else was doing. It was a big surprise to them that they were supposed to do their own [work]."[61] Changes in teaching style were gradual. As NIA instructor Nguyen-Duy Xuan noted, "the permission granted to students to express their own views and raise questions in class constitutes a somewhat radical transformation of pedagogical techniques in a country whose professors are accustomed to speaking from the podium without interruption from a docile audience."[62]

Poor relations between Michigan State's staff and NIA faculty also slowed the change from French to American teaching methods. Educated under the French juridical system and set in their ways, institute personnel resisted working with and accepting advice from the MSUG. Michigan State political scientists Fox and Scigliano noted that the Vietnamese were "understandably unwilling to sit in on classes taught by MSUG professors, and almost equally reluctant to offer courses jointly with them."[63] Interaction between the two groups was limited, and efforts at bridging the cultural gap often failed. Neither formal American-Vietnamese faculty seminars nor informal social gatherings generated much interest. About twelve MSUG members shared offices with NIA counterparts, but this occurred primarily during the project's early years. Nguyen-Duy Xuan argued that incompatibility was common in technical-assistance programs. Initially, "language barriers, cultural differences, and disparities in the standard of living are the main obstacles. . . As impediments these gradually recede into the background," he said, "although they remain present, for most advisers and advisees."[64]

Socioeconomic and cultural differences between the Americans and the Vietnamese hampered the institute throughout the seven years of the project. MSUG academic instruction specialist Montgomery wrote then-Chief Adviser Smuckler that the NIA's Vietnamese faculty was disinclined to visit Michigan State personnel at home on an informal basis. Montgomery commented that this evidently "develops a sense of obligation which is uncomfortable to the professors whose housing is inadequate to return such invitations."[65] The result was often a tense working atmosphere. Fox and Scigliano contended that most "MSUG-NIA contacts were restricted to business matters or superficial conversations."[66] The notable exception, the institute's library staff, was part of the MSUG, trained and paid by them. By 1959, the Vietnamese were operating the library without Michigan State's supervision.[67]

The library's success suggested that the NIA's faculty shortage could be resolved with greater U.S. influence over training. Michigan State supported this position and wished to send young NIA staff members and graduate students abroad for Ph.D.'s in public administration and related fields. An overseas doctoral program did not begin until late 1958, however; Diem's government and the United States Operations Mission (USOM) feared that gifted Vietnamese would not return if allowed to leave South Vietnam for extended periods. Between 1958 and 1962 the MSUG and the NIA together selected seventeen doctoral candidates, two of them sponsored by the USOM and fifteen by Michigan State. Many of the students attended American universities, including Michigan State.[68] The first Ph.D. candidates returned to South Vietnam in the early 1960s. Only eight of the original seventeen came back to NIA service. Of these, several earned bachelor's and master's degrees, but just one, Nguyen-Duy Xuan, obtained a doctorate. Under the joint auspices of Michigan State and the NIA, Xuan attended Vanderbilt University, where he graduated in 1963 with a Ph.D. in economics. By 1964, two other overseas students had received doctorates, but they chose to work for other government agencies. Xuan was unique among the Ph.D. returnees in that he both taught at the NIA and was South Vietnam's minister of national economy.[69]

The MSUG overseas program for NIA instructors was a long-range solution to an urgent problem, the shortage of qualified South Vietnamese civil servants. Another option, designed to produce faster results, was the in-service training program for government employees. Following Vietnam's partition and France's departure in the mid-1950s, there were few knowledgeable Vietnamese to provide administrative stability. Since the early 1900s, the French had co-opted Vietnam's civil service, taking over the upper-level management positions and the education system. The result was a lack of skilled Vietnamese bureaucrats.[70]

In October 1954, Michigan State's original inspection team, concerned about the dearth of capable administrators, recommended prompt action. Although the mission acknowledged the necessity of academic instruction, it argued that "high priority should be put on immediate in-service training."[71] The university's first South Vietnam contract provided for a "comprehensive program of training for public officials and employees already in office."[72] Diem appeared to support this position but never officially decreed "government-wide in-service training."[73]

In this instance, the Vietnamese president proved more pragmatic than Michigan State did, and in 1957 the university revised its initial proposition. As Scigliano and Fox noted, none of South Vietnam's agencies were "equipped to coordinate or prepare materials for such a grandiose scheme—not to mention the unwillingness of higher level officials to submit themselves to training, even under the guise of discussion seminars or conferences."[74] The new, less ambitious in-service program shied away from government-wide training, limited its activities mainly to the NIA, and allowed Michigan State to play primarily an advisory role. Together, the institute and the MSUG created piecemeal an approach that included a night school, an in-service newsletter, and a number of special programs for central and local government agencies.[75]

The availability of MSUG professors to teach evening courses permitted the NIA to create a night school in 1955. Most of the students were low-level bureaucrats, attempting to advance professionally by preparing themselves for civil service exams. Although the school did not originate as an in-service program, it evolved into one by allowing inexperienced government employees to attend classes after work. Initially, about five hundred people registered each semester, with those living outside the capital able to take correspondence courses. Several thousand individuals completed training by the early 1960s; afterward, numbers tapered off. When Michigan State departed from Vietnam in 1962, a scant thirty to fifty students were enrolled in evening classes. The MSUG's *Final Report* concluded that the night school had "served a valuable purpose, but unless the program is revamped or revitalized it probably should be discontinued."[76]

Aside from teaching at the NIA's night school, Michigan State did not want to be directly involved with in-service training. The university strived to remain a consultant and to conduct special programs only on a limited basis. For example, the MSUG assisted the institute in establishing a newsletter for civil servants and oversaw the construction of twenty-one provincial training centers throughout South Vietnam.[77]

The *In-service Training Newsletter*, a monthly publication, was created in 1958 by the MSUG and the NIA in order to compensate for Diem's failure to establish a national in-service training program. With a distribution of about six thousand copies, the newsletter provided government employees with some cohesion by informing them of current events, including new public administration training methods, such as case studies. By 1962, the newsletter had become journal-length and was renamed *Progress*. After Michigan State left Vietnam in 1962, the newsletter was terminated for lack of funding.[78]

The university's most noteworthy in-service program, the Presidential Lectures, provided for a number of speeches to be given by MSUG members during the spring of 1956. Sponsored by Diem, the series dealt with public administration management. About three hundred upper- and middle-level bureaucrats attended. The first presentation, held at Saigon City Hall, was given by Walter Mode and dealt with the "role of management in government." Mode had been a public administrator at the U.S. Social Security Administration prior to joining the MSUG. His lecture was translated from English into Vietnamese and included a question-and-answer period. Diem placed a great deal of emphasis on the event, going so far as to invite the participants and audience to the presidential palace for tea. Closing the reception with a short talk, he asserted that "the inaugural session for this series of conferences should have been held here in the Palace itself. For it was I who prescribed this program of study and who requested the Michigan State University Group to take the responsibility for conducting it."[79]

In 1958, the MSUG submitted a number of proposals for central and local government in-service training. The most significant were: (1) that departmental and semiautonomous agencies should establish training centers and outline courses of action; (2) that the Civil Service Directorate should enhance in-service training by providing leadership, evaluations, and regulations; (3) that an interdepartmental council on in-service training should interlace differing programs; and (4) that the NIA should provide guidance and research and prepare training materials.[80]

Although the South Vietnamese government did not issue any official proclamations, various MSUG suggestions were implemented. To bring attention to in-service training, the NIA held informational seminars with the Ministry of Interior and the Civil Service Directorate. Delegates from all of South Vietnam's provinces attended three interdepartmental conferences. While there, they officially recognized the need for in-service training and outlined individual programs to be conducted by their own instructors. The NIA gradually developed a curriculum for producing in-service training instructors. Classes included a "government training officer seminar, two organization and methods courses for upper-middle management, and an organization and methods course for selected civil servants from twenty different agencies."[81]

Over 23,000 government employees took part in in-service training before Michigan State left Vietnam in 1962. Among those, 4,500 were either section chiefs or in higher positions. New training materials and centers were placed in the provinces. Innovative educational methods and a group of instructors capable of assisting other public officials emerged. The MSUG *Final Report* concluded that the in-service program, taken together, "can be judged relatively successful."[82]

Near the end of Michigan State's Vietnam project, the NIA was its major concern. A number of incidents in the early 1960s affected Michigan State's relationship with the school. The MSUG's last two chief advisers, Lloyd D. Musolf and Fox, became increasingly concerned about the university's status both in the institute and in Vietnam. Two developments in the fall of 1960 were particularly significant. An unsuccessful military coup against Diem and the MSUG's deliberation about future NIA needs created an atmosphere of tension at the institute. Twice in December Musolf anxiously wrote Michigan State officials. On the fifth, he corresponded with Smuckler, then associate dean of international programs. Musolf warned that communist activity had greatly increased after the coup, causing "apprehensiveness for staff members and dependents."[83] In addition, he noted that upper-level South Vietnamese officials "cannot get it out of their heads that the Americans staged the coup."[84] Ten days later, he informed Vietnam project coordinator Ruben Austin that "virtually all decisions about the future depend upon what is to happen at the NIA. The fate of the NIA, in turn, is bound up not only with our current study (as yet uncompleted) but also with the larger question of what is to happen in GVN [Government of Vietnam]."[85]

The following year a new crisis further threatened the Vietnam project's existence. Outraged over two articles written in 1961 by former MSUG members, Diem threatened to terminate Michigan State's technical-assistance contract. Stressing the regime's repressive tactics, these pieces had criticized the Ngo family's oligarchic rule and predicted its downfall within eighteen months.[86] The Vietnamese president informed Michigan State that its contract would not be renewed unless the university guaranteed him that returning professors would not produce negative publications about his government.[87]

An impasse over academic freedom emerged between Diem and Michigan State. In late 1961, Chief Adviser Fox informed James B. Hendry, the Vietnam project's acting coordinator, that a new contract would be to "the benefit of the NIA and Vietnam. I believe also that MSU scholars could profit considerably by being here."[88] Nevertheless, Fox was not willing to sacrifice the university's freedom of expression in order to remain in Vietnam. He noted that "[u]nless we can get some definite understanding in writing, however, regarding 1) the publications by returning MSUG members and 2) Censorship of our studies published by staff members while they are in Vietnam, I do not believe it would be in the interest of the University to continue here."[89] Michigan State's administration reached a similar conclusion, and the MSUG departed Vietnam in June 1962.

Michigan State considered the establishment of the institute its greatest achievement in Vietnam, one of long-term value. A research library and campus were built and the MSUG's and NIA's primary objective was realized: approximately 23,500 civil servants received instruction through the academic and in-service training programs. Employment records indicate that an NIA education was valued. Based on figures through 1964, a study by the NIA's Social Services Bureau maintained that about 53 percent of the institute's graduates served in the provinces as chiefs of provincial services, district chiefs, and deputy district chiefs. Other alumni worked as administrative bureau chiefs and service chiefs in the central government's various branches, including the Ministry of the Interior, the Ministry of Finance, and the Ministry of National Education. Moreover, some former students achieved the rank of director, secretary-general, and cabinet director.[90]

In contrast, Scigliano and Fox admitted that "a number of MSUG's achievements at the NIA have a Potemkin-village quality of appearing to be more substantial than they are."[91] The two Michigan State advisers argued that many of the institute's accomplishments were questionable because they reflected the MSUG's efforts rather than the NIA's. For instance, the library deteriorated after Michigan State's departure, and most of the institute's research and training materials were generated by the MSUG's American and Vietnamese staff.[92]

Two factors are principally responsible for the NIA's shortcomings: Diem's heavy-handedness and the poor quality of the NIA faculty. Scigliano commented that under Diem the institute became a "dumping place for civil servants not wanted elsewhere."[93] Most of these bureaucrats, intensely loyal to the Vietnamese president, feared angering him and did not want to implement any new ideas without his approval. In addition, the vast majority of the institute's teachers, trained under the legalistic French education system, resisted American concepts of public administration. Thus, many NIA staff members refused to work with MSUG members and chose the status quo, to the NIA's detriment.[94]

Still, despite the obstacles, Michigan State established a modern civil servant training school based on French juridical and American public administration methods. The Institute continued to operate after the MSUG's departure and survived Diem's overthrow in 1963 by dissident South Vietnamese generals. As NIA instructor and Vietnamese government official Nguyen Duy Xuan correctly concluded, "given the nature of the leadership and political environment at that time, looking back to what the MSUG accomplished mostly as adviser and sometimes as operator at the NIA, one can certainly say that it was a 'good job.'"[95]

NOTES

1. Ralph Smuckler, interview by author, 13 May 1993.

2. Ronald H. Spector, *Advice and Support: The Early Years of the U.S. Army in Vietnam, 1941–1960* (New York: Free Press, 1985), 278–81, 305, 366–67, 378–79.

3. *Final Report of the Michigan State University Advisory Group,* 1962, 24–25, Michigan State University Vietnam Project Papers, Michigan State University Archives and Historical Collections, East Lansing, Michigan (hereafter cited as Vietnam Project Papers); Nguyen Duy Xuan, "Technical Assistance to a Public Administration Institute: The Vietnam Case," in *Development Administration in Asia,* ed. Edward W. Weidner (Durham, N.C.: Duke University Press, 1970), 374.

4. Nghiem Dang, "The National Institute of Administration," in *Viet-Nam: The First Five Years, An International Symposium,* ed. Richard Lindholm (East Lansing: Michigan State University Press, 1959), 162.

5. *Final Report,* 23.

6. *Agreement between the Government of Vietnam and Michigan State University,* 14 April 1955, Vietnam Project Papers, box 628, folder 28, p. 7.

7. *Enabling Arrete of the NIA,* 9 August 1955, Vietnam Project Papers, box 666, folder 13, p. 1; Nguyen Duy Xuan, "Technical Assistance," 380.

8. *Enabling Arrete of the NIA,* 5.

9. Robert Scigliano and Guy H. Fox, *Technical Assistance in Vietnam: The Michigan State University Experience* (New York: Praeger, 1965), 30–31; Xuan, "Technical Assistance," 380.

10. Fred Wickert, interview by author, 20 July 1992.

11. Xuan, "Technical Assistance," 367–71; John D. Montgomery, *Aftermath: Tarnished Outcomes of American Foreign Policy* (Dover, Mass., and London: Auburn House Publishing Co., 1986), 56–57.

12. Xuan, "Technical Assistance," 376, 379.

13. *Final Report*, 40, 62–63; Michigan State University Lists of Participants, 1955–61, box 667, folder 52, Vietnam Project Papers, pp. 2, 6, 9, 11; Scigliano and Fox, *Technical Assistance in Vietnam*, 36; Participants in the United States, 27 March 1962, box 667, folder 52, Vietnam Project Papers; *Michigan State University Magazine*, MSU Department of Information Services, February 1956, p. 11, Michigan State University Archives and Historical Collections.

14. *Final Report*, 40; Xuan, "Technical Assistance," 379; Scigliano and Fox, *Technical Assistance in Vietnam*, 32; Guy H. Fox, "Commentary on Nghiem Dang," in *Viet-Nam: The First Five Years, An International Symposium*, ed. Richard Lindholm (East Lansing: Michigan State University Press, 1959), 170; Michigan State University *State News*, 16 February 1956; *Michigan State University Magazine*, MSU Department of Information Services, February 1956, 11.

15. Scigliano and Fox, *Technical Assistance in Vietnam*, 37.

16. *Final Report*, 40; Scigliano and Fox, *Technical Assistance in Vietnam*, 37; Xuan, "Technical Assistance," 379.

17. Scigliano and Fox, *Technical Assistance in Vietnam*, 37; *Final Report*, 40–41.

18. Montgomery, *Aftermath*, 56–59; Xuan, "Technical Assistance," 375–76.

19. Fox, "Commentary on Nghiem Dang," 170.

20. Scigliano and Fox, *Technical Assistance in Vietnam*, 33; *Final Report*, 39–41.

21. Luther Allen and Pham Ngoc An, *A Vietnamese District Chief in Action* (Saigon: Michigan State University Vietnam Advisory Group and the National Institute of Administration, 1961); John D. Donoghue, *My Thuan: A Study of a Delta Village in South Vietnam* (Saigon: Michigan State University Vietnam Advisory Group, 1961); Lloyd W. Woodruff, *My Thuan: Administrative and Financial Aspects of a Village in South Vietnam* (Saigon: Michigan State Vietnam University Group, 1961).

22. Scigliano and Fox, *Technical Assistance in Vietnam*, 33, 37–38; Gerald C. Hickey assisted by Mr. Bui Quang Da, *The Study of a Vietnamese Rural Community: Sociology* (Saigon: Michigan State University Vietnam Advisory Group, 1960); Lloyd W. Woodruff assisted by Nguyen Ngoc Yen, *The Study of a Vietnamese Rural Community: Administrative Activity*, 15.196, 15.197? (Saigon: Michigan State University Vietnam Advisory Group, 1960), 1:iv.

23. Montgomery, *Aftermath*, 57.

24. Ibid.

25. John D. Montgomery and the NIA Case Development Seminar, *Cases in Vietnamese Administration* (Saigon: Michigan State Vietnam University Group, 1959), 55–57; *Final Report*, 72.

26. Nguyen Dinh Thuan to Vu Quoc Thong, 24 September 1958, box 664, folder 33, Vietnam Project Papers; *Final Report*, 38.

27. Scigliano and Fox, *Technical Assistance in Vietnam*, 33; Dang, "National Institute of Administration," 164–65; Xuan, "Technical Assistance," p. 387n. 33; Shou-Sheng Hsueh, "Technical Co-operation in Development Administration in South and Southeast Asia," in Weidner, *Development Administration in Asia*, ed. Edward W. Weidner (Durham, N.C.: Duke University Press, 1970), 357–58.

28. Scigliano and Fox, *Technical Assistance in Vietnam*, 37–38.

29. Thuan to Thong, 24 September 1958, Vietnam Project Papers; *Final Report*, 38.

30. Fox, "Commentary on Nghiem Dang," 169.

31. Xuan, "Technical Assistance," 387–88.

32. Scigliano and Fox, *Technical Assistance in Vietnam*, 31; Fox, "Commentary on Nghiem Dang," 171–72; Xuan, "Technical Assistance," 380–81; *Final Report*, 22; Vietnamese Press Release, 5 November 1960, box 665, folder 93, Vietnam Project Papers, pp. 1–2; Vu Quoc Thong, Speech Dedicating the National Institute of Administration, 23 August 1962, box 666, folder 62, Vietnam Project Papers, p. 12.

33. Fox, "Commentary on Nghiem Dang," 171–72; Thong, Speech dedicating the National Institute, 12.

34. John T. Dorsey to David L. Wood, USOM Public Administration Adviser, 8 April 1958, box 663, folder 91, Vietnam Project Papers.

35. John T. Dorsey to Gordon Brown, 10 April 1958, box 663, folder 91, Vietnam Project Papers.

36. *Final Report*, 24–25.

37. Scigliano and Fox, *Technical Assistance in Vietnam*, 7.

38. Fox, "Commentary on Nghiem Dang," 170.

39. Ralph H. Smuckler to Dr. Vu Quoc Thong, 25 April 1958, box 663, folder 91, Vietnam Project Papers.

40. Lloyd D. Musolf to Ruben Austin, 21 January 1960, box 664, folder 38, Vietnam Project Papers.

41. Ngo Dinh Diem, Address by the President of the Republic at the Dedication Ceremony of the New Building of the National Institute of Administration, 23 August 1962, box 666, folder 56, Vietnam Project Papers; Frederick Nolting, Speech at the NIA Opening, box 666, folder 57, Vietnam Project Papers; Thong, Speech Dedicating the National Institute, 12.

42. *Final Report*, 24–25.

43. Fox, "Commentary on Nghiem Dang," 166.

44. Ibid., 166–67; Xuan, "Technical Assistance," 383–84.

45. Scigliano and Fox, *Technical Assistance in Vietnam*, 31–32; MSUG *Final Report*, 26–27; Xuan, "Technical Assistance," 375.

46. Scigliano and Fox, *Technical Assistance in Vietnam*, 32; *Final Report*, 29; Xuan, "Technical Assistance," 167; Fox, "Commentary on Nghiem Dang," 167.

47. John T. Dorsey to Stanley K. Sheinbaum, 2 January 1959, box 664, folder 37, Vietnam Project Papers.

48. *Final Report*, 27; Xuan, "Technical Assistance," 375.

49. Howard Hoyt to Vu Quoc Thong, 15 April 1957, box 664, folder 32, Vietnam Project Papers.

50. *Final Report*, 29; Wesley Fishel to Vu Quoc Thong, 20 March 1957, box 664, folder 32, Vietnam Project Papers; Hoyt to Thong, 15 April 1957; Fox, "Commentary on Nghiem Dang," 168; Dang, "National Institute of Administration," 163.

51. Hoyt to Thong, 15 April 1957, Vietnam Project Papers.

52. Wesley Fishel to Vu Quoc Thong, 20 May 1957, box 664, folder 32, Vietnam Project Papers.

53. Ibid.

54. John T. Dorsey to Nghiem Dang, 9 September 1957, box 664, folder 28; Ralph Smuckler to Vu Quoc Thong, 4 November 1958, box, 664, folder 33; Ralph Smuckler to Vu Quoc Thong, 1 December 1958, box 663, folder 81, all in Vietnam Project Papers.

55. *Report of the Curriculum Committee*, April 1959, box 663, folder 81, Vietnam Project Papers.

56. Scigliano and Fox, *Technical Assistance in Vietnam*, 31–32; *Final Report*, 27–29; Xuan, "Technical Assistance," 375–76; *Report of the Curriculum Committee*.

57. Wickert, interview.

58. Ibid.; Scigliano and Fox, *Technical Assistance in Vietnam*, 34–36; Fox, "Commentary on Nghiem Dang," 167–68; Nghiem Dang, *Vietnam: Politics and Public Administration* (Honolulu: East-West Center Press, 1966), 343.

59. John Hunter, interview by author, 22 July 1992.

60. Scigliano and Fox, *Technical Assistance in Vietnam*, 34–36.

61. Hunter, interview.

62. Xuan, "Technical Assistance," 384; Scigliano and Fox, *Technical Assistance in Vietnam*, 37; Hunter, interview.

63. Scigliano and Fox, *Technical Assistance in Vietnam*, 35.

64. Xuan, "Technical Assistance," 384–85.

65. John D. Montgomery to Ralph Smuckler, 6 November 1958, box 664, folder 37, Vietnam Project Papers.

66. Scigliano and Fox, *Technical Assistance in Vietnam*, 35.

67. Ibid., 34–35; Fox, "Commentary on Nghiem Dang," 167.

68. Fox and Scigliano, *Technical Assistance in Vietnam*, 36.

69. *Final Report*, 25; Scigliano and Fox, *Technical Assistance in Vietnam*, 36; Weidner, *Development Administration in Asia*, xviii.

70. *Final Report*, 23, 30.

71. *Report of the Special FOA Mission from Michigan State College for Public Administration, Public Information Police Administration, and Public Finance and Economics*, 16 October 1954, p. 32, box 42, folder 48, John A. Hannah Papers.

72. *Agreement between the Government of Vietnam and Michigan State University*, 14 April 1955, Vietnam Project Papers, p. 2.

73. *Final Report*, 33; Fox, "Commentary on Nghiem Dang," 170–71; Xuan, "Technical Assistance," 376–77; Scigliano and Fox, *Technical Assistance in Vietnam*, 33.

74. Scigliano and Fox, *Technical Assistance in Vietnam*, 29.

75. Ibid.; *Final Report*, 30–34.

76. Fox, "Commentary on Nghiem Dang," 171; *Final Report*, 29; Scigliano and Fox, *Technical Assistance in Vietnam*, 32.

77. *Final Report*, 33; Scigliano and Fox, *Technical Assistance in Vietnam*, 24, 30.

78. Xuan, "Technical Assistance," 377; *Final Report*, 31–32; Scigliano and Fox, *Technical Assistance in Vietnam*, 33–34.

79. *Times of Viet Nam*, 19 May 1956, box 657, folder 50, Vietnam Project Papers; Edward W. Weidner to Milton E. Muelder, 9 April 1956, box 628, folder 97, Vietnam Project Papers; Scigliano and Fox, *Technical Assistance in Vietnam*, 30.

80. *Final Report*, 32; Xuan, "Technical Assistance," 377.

81. *Final Report*, 32–33; Xuan, "Technical Assistance," 377.

82. *Final Report*, 33; Xuan, "Technical Assistance," 378.

83. Lloyd D. Musolf to Ralph Smuckler, 5 December 1960, box 664, folder 39, Vietnam Project Papers.

84. Ibid.

85. Lloyd D. Musolf to Ruben V. Austin, 15 December 1960, box 677, folder 26, Vietnam Project Papers.

86. Adrian Jaffe and Milton C. Taylor, "A Crumbling Bastion: Flattery and Lies Won't Save Vietnam," *New Republic*, 144 (June 1961); Frank C. Child, "Vietnam—The Eleventh Hour," *New Republic*, 145 (December 1961).

87. Ralph Smuckler to Guy Fox, 19 February 1962, box 657, folder 78, Vietnam Project Papers; Associated Press RTT Newscast, 17 February 1962, box 656, folder 72, Vietnam Project Papers.

88. Guy Fox to James B. Hendry, 9 November 1961, box 656, folder 72, Vietnam Project Papers.

89. Ibid.

90. Nghiem Dang, *Vietnam: Politics and Public Administration*, 339; Xuan, "Technical Assistance," 378, 392.

91. Scigliano and Fox, *Technical Assistance in Vietnam*, 38.

92. Ibid., 37–38.

93. Robert Scigliano, *South Vietnam: Nation Under Stress* (Boston: Houghton Mifflin Co., 1963), 65.

94. Scigliano and Fox, *Technical Assistance in Vietnam*, 37–38.

95. Xuan, "Technical Assistance," 386.

CHAPTER 4

MICHIGAN STATE UNIVERSITY AND POLICE ADMINISTRATION

"I studied law enforcement at Michigan State," commented a Thai police colonel as he guided "reckless, seasoned secret agent" Jerry Westerby through the countryside.[1] Westerby is the central character in spy novelist John le Carré's best-selling thriller *The Honourable Schoolboy* (1977). As this fictional passage indicates, Michigan State University's school of criminal justice became internationally recognized during the cold war era, training policemen from nations all over the world, including Germany, Indonesia, Korea, Thailand, and Vietnam.[2]

At the close of the Second World War, the U.S. government called on Arthur Brandstatter, chairman of Michigan State's law enforcement department, to undertake a ninety-day tour of Germany to inspect American and British occupation zones. Upon his return, U.S. officials approached Michigan State about instructing German policemen on public safety in democracies. Under the university's auspices, German officers stayed in the United States for three-month periods, receiving both academic and on-the-job training. The program lasted approximately four to five years, and afterward Michigan State's police administration division accepted additional foreign aid projects.[3]

The most significant of these projects, the Michigan State University Group (MSUG), assisted U.S. nation-building efforts in Vietnam. The MSUG's police administration staff provided material aid, training, and consultation to the South Vietnamese law enforcement agencies assigned to internal security: the sureté, municipal police, and civil guard. Michigan State achieved mixed results. The university staff successfully introduced modern criminology equipment and techniques, but also became involved in bureaucratic infighting with South Vietnam's president, Ngo Dinh Diem, and two American agencies, the United States Operations Mission (USOM) and the Military Assistance Advisory Group (MAAG). Michigan State disagreed with Diem and MAAG over the role of the

civil guard and clashed with the USOM over the development of a police communications system. In addition, the university faced accusations that from 1955
to 1959 it was a front for activities by the Central Intelligence Agency (CIA) in
South Vietnam.

As campus consultant to the MSUG's police administration branch,
Brandstatter recruited advisers to work in Vietnam. Eight men were in the first
MSUG police contingent. Not surprisingly, most came from Michigan law
enforcement agencies. Howard Hoyt, the group leader, was the former chief of
police in Kalamazoo. Other Michiganders included Midland police chief Richard
Rogers, Detroit police officer Gilbert Shelby, and State Police fingerprint expert
Corey Dymond. Jack Ryan, previously with the FBI, was a Michigan State professor of police administration. Charles Sloane had been a police examiner with the
New York State Department of Civil Service, Royce Williams was a radio engineer
from the Federal Civil Defense Administration, and Louis Boudrias was an
employee of the U.S. Central Intelligence Agency (CIA).[4]

When the MSUG arrived in Vietnam in May 1955, police operations were in
disarray. Using the national army, Diem had recently subdued the Binh Xuyen, a
gang of bandits and river pirates who ran gambling, prostitution, and the opium
trade in Saigon and its suburb, Cholon. Bao Dai, Vietnam's absentee emperor, had
sold the nation's police and security forces to the Binh Xuyen in 1953 to maintain
his hedonistic lifestyle on the French Riviera. Under the Binh Xuyen, law enforcement deteriorated. Many policemen were corrupted, broken equipment went unre-
paired, and facilities became outdated.[5]

Michigan State's effectiveness in police administration hinged on maintaining
Diem's favor and on its ability to dispense aid. Obsessed with security, the South
Vietnamese president routinely asked the United States for additional help for his
country's army and law enforcement agencies. During the MSUG's second contract
period, 1957–59, the greatest personnel increases occurred in police administration.
As early as October 1955, the International Cooperation Administration (ICA),
the U.S. government agency through which Michigan State held its Vietnam contract, approved additional MSUG police advisers, increasing the number to twenty-
two within two years. Although it did not provide the money itself, Michigan State
determined which security programs received funding. The USOM, the U.S. economic assistance bureau in Vietnam, lacked a public safety division until 1959 and
depended on MSUG experts to administer police projects.[6]

Progress in police training was inextricably tied to equipment distribution.
Michigan State police advisers were busiest from 1956 to 1958, when the bulk of

the law enforcement materials, such as firearms, tear gas, and fingerprint classification equipment, arrived. Language difficulties hindered classroom work. Since equipment demonstrations were more "concrete" and had a "lower cultural barrier to cross," they proved the most productive. A Michigan State faculty member and former FBI agent, MSUG training specialist Paul Shields, recalled that "[i]t was difficult to teach using an interpreter." One could not always determine from either "[l]ooking at their faces" or "the questions they asked" whether the Vietnamese were "getting the message."[7]

Philosophical and cultural differences between America and Vietnam made lecturing over law enforcement procedures useless. In situations where verbal communication and methodology were less important, training was more effective. Shields asserted that since the "Vietnamese were interested in anything technical," he avoided "anything political." Emerging from colonialism and facing an increasingly powerful communist insurgency, the sureté resented the export of the United States' "constitutional and legal norms" to South Vietnam. Shields noted that the sureté "had no trouble in accepting equipment such as revolvers, ammo, [and] communication equipment but being receptive to American democratic principles, that's something else." On a visit to the countryside, Shields was presented with the following scenario by a policeman. "[O]ne morning," the village flag pole "had a Viet-Cong flag flying" with a "hand grenade attach[ed] to it . . . If you pulled the lanyard it would blow up, how do you take it down, without 'losing face.'" Shields maintained that the "police were more interested in this kind of a dilemma," and not in American criminal justice concepts.[8]

For practical reasons, the MSUG focused more attention on the sureté than on either the municipal police or the civil guard. A national law enforcement agency also called the Vietnamese Bureau of Investigation (VBI), the sureté numbered some three thousand plainclothes officers and had jurisdiction in customs, immigration, revenue, and major criminal offenses. Its wide range of responsibilities necessitated that it obtain the bulk of the material aid and training. Sureté agents generally exercised greater authority than local policemen and in some cases doubled as city police chiefs. As a result, equipment intended for municipal forces often went to the VBI.[9]

Under French rule, the sureté did little criminal investigative work but concerned itself with "political control." Dennis J. Duncanson, who served on the British advisory mission in Vietnam from 1961 to 1965, asserted that the sureté "were never concerned with safeguarding the personal safety and private property of Vietnamese villagers," but primarily served as "a network of agents to watch over the interests of the French state." Furthermore, to achieve its ends, the VBI used extreme methods that violated civil rights.[10]

This attitude continued under Diem's regime. For example, MSUG Police Division Chief Hoyt told of an incident involving the police in Dalat, a city northeast of Saigon, in which a woman "became involved in a brawl at the market one morning. When the police were called, she tore one of the policemen's uniform. She was arrested, taken to headquarters and beaten so badly that she had to be hospitalized."[11] Although a number of MSUG personnel disagreed with using oppressive methods, the university was in South Vietnam at Diem's behest and could do little more than protest such cases of police brutality. Other Michigan State faculty members, such as MSUG Chief Adviser Wesley Fishel, rationalized the government's use of force, while some entirely avoided taking a political stand. Eventually, however, the issue would lead to the university's departure from Vietnam.

Diem approved of using repressive tactics to purge political rivals and communists from South Vietnam and enlisted Michigan State's aid in doing so. He began an Anti-Communist Denunciation Campaign in 1955, and one year later called "for the arrest and detention of persons deemed dangerous to the state," and suspended all habeas corpus laws.[12] As journalist Frances Fitzgerald noted, the edict "gave legal grounds for the creation of political prison camps throughout" South Vietnam.[13] In a 1959 article, "Vietnam's Democratic One-Man Rule," Fishel defended Diem's actions as necessary to the nation's survival. "It may seem paradoxical to some that out of strong governmental power may come individual freedom," he conceded. "But considering the context in which Vietnam exists, can one think of a more dependable method of assuring it?"[14] Critical of Fishel, Fitzgerald characterized the essay as an "heroic Houdini-like attempt."[15] Later scholars such as historian George C. Herring agreed with Fitzgerald's assessment and labeled Fishel an "apologist."[16]

In 1955, the sureté was extremely disjointed. Having defeated the Binh Xuyen that spring, Diem officially terminated the Binh Xuyen's control of the VBI and dismissed a number of dishonest officers. When the Binh Xuyen left, they took arms, ammunition, vehicles, and numerous files on people and political organizations. Although Diem rehired former agents discharged by the Binh Xuyen, the agency needed reorganizing, training, and material. Michigan State supplied these things.[17]

Two different MSUG departments assisted the VBI: a CIA group provided counterespionage (CE) training and a university-sponsored staff offered instruction in such areas as firearms and fingerprinting. Although housed by the Michigan State project, the CIA group was essentially autonomous. According to Scigliano and Fox, the unit "reported and [was] responsible only to the American Embassy in Saigon."[18] In a 1993 interview, former MSUG Chief Adviser Ralph Smuckler contradicted this statement, arguing that the university group maintained ultimate control over the intelligence agents. The truth lies somewhere in between. Most of the MSUG personnel were unaware of the CIA's activities. However, CIA adviser Boudrias valued Hoyt's opinion and notified the police leader of his progress. Boudrias also continually referred to himself as a "MSU Police Team member" in his reports.[19]

From 1955 to 1956, Boudrias established a "Clearing House," where South Vietnam's police forces went through a security check in order to ferret out "subversive elements" and also received training. Completed in fall 1955, the facility had a polygraph center, a microfilming department, and bugged prisoner cells. The first inmates were a married couple, "suspected of belonging to a subversive net operating in South Vietnam." The "husband claims to be stone deaf," Boudrias noted. "It is hoped that the microphones will prove that claim to be false."[20]

CE training progressed slowly. The one month allotted for preparing individuals either to spy or to be an interrogator was not enough, Boudrias argued. "I still am training photographers to cover . . . clandestine meetings of opposition agents, in order . . . to simplify our chore of identifying [them] . . . I have had many heartbreaks in that endeavor but I am not ready to give up."[21] To remedy the situation, Boudrias advocated creating a training facility like those used by the American Office of Strategic Services (OSS). Established during the Second World War, the OSS was the predecessor to the CIA. Boudrias asked Hoyt to present the idea to MSUG Chief Adviser Fishel, "with a view to bringing it to the attention of President Ngo Dinh Diem."[22] Adamant, Boudrias asserted that the CE department of the VBI desperately needed loyal individuals "thoroughly trained in the rather complicated niceties and modern techniques of this work." "The agents of the opposition have had a picnic of it, here," he asserted, "[and] it is high time to put a stop to their gnawing."[23]

Near the end of Boudrias's Vietnam tour in late 1956, CE training remained tenuous. Although the MSUG consolidated sureté operations at a former French army installation in Saigon, Camp des Mares, the CE headquarters there suffered from mismanagement. After visiting Camp des Mares in the fall, Boudrias noted, "I realized that despite the changes and promotions mentioned to me by the Director General of the VBI . . . the [c]ompound was in the same awful mess" as before. "I pointed out again to the General that as long as the present conditions remain, there was no use for me to even think of trying to establish" a CE division.[24]

Although Boudrias was skeptical of its capabilities, CE contributed to Diem's political purge of opponents and suspected communists. As Vietnamese specialist Joseph Buttinger pointed out, once South Vietnam's "military and police apparatus was sufficiently developed," a "manhunt" began in 1956 against the government's supposed enemies.[25] That September, Boudrias informed Hoyt that CE had started six new investigations that resulted in nine arrests.[26] Historian George C. Herring has written that the "Vietnam Bureau of Investigation rooted out suspected subversives in a manner that would have made J. Edgar Hoover blanch."[27] By 1956, Diem's administration had jailed at least 20,000 individuals, both "Communists and non-Communists."[28]

Most MSUG advisers were not involved with the VBI's CE department, but instead provided equipment instruction and helped establish law enforcement schools like the National Police Academy. Ralph Turner, a university faculty member and the MSUG's last police division chief, recently recalled that he "had no *personal* knowledge or experience with oppressive tactics used by the police." However, "[r]umours of such tactics abounded."[29] Tailoring curriculum and methods to each situation, MSUG training "took many forms, ranging from short, intensive courses of a few days or weeks to some lasting as long as six months."[30] The university's goal was for the Vietnamese quickly to assume responsibility for training. In the fall of 1957, the MSUG visited numerous provinces to demonstrate the use of new items such as revolvers, handcuffs, tear gas grenades, and tear gas masks. Hoyt happily observed that the MSUG found in a number of localities graduates from the National Police Academy being used as instructors. According to Scigliano and Fox, "[t]raining was MSUG's brightest and most lasting achievement in the police field."[31]

Working with Vietnam's head of internal security, Minister of Interior Bui Van Tinh, Michigan State established the National Police Academy. Located in Saigon, the school opened in the fall of 1955 and trained individuals from all South Vietnamese law enforcement agencies. In September, Tinh's office asked the MSUG to develop an intelligence test to evaluate the capabilities of incoming trainees. In particular, MSUG members and Vietnamese officials sought to determine which policemen were qualified to become training instructors. Most officers possessed an elementary school education, so Michigan State psychologist Fred Wickert created a sixth-grade-level examination with forty arithmetic and one hundred language questions.[32]

Constructing an appropriate language test proved difficult. Vietnamese is a peasant's language made up of monosyllables. Complicated abstract ideas are communicated by linking several monosyllables together. "Luckily," Wickert commented, *"Reader's Digest* was published in Vietnamese and so I could get items for a test."[33] The journal's Far East edition contained a multiple-choice vocabulary section. Often processed in less than a day, the test's results served two purposes: instructor selection and identification of individuals in need of remedial training.[34]

One hundred and thirty policemen initially took the exam; three-fifths were municipal officers, two-fifths sureté agents. Graduating from the academy in December 1955, the first group of students attended training sessions and classes for police instructors. MSUG advisers taught all courses, including homicide investigation, police records, firearms, investigation of auto theft, transportation of prisoners, public relations, crime scene investigation, fingerprint classification, driver training, traffic control, mechanics of arrest and raid, low-echelon radio maintenance, and audio-visual equipment maintenance. The academic program paralleled the one at Michigan State's School of Police Administration and Public Safety. The first year 606 policemen, representing thirty-seven of South Vietnam's forty provinces, attended the school. By 1958, the academy had graduated 1,537 and relocated to a larger facility at Rach Dua, outside of Saigon. At this time, the sureté assumed operation of the institute, and the MSUG devised new curricula. Emphasizing the need to produce more sophisticated policemen, American and Vietnamese officials added courses like criminal law and criminal prosecution, politics, and the history of Vietnam.[35]

After arriving in Saigon in late October 1955, Deputy Division Chief Ryan devoted most of his time to examining the VBI's administrative structure and procedures.[36] In November, he wrote his colleagues in Michigan that "[t]he magnitude of the job to be done in the police field here is staggering. I'm sure that the best we can hope to do in two years is to scratch the surface."[37] On a certain level Ryan was correct. Although reasonably successful in demonstrating the use of new equipment, the MSUG often failed to implement procedural reforms. As Scigliano and Fox noted, "[t]he Vietnamese were understandably more willing to be instructed in the use of tear gas or the maintenance of motor vehicles than to be told how they should gather evidence or treat suspects."[38] The week before Christmas, Ryan contacted Chairman Brandstatter about MSUG-VBI relations. "Last week, nearly all of us lectured a class of Vietnamese police instructors," he remarked. "I believe the thing went well." He observed, however, that the lower-level Vietnamese officers had "heard of our Negro problem, and they've been told by certain French that we would treat them exactly as we treat Negroes down South."[39] Ryan closed by saying that once the Vietnamese "get to know us, they find that this is not true."[40]

Geographically scattered throughout Saigon, VBI offices suffered from bureaucratic inefficiency. In 1956, Michigan State consolidated sureté operations at Camp des Mares, a former French army installation in Saigon. Police Division Chief Turner noted that once the "[s]ureté was gathered together in a central location work progressed with fewer inconveniences."[41] Using U.S. funds, the MSUG renovated the camp's existing structures and constructed new ones to house an interrogation center, detention center, vehicle maintenance garage, identification center, crime detection laboratory, and communications center. Camp des Mares also accommodated a VBI officers and firearms school where Michigan State advisers and MSUG-trained sureté instructors taught.[42]

In addition to supervising Camp des Mares's physical plant construction, the MSUG also outfitted and trained personnel for the identification bureau, crime detection laboratory, and communications system. The university replaced obsolete French methods and outdated equipment. In each case, Michigan State was partly successful.

Between 1955 and 1958 a Central Identification Bureau emerged at Camp des Mares. Michigan State, along with the sureté and South Vietnam's other security forces, established the bureau, which contained a fingerprint division and a National Identity Card program (NIC) for South Vietnamese citizens. Police files needed revamping because the Binh Xuyen had confiscated many of the reports when they departed, and no central repository existed. Written in longhand and stored in poorly ventilated rooms, criminal records (including fingerprint cards) were hard to access and in some instances "moldy." According to a 1957 Michigan State report, the filing system "contained too much duplicated information and searches were difficult."[43]

Vietnam utilized two different fingerprint classification systems, the Parisian and Pottecher, which most Western law enforcement agencies considered antiquated. The police kept fingerprints at four different locations: one each at Hue and Dalat, and two in Saigon. Hue and Dalat employed the Parisian system, a simple procedure designed for a small number of cards. Yet Vietnam's files numbered over four million. One Saigon office used the Pottecher system, originated about 1900 in France, and the other used both the Parisian and Pottecher. Neither system permitted easy exchange of information with Southeast Asia's major law enforcement departments, which used the Henry system.[44]

In late 1955, Michigan State assisted the Vietnamese in modernizing their fingerprint operations through adoption of a variation of the Henry system. Introduced in 1901 by Sir Edward Richard Henry of England's Scotland Yard, the procedure separated fingerprints into eight types of identification patterns. Simpler and more comprehensive than previously used procedures, the technique became the generally accepted form for classifying fingerprints, and most of the world's police forces quickly adopted it. Consequently, switching to the Henry system streamlined Vietnam's record keeping and made their records compatible with those of Southeast Asia's major security agencies.[45]

Initially, the MSUG trained thirty police technicians in the English language, filing, typing, and standard fingerprinting. From this corps, a larger staff evolved that filed and classified about 16,000 fingerprint cards for the VBI's Central Identification Bureau. Nevertheless, resistant to change, the Vietnamese preferred the Parisian and Pottecher systems to the Henry system. Citing the compatibility argument, Michigan State urged Vietnamese officials to make the conversion. Turner recalled that MSUG's police advisers wanted to "get Vietnam in the mainstream" by enabling Saigon's police to communicate with counterparts in Singapore and Hong Kong.[46] Michigan State argued that using the Henry system would make it easier for the police to combat such regional problems as drug trafficking.[47]

University lobbying efforts proved effective in late 1957 when Diem ordered the nation's police forces to use the Henry system. The government placed the Dalat, Hue, Saigon, and Immigration Service files under the director general of the sureté, Lt. Colonel Pham Xuan Chieu. To avoid disrupting police activities, however, the MSUG and VBI only gradually eliminated the Pottecher and Parisian classification systems.[48]

Michigan State experienced difficulties in implementing the Henry system. Classification and filing inaccuracies abounded. Although obstacles often hamper many new programs, a two-year lull, from 1958–60, during which the MSUG could not find a fingerprint specialist, compounded the problem. Corey Dymond, the first MSUG adviser to work with the Central Identification Bureau, was a fingerprint expert from the Michigan State Police. Arriving in August 1955, he conducted training sessions on the Henry system. Two years later he produced a textbook on the topic and then departed Vietnam. During 1958, Everett A. Chamberlin provided "intermediate supervision" of the program. The next adviser, Elmer Adkins, arrived two years later. A former FBI agent and an identification specialist with the Miami Beach, Florida, Police Department, Adkins inspected the fingerprint files and found numerous mistakes. In a 1960 status report, Turner noted that some of the classification difficulties were "due to carelessness and improper supervision by the Vietnamese. Other mistakes seem to be . . . errors due to having been given wrong information, or having interpreted some instruction in an incorrect manner."[49] In response, Adkins conducted retraining and made corrections. Starting in 1961, the MSUG and the Central Identification Bureau accelerated conversion of the Parisian and Pottecher systems into the Henry. Using the new procedure, Vietnamese police reclassified about 600,000 fingerprint cards.[50]

To help ferret out suspected communist agents living in South Vietnam, the Central Identification Bureau in 1958 created a National Identity Card program (NIC). Michigan State provided advice and equipment to this project, which furnished an ID for every Vietnamese citizen eighteen years of age and older. Diem's government requested Michigan State's assistance in this project because the current IDs, made of photographs and mimeographed pieces of paper, disintegrated easily. Turner has recalled that the NIC was the only project that the United States did not "ram down the throat of the Vietnamese."[51] In 1959, with a limited amount of equipment, four "mobile teams" started operating in Saigon and surrounding provinces.[52]

As adviser to the Central Identification Bureau, Elmer Adkins oversaw NIC activities. To facilitate matters, he initiated plans for rapid expansion of the bureau and obtained the necessary equipment (cameras, flashguns, tripods, filing cabinets, typewriters, and plastic lamination machines). In a July 1960 report, Turner complimented the new adviser's efficiency. He remarked that "[e]ver since his arrival, Adkins has taken a firm hold of this project and things seem to be moving quite well." Headway was being made "in Saigon with teams handling the city precinct by precinct."[53] The NIC captured a number of communists who provided military intelligence. In one case, Adkins reported, the interrogation of a prisoner led to a "military operation, killing 3 VC and capturing 2 MAS machine-guns, 1 Chinese compass and propaganda materials."[54] By June 1962, a total of 3,023,947 identification cards had been issued. According to the MSUG's *Final Report*, this "directly resulted in the arrest of 50 Viet Cong and 163 military deserters, and has revealed 4,440 instances of faulty or erroneous identity papers."[55]

NIC success prompted the Viet Cong to respond violently. By 1959, the mounting insurgency threatened Diem's regime and hindered the ID program's effectiveness. Poor security conditions "repeatedly delayed" NIC operations. Communist agents intimidated the rural population, stole IDs, and then made

Wesley R. Fishel (left) exercised great power in South Vietnam during the mid-1950s because of his friendship with Ngo Dinh Diem and because of American concern over communist expansion in Southeast Asia.

John Hannah (second from left) took a nineteen-month leave of absence from Michigan State during 1953–54 to serve as President Dwight Eisenhower's assistant secretary of defense for manpower and personnel. Throughout his career, Hannah relished his strong ties to the federal government.

In the wake of Diem's request for aid from the United States, a delegation of Michigan State administrators and faculty embarked in 1954 on a whirlwind tour of the Far East to determine whether a technical-assistance program would benefit both the university and South Vietnam. Meeting with the American Ambassador in Saigon, Donald R. Heath (fourth from left), were Charles C. Killingsworth, Arthur Brandstatter, Edward W. Weidner, Wesley R. Fishel, and James H. Denison.

Wesley Fishel and his family took up permanent residence in Saigon in March 1956, when he became head of the MSUG Project.

Like other U.S. policy makers, Fishel (right) conceded that Diem had faults, but supported
him because he was considered the best—and possibly only—choice to represent American
interests in the post-World War II period.

President Diem returned to the Michigan State campus on 15 May 1957, and addressed some four thousand faculty and students. He termed the visit "a home-coming for me—a very pleasant and warming home-coming."

Michigan governor G. Mennen Williams proclaimed 15 May 1957 "Ngo Dinh Diem Day" to celebrate the Vietnamese president's return to the Michigan State campus. The governor presented the honoree a bow tie in honor of the occasion.

Michigan State president John A. Hannah enthusiastically endorsed the MSUG because it combined his love of institution building and his dislike of communism. Here he meets with President Diem during a visit to Saigon.

MSUG project members Guy Fox (left) and Stanley Sheinbaum (center) attended a Vietnamese Constitution Day celebration in Saigon, 26 October 1958.

Although critics later alleged that members of the MSUG team enjoyed an opulent lifestyle in Saigon, the personnel typically lived in more modest accommodations, such as this two-bedroom duplex.

Wesley Fishel with General William C. Westmoreland.

Like John Hannah and Hubert H. Humphrey (front row, center), most Americans believed the "menacing cloud of communism" threatened to engulf the world and had to be contained.

Following Hannah's resignation in 1969, Walter Adams served as interim president of Michigan State. Years later Adams observed, "In my view we haven't had a president since John Hannah—of his stature. But the Vietnam project, I think, was a sad mistake."

The exposé of the MSUG project that appeared in *Ramparts* magazine fueled the antiwar movement on the campus at East Lansing.

Interim president Walter Adams, in his trademark bow tie, marched at the head of a campus rally for peace, November 1969.

counterfeit ones. Following a 1960 MSUG field trip to Vinh Long, an area south-west of Saigon, the province chief was assassinated. For a period afterward, trips to that area were prohibited. The MSUG *Final Report* stated that the communists threatened entire villages with reprisals, used hand grenades to ambush identity card teams, and killed security agents. Adkins expected the NIC to provoke the Viet Cong. In the spring of 1962 he noted that "[t]hings are getting pretty hot out this way and I don't mean the weather. I think we are beginning to hurt them and retaliation is inevitable . . . but we'll keep plugging."[56]

In July 1959, the USOM created its own public safety department and began assuming the MSUG's police responsibilities. One year later, the MSUG's main concerns were the NIC and the sureté crime laboratory. In April 1962, 5,732,099 IDs still needed to be issued, but by this time Adkins was primarily a USOM employee. Although the NIC experienced some success, Scigliano and Fox have argued that the program was limited by "guerrilla interference in the sizable areas under strong Communist influence and was never carried to completion."[57]

In 1955, Michigan State found the VBI's Saigon crime laboratory run down and the Vietnamese personnel unskilled. MSUG Deputy Division Chief Ryan labeled the facility a "mess," and remarked that the "equipment they have to work with was old when Leif Erickson landed in North America."[58] Left unattended, materi-als like the photographic equipment had been spoiled by fungus and bacteria in Vietnam's tropical climate. The lab's primary and secondary power sources were outdated and unreliable. Before departing Vietnam in 1955, French technicians had failed to train replacements; the Vietnamese were thus unable to operate the facility.[59]

To remedy the situation, Michigan State selected a Vietnamese student for lab training in East Lansing and sent to Vietnam two criminalistics consultants from the university faculty: Ralph Turner and Joseph Nicol. Turner went to Saigon in the summer of 1956 and developed a guide specifying the lab's training and equip-ment needs. Based on his suggestions, the MSUG sent ten VBI agents between 1958 and 1960 to the United States for instruction. In late 1959, furthermore, Michigan State began renovating Camp des Mares's old jail, with U.S. funding, to house the new crime detection laboratory.[60]

Nicol's arrival in Vietnam in July 1960 coincided with the completion of con-struction of the laboratory. He conducted in-service training, held instructional seminars for technicians, and oversaw installation of equipment, which included such items as a comparison microscope and a bullet recovery box. Nicol noted that the "quarters at Camp des Mares should be sufficient for any foreseeable future

73

growth . . . It is in the area of laboratory personnel that maximum attention should be given."[61] The lab contained the essentials for criminalistics investigation, but additional "stateside training" was necessary in order to introduce more sophisticated equipment. "Thus in one sense of the word," Turner concluded, "the laboratory project can be regarded as completed, if one is not too demanding insofar as excellence and quality of work are concerned."[62]

Michigan State's work on a police communications system proved more troublesome than the establishment of a crime laboratory. Working primarily with the sureté and Saigon's municipal police, the MSUG established a nationwide communications network, which included constructing and equipping various installations in South Vietnam. In addition, the MSUG helped Diem's administration prepare for the 1957 Colombo Powers Conference, a convention at which representatives from twenty-one countries and colonies of "free Asia" met from 7–23 October in Saigon to evaluate the region's economic and technical needs. Michigan State supervised police communications from 1955 to 1960, when the USOM's newly created Public Safety Division assumed control.[63]

In 1955, Vietnam had limited communication capabilities. The Indochina War between France and the Vietminh had ravaged facilities. The combatants demolished a number of telephone centers and severed transmission lines. Few Vietnamese cities enjoyed extensive phone service, radio operations were crude, and most provincial capitals had electricity "only from sunset to sunrise." Communication took place "frequently by courier."[64]

Radio engineer Royce Williams, the first MSUG communications specialist, worked in Saigon for less than three months. In January 1956, he died of a kidney disease. His position remained vacant for just over a year and a half. Lyman M. Rundlett arrived in April 1957 and was joined seven months later by Jerome H. Hemmye, an electrical engineer and a Michigan State faculty member. The bulk of the MSUG's communications activity occurred during their tenure.[65]

Following his arrival, Rundlett served as a consultant to Vietnamese officials preparing for the Colombo Powers Conference. Washington cautioned Michigan State to remain in the background because U.S. policy makers wanted to portray the event as "a Vietnamese affair."[66] Fishel, however, advised Diem on various preparations for the conference, including housing, immigration, and sightseeing for guests. The university also sent one of its senior conference specialists, Milton Hagelberg, to organize public relations training for local conference workers. As host, Diem erected a two-story convention hall and doubled security patrols. Rundlett flew to the United States and Singapore to assist in the purchase of police radios (four base and forty mobile units) and an electronic device that provided multilingual translations to delegates simultaneously. In addition, he helped expand telephone service for the event and supervised installation of the Saigon municipal police's radios. In his report to Chief Adviser Fishel, Police Division Head Hoyt remarked that the police "equipment was delivered and installed on schedule and functioned throughout the conference without difficulty."[67] Three years later, Turner noted that the radios were still "working quite well," but that further improvement depended "upon the amount of money which either the American [a]id program or GVN wishes to put into the system."[68]

The last phase of the MSUG's communications project, during 1959–60, proved controversial. Turner commented that during this period the group was "attacked, criticized, questioned, [and] probed."[69] The university became embroiled in the Colegrove congressional investigations and subsequently had a falling-out with the USOM. Also during this period, however, much-anticipated teletype equipment arrived, linking South Vietnam's southern, central, and northern regions at Saigon, Banmethuot, and Hue. The teletype hookup was a significant advancement that offered police a means of sharing information quickly.[70]

During the summer of 1959, journalist Albert M. Colegrove wrote six articles for the Scripps-Howard newspapers alleging that gross financial waste and corruption permeated U.S. nation building in Vietnam. According to historian David L. Anderson, "[m]uch of Colegrove's evidence was vague and circumstantial." However, "appearing in the wake of the 1958 best-selling novel *The Ugly American*, which purported to unmask the hypocrisy of U.S. policy in developing areas," the columns prompted a congressional inquiry.[71]

Although the 1959 investigation produced no real evidence to support Colegrove's accusations, an incriminating incident surfaced that same year involving the MSUG communications project. The so-called Rundlett Affair placed the university in a compromising position that detracted from its efforts. In late October, Scripps-Howard writer Jack Steele reported that U.S. Justice Department officials were pursuing allegations of misconduct on the part of Michigan State's Rundlett. Allegedly, he had contracted with Motorola Communications and Electronics, Inc., to provide Vietnam's police radio equipment in exchange for financial "kickbacks." Standard Electric A.S. of Copenhagen, a subsidiary of International Telephone and Telegraph Co., charged that the bidding specifications were written so that only Motorola could meet them.[72]

The International Cooperation Administration (ICA), the U.S. agency through which Michigan State held its Vietnam contract, asserted that the university was "blameless" in the affair. However, the episode damaged the MSUG's reputation, affecting its relationship with the USOM. Although Rundlett was not charged, he resigned from the MSUG, reportedly for "personal reasons," and left Vietnam in June. The incident exacerbated an already tense situation by appearing to give Colegrove's charges some validity. As a result, the USOM became resentful and suspicious of the MSUG. Seven months later, Turner wrote Brandstatter that he understood that "back in East Lansing all parties concerned do not view the Rundlett matter as very serious," but in Vietnam the "affair has put us on one hell of a spot and it will take careful timing along with superior personnel to help us work out of this one."[73]

Relations between the MSUG and the USOM deteriorated because of the Scripps-Howard episode, as well as professional differences over the communications project. In 1959, the USOM established its own Public Safety Division (PSD). According to a March 1960 Michigan State report, conflicts were inflamed by both personality differences and overlapping responsibilities. Turner contended that USOM director Arthur Z. Gardiner probably harbored ill feelings toward the university because he felt that Ryan had provided reporters and congressional investigators with information concerning the Colegrove incident. MSUG campus police consultant Brandstatter maintained that "I am thoroughly convinced that Frank Walton, Chief of the Public Safety Division in Saigon, is embarked on a program of harassment and an attempt to embarrass the university program, if possible."[74]

Having established its own police division, the USOM wished to replace the MSUG. Turner recalled that USOM PSD director Byron Engle was "in direct competition with Brandstatter to recruit" police advisers.[75] In Vietnam, the two police agencies also were in conflict. Michigan State disagreed with PSD's decision to create a more complex telecommunications system integrating the civil guard with the sureté and the Saigon municipal police. According to Turner, the USOM cited university objections to the plan as instances of noncooperation. In June 1960, MSUG chief adviser Lloyd D. Musolf wrote project coordinator Ruben V. Austin that it distressed him that Gardiner believed "there is a basic problem in USOM-MSUG relations centering in the police group of MSUG . . . One might say that both Gardiner and [Acting USOM Director] Coster seem ready to accept very flimsy evidence as a basis for the charge of noncooperation."[76] Moreover, Musolf commented that Emil Simek, one of the PSD's two communications advisers, informed Michigan State that Walton instructed him and his colleague "not to associate with" MSUG communications consultant Jerome H. Hemmye.[77]

After Hemmye completed his service in October 1960, the ICA phased out the MSUG's role in the communications program and the PSD took over.[78]

The establishment of a nationwide teletype system connecting Vietnam's three primary regions was Michigan State's most significant contribution in communications. The university's assistance during the Colombo Powers Conference was also of some importance. The MSUG might have accomplished more, but several difficulties hampered the project, including personnel problems, congressional investigations, and bureaucratic infighting.

In most instances, like the communications project, Saigon's police department secured more financial assistance than other local law enforcement agencies, but it received proportionately less than the sureté. Traffic control was an exception. Population growth necessitated that the MSUG focus its efforts almost entirely on Saigon. In less than a decade, the city's number of inhabitants tripled, from 600,000 to 1,800,000.[79]

Like any rapidly developing overcrowded city, Saigon experienced "chaotic traffic conditions." In 1957, a total of 10,378 accidents occurred there, involving cars, trucks, pedicabs, bicycles, motorbikes, and horse-drawn carriages. Michigan State recruited two consultants who, for various reasons, could not carry the project to completion. The first, traffic engineer Joseph S. Marlow, remained in Vietnam for less than a year because of health reasons. His replacement, Jerome D. Franklin, a traffic engineer from Grand Rapids, Michigan, worked in Saigon from 1957 to 1959 and volunteered to come back a second time, but "inordinate delays" by the Vietnamese government in trying to define his future services prevented his return. For a number of months, Vietnamese officials vacillated over whether to retain a traffic engineer. In April 1959, Nguyen Dinh Thuan, the secretary of state at the presidency, terminated the position. Yet, one month later, Vietnam's Department of Public Works again requested Franklin's assistance. Having already returned to the United States, however, he declined.[80]

Although the university suffered from personnel difficulties, progress occurred during Franklin's tour of duty. Under the MSUG's guidance, Saigon's municipal police and Public Works Department painted traffic lines, created one-way streets, and installed new automatic traffic signals. In late 1957, division head Hoyt remarked that the "first thru-streets in the history of Saigon were approved by the [m]ayor and put into effect. Paint received under the American [a]id program has been used to further mark streets and for zebra cross walks."[81] Conducting training courses in public relations, courtesy, and traffic control, the MSUG encouraged the municipal police to act professionally and treat the public politely. Scigliano

77

and Fox noted that university efforts resulted in a "marked improvement in the deportment of the Saigon police."[82] After Franklin departed Vietnam in April 1959, the USOM's Public Safety Division began planning for its own traffic advisory program.[83]

In contrast to its work with the sureté and Saigon's municipal police, Michigan State's association with the civil guard proved a failure. In April 1955, Diem officially organized the guard into a sixty-thousand-man paramilitary organization. An impasse emerged a year later when the MSUG, going against Diem and the MAAG's wishes, tried to alter the guard's role. Michigan State wanted to convert the organization into a civil agency operating on the village level and equipped with simple weaponry. Comparing it to a state police outfit in the U.S., the MSUG advocated training it to handle burglaries and homicides in Vietnam's countryside. The Vietnamese president and the MAAG wanted to maintain the guard as a paramilitary unit capable of exercising national police duties and providing support for the South Vietnamese Army. The result of the conflict, historian Ronald Spector noted, was bureaucratic infighting and unpreparedness when insurgency threatened the South in 1959.[84]

Initially, Michigan State itself seemed split over the guard issue. In November 1955, MSUG political scientist Ralph Smuckler and Deputy Division Chief Ryan presented differing views. Having visited the settlements of Tra Vinh, Vinh Long, and Catho early in the month, Smuckler observed that the guard generally acted as a military group, patrolling villages and manning guard posts. Asserting that this was probably "due to the fact that the need at present is for semi-military rather than police units," he held that the guard "is doing a big job . . . pretty well given their obvious personnel and equipment limitations."[85] In contrast, Ryan appeared critical of Diem's regime, commenting that Vietnamese officials treated the guard "like a bast—d at a family reunion."[86] The government wanted "a strong gendarmerie, under army control," he said, "with no civilian rural police at all. This matter will have to be decided by Diem himself, since he still hasn't learned or doesn't want to delegate authority." In closing, Ryan commented that "[a]nyone who says that this country is a true democracy at this moment is kidding himself!"[87]

In late 1957, anxiety over the guard's future increased. Specifically, Diem and the top U.S. officials in Vietnam, the Country Team, including Ambassador Elbridge Durbrow, MAAG chief Lt. General Samuel Williams, USOM director Leland Barrows, and MSUG division head Wesley Fishel, expressed growing dissatisfaction. In mid-October, Williams informed the U.S. Pacific commander in chief, Admiral Felix B. Stump, that Diem did not believe Michigan State understood the concept of a civil guard.[88] Moreover, Williams told the admiral of the Vietnamese president's complaint that "MSU and USOM seemed to think that the same organizations could be used in Vietnam as the ones being used in Michigan and this was not valid reasoning. With all the piracy and terrorism in areas of Vietnam, this was not peace but war."[89]

Like Diem, the MAAG disliked Michigan State's handling of the guard. In December, Colonel James I. Muir, a MAAG adviser assisting South Vietnam's Ministry of Defense, warned Williams that the MSUG "knows no more about the [c]ivil guard than do we—perhaps not as much." Muir criticized university indecision over the guard's organizational structure. The MSUG "once recommended that C.G. [c]ompanies should consist of 150 men instead of two hundred, but only because 'New York State Police have companies of 150 men, and that seemed like a good figure.'" In closing, he labeled working with Michigan State a "frustrating" experience.[90]

Unable to compromise in 1957, the Country Team suspended support of the guard. Large-scale aid did not resume until two years later, when the PSD assumed control of the operation. During that interval, Michigan State continually lobbied to make the guard a civil police agency. The university also distributed limited amounts of aid, such as one hundred U.S. jeeps, and established two training facilities, a noncommissioned officers school at Quang Trung, near Saigon, and a high officers school south of the capital at Cape St. Jacques. Although they do not describe course offerings, the MSUG records maintain that roughly 19,000 guardsmen graduated from Quang Trung and 344 from Cape St. Jacques.[91]

The years from 1957 to 1959 were a period of deceptive calm in South Vietnam. Security conditions had improved as remnants of "dissident guerrilla activity were being wiped out and it was possible to travel the length and breadth" of the country safely.[92] In this environment, Michigan State "continued to press for the creation of a truly democratic and civil police agency."[93] By 1959, however, insurgency again imperiled the South. The "[r]eported deaths of Viet Namese, both civil and military increased from 30–40 per month in 1958 to nearly 400 per month during the last quarter of 1960."[94] As a result of bureaucratic delays and indecision, the guard was not prepared to handle the situation. In retrospect, a number of MSUG advisers admitted misjudging the situation. In February 1961, Brandstatter wrote: "I am not certain whether I would have agreed in 1958 or 1959 that the Civil Guard should have been transferred to the military forces of Vietnam, but I certainly would have modified its training and provided the arms and equipment necessary to cope with the Viet Cong."[95] Agreeing with him, Turner remarked in a 1992 interview that "in hindsight, obviously the Vietnamese were right" in wanting a paramilitary unit.[96]

Neither the MSUG nor the PSD, however, had the training to undertake such an endeavor. Turner visited PSD chief Walton several years after Michigan State had departed Vietnam. Walton was a former student of Turner at the University of Southern California, and the two had remained friends. Turner jokingly noted that the civil guard situation frustrated his former pupil so much that Walton ended up "talking to himself." The PSD advised the guard for only approximately sixteen months. In November 1960, the MAAG assumed control of it.[97]

During the early 1960s, relations between Diem and Michigan State became increasingly strained. In the Vietnamese president's mind, Michigan State had probably outlived its usefulness. The university's refusal to train the guard as a paramilitary unit and the publication of two articles written by former MSUG members prompted Diem in 1962 not to renew Michigan State's technical assistance contract. The two articles castigated Diem's antidemocratic methods, prophesied his overthrow in less than two years, and chided other MSUG members for not speaking out against him.[98]

MSUG police advisers did not write the articles. From the project's beginning, however, Ryan had been privately critical of Fishel and his friend Diem. In June 1956, he wrote Brandstatter: "I don't trust Fishel . . . and if ever Diem was pitched-out, Mr. Fishel's affiliations with that gentleman would really hurt us with the new team."[99] Five months later, Ryan noted that MSUG and USOM members believed "brother Fishel is unqualified . . . He lacks stability, wisdom, and tact. He is too closely associated with Diem," which could damage U.S. efforts because "Diem is not as popular as American and Vietnamese propaganda would have us believe."[100]

Hoyt also confided to Brandstatter that Fishel's self-importance undermined operations in Vietnam. In the fall of 1957, he remarked that Fishel "likes to play policeman, junior 'G' man, or junior cloak and dagger operator. He has a ready answer for any situation involving police. . . .We are constantly running into cases where he has given advice contrary" to the MSUG's recommendations.[101] Fishel's close friendship with Diem allowed him to intervene in a wide range of matters, annoying the Country Team. He was scheduled to leave Vietnam in April 1958; until then, Hoyt anxiously tried to avoid an incident. He told Brandstatter that "we are sitting on the lid of the powder keg as tightly as we can and hope to keep it from blowing before Wes's departure date."[102] Before returning to the United States, however, Fishel offended both Ambassador Durbrow and General

Williams. In one instance, he "took it upon himself" to arrange a meeting between Diem and the ambassador's houseguest, American singer Marian Anderson. On another occasion, Fishel informed Williams that the Vietnamese president had told him that he was receiving bad military advice and that South Vietnam's Army "stunk."[103]

Fishel's replacement as chief adviser, Ralph Smuckler, served the MSUG from 1955 to 1956 as research coordinator and acting and assistant chief adviser. In 1958, the dean of international programs, Glen Taggart, instructed Smuckler to end the MSUG's police responsibilities. According to Smuckler, Taggart informed him that "everybody was uncomfortable with the notion that we had too many people in police administration who were not from our own campus."[104] Because the police project's demands necessitated that Michigan State recruit from outside the school, only four of the thirty-three MSUG police advisers originated from the university. Although Michigan State had a nationally recognized law enforcement department, the university could not sufficiently staff both the home campus and the MSUG. In addition, in certain fields such as paramilitary and counterinsurgency training, Michigan State did not have qualified personnel.[105]

Four years after the project's termination, Michigan State's willingness to accept assignments unsuitable for its staff resulted in trouble. In April 1966, a story broke in *Ramparts*, a liberal West Coast Catholic magazine, asserting, among other things, that the MSUG had equipped Diem's police forces, including the "dreaded" sureté, and from 1955 to 1959 was a front for covert CIA operations in South Vietnam. An embarrassing controversy ensued that debated the propriety of academia in foreign aid projects.[106]

Although it had some basis in fact, the *Ramparts* piece was written in a sensationalized manner, distorting the truth. Attempting to portray the MSUG in a sinister light, *Ramparts* asserted that the university "helped secure Diem's dictatorship" by providing the "base and the arms" for his secret police.[107] In theory, these allegations were true. The MSUG housed a CIA unit that trained the VBI's counterespionage division, while the sureté used the National Identity Card program to eliminate suspected communists and subversives. In contrast to the journal's allegation, Michigan State had emphasized the need for democratic principles in law enforcement and had tried to develop South Vietnam's police forces along the lines of American ones. The university was not in a position to impose its views, however, and rarely succeeded in such efforts. One notable exception was the professional attitude Saigon's municipal police adopted in dealing with the public. In 1959, the university "refused to provide cover" any longer for the CIA.[108]

Michigan State officials asserted that the university issued police materials such as ammunition, handguns, riot guns, handcuffs, jeeps, and tear gas, but resisted purchasing larger military arms for South Vietnamese policemen. *Ramparts* took the school to task on this point, producing a 1955 inventory sheet from the MSUG *Final Report*, which listed heavy-duty combat weapons, such as mortars and rocket launchers. Whether or not MSUG personnel approved such a purchase is debatable. Michigan State president John Hannah charged that the inventory was fake. In contrast, at least one scholarly source contends a student photocopied the evidence and sent it to *Ramparts*. The infamous page is not in the current MSUG *Final Report*. An internal history of the Vietnam project and MSUG property receipts housed in the Michigan State archives does not indicate that the university bought the items in question. However, documentation does exist showing that the MSUG purchased Thompson submachine guns for the sureté. Police supplies came from the USOM and from old stockpiles left by the French Expeditionary Corps. Initially, the USOM lacked a police advisory unit, so Michigan State ordered equipment and trained the Vietnamese. The MSUG and the USOM never had "operational control" of security forces, though Diem dictated policy and the Americans served as advisers. The university's refusal to organize the civil guard as a paramilitary organization with heavy armaments was one of the reasons the Vietnamese president terminated the Michigan State project. Turner stated that "regardless of what has been said, the MSU advisers never recommended weaponry above 45 caliber."[109] The university wanted the guard to resemble American state police.[110]

At a press conference on 22 April 1966, Hannah denied the CIA allegations. He remarked that the school "did *not* have a spy operation within its Vietnam Project. It did *not* have CIA people operating under cover provided by the University, or in secret from the Vietnamese government."[111]

Nevertheless, the charges of CIA involvement within the MSUG were correct. Several different sources, including Michigan State representatives and the former inspector general of the CIA, Lyman Kirkpatrick, confirmed the story. Theoretically, however, Hannah's rebuttal was also accurate. Although approximately five to eight CIA agents worked within the MSUG group, they did so as sureté advisers and were not supposed to be involved in spying. In addition, both the South Vietnamese and United States governments were aware of the intelligence group's presence. In a 1993 interview, Smuckler recalled that his boss, Dean Milton E. Muelder, notified him of the U.S. government's desire to expand the MSUG police branch. Specifically, Washington wanted the university to train the sureté to handle Vietnamese subversives. Since the MSUG had no counterinsurgency experts, Smuckler said that Michigan State recruited people from "U.S. intelligence circles." The MSUG assured Diem that the police division's chief adviser would supervise activities and that these individuals would only assist the sureté and "not be running around as agents working for the C.I.A."[112]

According to Smuckler, "there was a kind of openness about this whole thing [CIA] which later *Ramparts* portrayed as . . . a deep dark secret that they were revealing." Anyone in a position of authority knew of the agents' existence, he said, and "anybody who was on the [MSUG] team had a sense of it."[113] By 1956, Ryan was aware of the CIA contingent. Writing Brandstatter that January, he noted that "I am not at all impressed by the attempt of Boudriàs and the outfit he represents to use us as their damned cover. It sure is a pity that 'bubble-head' [Harry] Truman pulled the Bureau [FBI] boys out of that operation! These guys couldn't hold a candle to the laddies I've known in the Bureau!"[114]

In 1965, two publications discussing the CIA link appeared. Robert Scigliano and Guy Fox mentioned the CIA involvement in their "official volume" on the project, *Technical Assistance in Vietnam: The Michigan State University Experience*. In his capacity as Michigan State's associate dean of international programs, Smuckler helped fund the book. Also in 1965, Robert Scheer, the foreign editor for *Ramparts*, produced a booklet entitled "How the United States Got Involved in Vietnam." In it, he charged that a CIA connection to Michigan State existed. At the time there were no sizable consequences because few people had an opportunity to read the story. Scheer estimated that only about sixty thousand copies were in circulation. However, material from the publication was used in the 1966 *Ramparts* article. In retrospect, the university should have discussed the CIA involvement with the media, Smuckler said, and made a "splash" by doing a couple of interviews. "That would have prevented the type of onslaught that we had to deal with when *Ramparts* came along."[115]

South Vietnam's security needs during the 1950s were too demanding for Michigan State to handle alone. Rather than recruit heavily from outside the campus, the university should have refused certain assignments. This mistake resulted in a number of difficulties, including the *Ramparts* exposé and bureaucratic infighting with the USOM and the MAAG. In the civil guard's case, the ramifications were severe, as the unit did not receive any appreciable training or equipment until 1959.

When working within its areas of expertise, Michigan State proved capable. As advisers to Saigon's municipal police and, in some cases, to the sureté, the MSUG effectively modernized facilities and introduced up-to-date methods. The university assisted in the development of an identification bureau, a crime detection laboratory, and a communications network by providing training and equipment. In addition, Michigan State helped establish several police academies and short-term instructional courses that enabled the Vietnamese to train their own police forces.

The MSUG was unable to make any significant changes within the sureté that could have expanded support for Diem's regime, however. In many instances, the VBI alienated South Vietnam's population by utilizing MSUG programs such as the National Identity Card program for oppressive purposes. This situation demonstrated why nation building failed. The United States provided Diem with substantial technical assistance but could not persuade him to implement the necessary political or economic reforms to establish a viable government.

NOTES

1. John le Carré, *The Honourable Schoolboy* (New York: Bantam Books, 1977), 407.
2. Arthur Brandstatter, interview by author, 17 July 1992.
3. Ibid.; Ralph Turner, interview by author, 9 July 1992.
4. *Michigan State University Magazine,* February 1956, 10; *Final Report of the Michigan State University Advisory Group,* 61–62; Jack Ryan to Art Brandstatter, 11 January 1956, box 680, folder 2, Vietnam Project Papers; MSU News Release, Saigon, 28 January 1956, box 657, folder 67, Vietnam Project Papers; Turner, interview; Royce A. Williams, Personnel File, box 655, folders 55–57, Vietnam Project Papers. In places where a MSUG police member does not have biographical information listed, the author was denied access to personnel files in keeping with federal and state law. The director of Michigan State University Archives and Historical Collections, Dr. Fred Honhart, letter to author, 19 January 1994.
5. Michigan State University Contribution to the Vietnamese Sureté, box 684, folder 36, Vietnam Project Papers, pp. 7–9; Robert Scigliano, *South Vietnam: Nation Under Stress* (Boston: Houghton Mifflin Company, 1963), 20–21.
6. Robert Scigliano and Guy H. Fox, *Technical Assistance in Vietnam: The Michigan State University Experience* (New York: Praeger, 1965), 3–4, 6–8.
7. Paul Shields, letter to author, 5 April 1994; Scigliano and Fox, *Technical Assistance in Vietnam,* 18–19.
8. Paul Shields, letter to author, 5 April 1994; Scigliano and Fox, *Technical Assistance in Vietnam,* 18–19.
9. Scigliano and Fox, *Technical Assistance in Vietnam,* 14–19; *Final Report,* 47; "Report on the Police of Vietnam," box 681, folder 33, Vietnam Project Papers.
10. Dennis J. Duncanson, *Government and Revolution in Vietnam* (New York and London: Oxford University Press, 1968), 99; Richard Critchfield, *The Long Charade: Political Subversion in the Vietnam War* (New York: Harcourt, Brace and World, 1968), 10.
11. Howard Hoyt to Jack Ryan, 31 October 1956, box 680, folder 2, Vietnam Project Papers.

12. Frances Fitzgerald, *Fire in the Lake: The Vietnamese and the Americans in Vietnam* (New York: Random House, 1972), 89.

13. Ibid.

14. Wesley Fishel, "Vietnam's Democratic One-Man Rule," *New Leader*, 2 November 1959.

15. Fitzgerald, *Fire in the Lake*, 89.

16. George C. Herring, *America's Longest War: The United States and Vietnam, 1950–1975*, 2d ed. (New York: Alfred A. Knopf, 1986), 66.

17. MSU Contribution to Sureté, Vietnam Project Papers, 8–9; Jack Ryan to Howard Hoyt, "Brief History of the Sureté in Indo-China," 8–9, box 682, folder 9, Vietnam Project Papers.

18. Scigliano and Fox, *Technical Assistance in Vietnam*, 21.

19. Ralph Smuckler, interview by author, 13 May 1993; Louis Boudrias to Howard Hoyt, 27 July, 31 August, 1 September, 21 November 1955, and 12 April, 28 June, 27 September, 2 October 1956, box 685, folders 26–27, Vietnam Project Papers.

20. Boudrias to Hoyt, 21 November, 27 July 1955.

21. Ibid., 12 April 1956.

22. Ibid., 28 June 1956.

23. Ibid.; William Colby and Peter Forbath, *Honorable Men: My Life in the C.I.A.* (New York: Simon and Schuster, 1978), 26.

24. Boudrias to Hoyt, 2 October 1956, Vietnam Project Papers; *Final Report*, 47–48, 61; MSU Contribution to Sureté, Vietnam Project Papers, pp. 1–9.

25. Joseph Buttinger, *Vietnam: A Dragon Embattled*, vol. 2, *Vietnam at War* (New York: Frederick A. Praeger, 1967), 2:975.

26. Boudrias to Hoyt, 27 September 1956, Vietnam Project Papers.

27. Herring, *America's Longest War*, 65.

28. Ibid., 65–66; Boudrias to Hoyt, 27 September 1956, Vietnam Project Papers.

29. Ralph Turner, letter to the author, 26 March 1994.

30. Ralph Turner's Report to the Minister of Interior, box 680, folder 9, Vietnam Project Papers, p. 7.

31. *Final Report*, 45; Scigliano and Fox, *Technical Assistance in Vietnam*, 18–19; First Report of the Michigan State University Vietnam Team, Saigon, 19 August 1955, box 675, folder 74, Vietnam Project Papers; Howard Hoyt to Colonel Pham-Xuan-Chieu, Director General of Police and Security Forces, 25 November 1957, box 690, folder 47, Vietnam Project Papers.

32. First Report of the Michigan State University Vietnam Team; Frederic R. Wickert, "An Adventure in Psychological Testing Abroad," *American Psychologist* (February 1957): 86–88; Michigan State University *State News*, 15 February 1956, box 657, folder 39, Vietnam Project Papers; *Lansing State Journal*, 13 February 1957, box 657, folder 38, Vietnam Project Papers.

33. Fred Wickert, interview by author, 20 July 1992.

34. Wickert, "Adventure in Psychological Testing Abroad," 86–88.

35. Michigan State University *State News*, 15 February 1956, box 657, folder 39, Vietnam Project Papers; *Michigan State University Magazine*, February 1956, 10, box 657 folder 29, Vietnam Project Papers; *Final Report*, 45; Michigan State University *State News,* 17 October 1956; Wickert, "An Adventure in Psychological Testing Abroad," 87–88; Michigan State University Viet-Nam Semi-Annual Report, 30 December 1957, Box 683, Folder 56, Vietnam Project Papers, p. 7; Michigan State University News Bulletin, May 1960, International

Studies and Programs, Box 1, Folder 5, Michigan State University Archives and Historical Collections, East Lansing, Michigan, 5–6; Scigliano and Fox, *Technical Assistance in Vietnam*, 21; Rach Dua Basic Training Center Training Program, August 1959, box 694, folder 38, Vietnam Project Papers, pp. 6, 8–9, 14–15; Do-Van-Ro to Secretary of State for Interior, undated, box 691, folder 9, Vietnam Project Papers; Training for the VBI, October 1957, box 686, folder 11, Vietnam Project Papers; *Michigan State College Catalog, 1955–56*, 110–12, 306–8; *Michigan State University Catalog, 1960–61*, 112–16, 125–26.

36. MSU News Release, 28 January 1956, box 657, folder, 67, Vietnam Project Papers.
37. Jack Ryan to MSU Department of Police Administration, 9 November 1955, box 680, folder 2, Vietnam Project Papers.
38. Scigliano and Fox, *Technical Assistance in Vietnam*, 19.
39. Jack Ryan to Arthur Brandstatter, 17 December 1955, box 680, folder 2, Vietnam Project Papers.
40. Ibid.
41. Turner Report to the Minister of the Interior, Vietnam Project Papers, pp. 8–9.
42. *Final Report*, 47–48; MSU Contribution to Sureté, Vietnam Project Papers, pp.1–9.
43. MSU Contribution to Sureté, 3–6, 13; *Final Report*, 48–49; Turner's Report to the Minister of the Interior, Vietnam Project Papers, 17.
44. MSU Contribution to Sureté, 3–4; Turner Report to the Minister of the Interior, 15.
45. Scigliano and Fox, *Technical Assistance in Vietnam*, 21; *Final Report*, 48; *Encyclopedia Americana* (Danbury, Conn.: Grolier, 1992), 11:216; *New Encyclopaedia Britannica* (Chicago: Encyclopaedia Britannica, 1991), 4:781.
46. Turner, interview.
47. Ibid.; *Final Report*, 48; MSU Contribution to Sureté, Vietnam Project Papers, pp. 4–5; Police Administration Division Michigan State University Viet-Nam Advisory Group, Semi-Annual Report, June 1957, box 683, folder 55, Vietnam Project Papers, p. 6.
48. *Final Report*, 48; MSU Contribution to Sureté, pp. 4–5; Memo from Howard Hoyt to Wesley Fishel, 9 December 1957, box 680, folder 39, Vietnam Project Papers.
49. Project Status Report, 29 July 1960, box, 680, folder 5, Vietnam Project Papers, pp. 2–3.
50. *Final Report*, 48, 71; Turner Report to the Minister of the Interior, Vietnam Project Papers, p. 16; Project Status Report, 29 July 1960, 2; E. H. Adkins, "An Idea for a Foreign Police Academy," *Police Magazine*, (March-April 1962, pp. 2–3), box 680, folder 14, Vietnam Project Papers; author's conversation with Ralph Turner, 16 March 1994, East Lansing, Michigan; E. H. Adkins to Arthur Brandstatter, 3 April 1961, box 680, folder 13, Vietnam Project Papers.
51. Ralph Turner, conversation with author, 16 March 1994.
52. Ibid.; *Final Report*, 49; Turner Report to the Minister of the Interior, Vietnam Project Papers, p. 17; Scigliano and Fox, *Technical Assistance in Vietnam*, 21.
53. Project Status Report, 29 July 1960, Vietnam Project Papers, p. 2.
54. E. H. Adkins to Frank E. Walton, 17 April 1962, box 680, folder 14, Vietnam Project Papers.
55. *Final Report*, 49; Turner Report to the Minister of the Interior, Vietnam Project Papers, pp. 16–17; Project Status Report, 29 July 1960, Vietnam Project Papers, p. 2; E. H. Adkins Jr., "Monthly Report," July 1961, box 680, folder 13, Vietnam Project Papers, p. 1.
56. E. H. Adkins to James Hendry, 5 May 1962, box 680, folder 14, Vietnam Project Papers; Ralph Turner to Lloyd D. Musolf, 20 December 1960, box 696, folder 46, Vietnam Project

Papers; Lloyd D. Musolf to John Murtha, USOM, 21 December 1960, box 696, folder 46, Vietnam Project Papers; *Final Report*, 49; Ralph Turner, conversation with author.

57. Scigliano and Fox, *Technical Assistance in Vietnam*, 21, 10–11; *Final Report*, 49, 61–62; Adkins to Walton, 17 April 1962, Vietnam Project Papers.

58. Ryan to Brandstatter, 17 December 1955, Vietnam Project Papers.

59. MSU Contribution to Sureté, Vietnam Project Papers, p. 12.

60. *Final Report*, 62, 80; Turner Report to the Minister of the Interior, Vietnam Project Papers, p. 20; MSU Contribution to Sureté, 12; Michigan State University Participants, 1955–61, box 667, folder 52, Vietnam Project Papers; Report on MSUG Police Participant Program, 1960, box 692, folders 14–15, Vietnam Project Papers, p. 73.

61. Turner Report to the Minister of the Interior, 20.

62. Project Status Report, 29 July 1960, Vietnam Project Papers, p. 6; MSU Contribution to Sureté, Vietnam Project Papers, p. 12; Turner Report to the Minister of the Interior, 19–21.

63. *Final Report*, 50; Turner Report to the Minister of the Interior, 14; Scigliano and Fox, *Technical Assistance in Vietnam*, 16–17; *New York Times*, 29 September 1957.

64. A Study of Police Communications in Viet Nam, 1957, box 696, folder 7, Vietnam Project Papers; MSU Contribution to Sureté, Vietnam Project Papers, p. 14.

65. Royce Williams's Obituary, box 648, folder 91, Vietnam Project Papers; Project Status Report, 29 July 1960, Vietnam Project Papers, pp. 3–4; Turner Report to the Minister of the Interior, p. 14; Ralph Turner, conversation with author.

66. Glen L. Taggart to Wesley Fishel, 19 June 1957, box 629, folder 9, Vietnam Project Papers.

67. Howard Hoyt to Wesley Fishel, Semi-Annual Report, Police Administration Program, 30 December 1957, box 683, folder 56, Vietnam Project Papers, p. 12.

68. Project Status Report, 29 July 1960, Vietnam Project Papers, p. 4; *New York Times*, 29 September 1957; Howard Hoyt to Wesley Fishel, Semi-Annual Report, 30 December 1957, 12; Lyman M. Rundlett to Wesley Fishel, 21 June 1957, box 660, folder 89, Vietnam Project Papers; Wesley Fishel to Elbridge Durbrow, 26 July 1957, box 660, folder 90, Vietnam Project Papers; Wesley Fishel to Ngo Dinh Diem, 24 May 1957, box 660, folder 89, Vietnam Project Papers; Wesley Fishel to Stanley K. Sheinbaum, 24 June 1957 box 660, folder 89, Vietnam Project Papers; Milton Hagelberg to Wesley Fishel, 30 July 1957, box 660, folder 90, Vietnam Project Papers; Wesley Fishel to Elbridge Durbrow, 8 August 1957, box 660, folder 90, Vietnam Project Papers.

69. Project Status Report, 29 July 1960, 4.

70. Ibid.; *Final Report*, 50.

71. David Anderson, *Trapped by Success: The Eisenhower Administration and Vietnam, 1953–1961* (New York: Columbia University Press, 1991), 180–81.

72. Ibid., 181; Ralph Turner to Arthur Brandstatter, 10 December 1959, box 695, folder 31, Vietnam Project Papers; *San Francisco News-Call Bulletin*, 28 October 1959, box 657, folder 49, Vietnam Project Papers; *Grand Rapids Press*, 29 October 1959, box 657, folder 49, Vietnam Project Papers.

73. Turner to Brandstatter, 10 December 1959; *Grand Rapids Press*, 29 October 1959; Resume of MSU-USOM Relationships, 1960, box 695, folder 2, Vietnam Project Papers; Ralph Turner to Lloyd D. Musolf, 28 January 1960, box 686, folder 15, Vietnam Project Papers.

74. A. F. Brandstatter to Ruben Austin, 8 June 1960, box 681, folder 8, Vietnam Project Papers; Resume of MSU-USOM Relationships, 3–4; Evaluation of Current Situation in Vietnam As it Applies to the MSUG Program March 1960, box 695, folder 2, Vietnam Project Papers, p. 2.
75. Ralph Turner, conversation with author, 16 March 1994.
76. Lloyd D. Musolf to Ruben Austin, 10 June 1960, box 681, folder 4, Vietnam Project Papers.
77. Ibid.
78. Resume of MSU-USOM Relationships, Vietnam Project Papers, Vietnam Project Papers, p. 3; Project Status Report, 29 July 1960, Vietnam Project Papers, pp. 3–4; Turner Report to the Minister of the Interior, Vietnam Project Papers, p. 14; Ralph Turner, conversation with author, 16 March 1994.
79. Scigliano and Fox, *Technical Assistance in Vietnam*, 21–22; Tran Van Tu, "Solving the Traffic Problem in Saigon, Capital of the Republic of Vietnam," 1959, box 685, folder 23, Vietnam Project Papers.
80. Turner Report to the Minister of the Interior, Vietnam Project Papers, pp. 21–22; *Final Report*, 46, 62; Nguyen Dinh Thuan to Ralph Smuckler, 22 April 1959, 11 May 1959, box 672, folder 58, Vietnam Project Papers; Ralph Smuckler to Nguyen Dinh Thuan, 27 July 1959, box 672, folder 59, Vietnam Project Papers; Ralph Turner, conversation with author; "Domestic News," 24 November 1958, box 685, folder 21, Vietnam Project Papers.
81. Howard Hoyt to Wesley Fishel, Semi-Annual Report, 30 December 1957, Vietnam Project Papers, p. 12.
82. Scigliano and Fox, *Technical Assistance in Vietnam*, 21.
83. *Final Report*, 46–47; Turner Report to the Minister of the Interior, Vietnam Project Papers, p. 22.
84. Ronald H. Spector, *The United States Army in Vietnam: Advice and Support: The Early Years, 1941–1960* (Washington, D.C.: U.S. Government Printing Office, 1983), 375–78; Turner Report to the Minister of the Interior, 6; Analysis of the Role of Security Services, box 680, folder 8, Vietnam Project Papers, pp. 2–3; Turner, interview.
85. Ralph Smuckler to Howard Hoyt, November 1955, box 679, folder 44, Vietnam Project Papers, pp. 2–3.
86. Ryan to MSU Department of Police Administration, 9 November 1955, Vietnam Project Papers.
87. Ibid.; Smuckler to Hoyt, November 1955, Vietnam Project Papers.
88. Telegram from MAAG chief Samuel Williams to the Pacific Commander in Chief Admiral Felix B. Stump, 14 October 1957, *Foreign Relations of the United States, 1955–1957, Volume I Vietnam* (Washington, D.C.: U.S. Government Printing Office, 1985), pp. 849–50; Samuel Williams to Felix B. Stump, 18 October 1957, and attached Memo of a Conversation between Diem and Williams dated 13 October 1957, ibid., 850–52.
89. Memo of a Conversation between Diem and Williams, 852; Analysis of the Role of Security Services, Vietnam Project Papers, p. 3.
90. James I. Muir memorandum for Chief MAAG, 10 December 1957, box 2, Samuel L. Williams Papers, U.S. Military History Institute Archives, Carlisle Barracks, Pennsylvania.
91. Turner Report to the Minister of the Interior, Vietnam Project Papers, pp. 6–7; Analysis of the Role of Security Services, Vietnam Project Papers, p. 3; Police Administration Division, Michigan State University Viet-Nam Advisory Group, Semi-Annual Report, June 1957, box 683, folder 55, Vietnam Project Papers, pp. 3–5; Hoyt to Fishel, Semi-Annual Report, 30

December 1957, Vietnam Project Papers, p. 7; *Final Report*, 48; Scigliano and Fox, *Technical Assistance in Vietnam*, 22.

92. Analysis of the Role of Security Services, 3.

93. Ibid.

94. Ibid., 4.

95. Arthur Brandstatter to Ralph Turner, 3 February 1961, box 680, folder 48, Vietnam Project Papers.

96. Turner, interview; Analysis of the Role of Security Services, Vietnam Project Papers, p. 4.

97. Ralph Turner, conversation with author; Analysis of the Role of Security Services, 4; Scigliano and Fox, *Technical Assistance in Vietnam*, 11.

98. Scigliano and Fox, *Technical Assistance in Vietnam*, 12; Frank C. Child, "Vietnam—The Eleventh Hour," *New Republic*, 145 (December 1961): 14–15; Adrian Jaffe and Milton C. Taylor, "A Crumbling Bastion: Flattery and Lies Won't Save Vietnam," *New Republic*, 144 (June 1961): 19; Turner, interview.

99. Jack Ryan to Arthur Brandstatter, 16 June 1956, box 680, folder 2, Vietnam Project Papers.

100. Jack Ryan to Arthur Brandstatter, 14 November 1956, box 680, folder 2, Vietnam Project Papers.

101. Howard Hoyt to Arthur Brandstatter, 30 October 1957, box 680, folder 1, Vietnam Project Papers.

102. Ibid.

103. Ibid.

104. Smuckler, interview.

105. Ibid.; Scigliano and Fox, *Technical Assistance in Vietnam*, 40, 60–61; Anderson, *Trapped by Success*, 144–45; *Final Report*, 61, 64.

106. Anderson, *Trapped by Success*, 144; "MSU: The University on the Make," *Ramparts* 4 (April 1966): 14, 20.

107. "University on the Make," 20.

108. Scigliano and Fox, *Technical Assistance in Vietnam*, 11, 19, 21; Anderson, *Trapped by Success*, 143–46.

109. Turner, interview.

110. Ibid.; Anderson, *Trapped by Success*, 144–47; "University on the Make," 20; Scigliano and Fox, *Technical Assistance in Vietnam*, 16; Kenneth J. Heineman, *Campus Wars: The Peace Movement at American State Universities in the Vietnam Era* (New York: New York University Press, 1993), 137; Memo, "38 cal. Smith & Wesson Revolvers and Thompson Submachine Guns, box 696, folder 7, Vietnam Project Papers; Property Receipts 1955–58, box 689, folders 42–52, Vietnam Project Papers.

111. Statement by John A. Hannah, 22 April 1966, box 55, folder 50, John A. Hannah Papers, Michigan State University Archives and Historical Collections, East Lansing, Michigan.

112. Smuckler, interview; Anderson, *Trapped by Success*, 144–45; Irving D. Horowitz, "Michigan State and the C.I.A.: A Dilemma for Social Science," *Atomic Scientist* 22 (September 1966): 27.

113. Smuckler, interview.

114. Jack Ryan to Arthur Brandstatter, 11 January 1956, box 680, folder 2, Vietnam Project Papers.

115. Smuckler, interview; *Detroit News*, 28 November 1965, box 1, folder 23, International Studies and Programs, MSU Archives and Historical Collections, East Lansing, Michigan.

CHAPTER 5

MICHIGAN STATE UNIVERSITY AND THE PARTICIPANT PROGRAM

From 1955 to 1961 the Michigan State University Group (MSUG) selected 179 Vietnamese to be educated in various foreign countries, including the United States, the Philippines, Japan, and Malaya. Working closely with the MSUG, the United States Operations Mission (USOM) also sponsored a number of Vietnamese. The participant program sought to improve South Vietnam's government by exposing its civil servants and police forces to modern administrative and law enforcement methods. In addition, gifted students were given the chance to pursue advanced academic degrees. Specifically, the National Institute of Administration (NIA), the civil servant training school that the MSUG helped establish in 1955, brought promising graduates and faculty members to the United States to obtain doctorates.[1]

Only partially successful, the participant program suffered from a lack of well-defined objectives and was constantly reevaluated by MSUG personnel. Contributing to this problem was the inability of the South Vietnamese government to communicate effectively with the two U.S.-supported agencies, the MSUG and the USOM. As a result, inconsistent programming emerged in an ad hoc fashion. In addition, English-language difficulties and homesickness on the part of the participants hindered progress. As the MSUG *Final Report* noted, the participants who benefited the most were "those who came for specific degree objectives and who expected the training received to be immediately useful to them in their careers upon return" to Vietnam.[2]

Although most MSUG-sponsored participants (116) went to the United States, a significant number (63) received training in Southeast Asian countries. The MSUG often utilized this option to address Vietnamese personnel shortages quickly. The period of instruction was typically brief, ranging from several weeks to a few months. The principal exception was the NIA's head librarian, Tang Thi Ty, who studied in the United States for nine months and later obtained a bachelor's degree in library science from the University of the Philippines in Manila.[3]

Over half of the MSUG participants who did not go to the United States studied in the Philippines. Having been under American control from 1902 to 1946, the islands were partly Americanized. In addition, under the leadership of President Ramón Magsaysay, the Philippine government in 1951 had defeated the communist-led "Huk" movement. The long-established U.S. presence there, the Filipinos' experience in handling communist insurgents, and the islands' proximity to Vietnam made the Philippines a logical place to educate participants.[4]

Moreover, Michigan State had established a special rapport with Magsaysay. In the fall of 1954, the university sent a four-member exploratory team to South Vietnam to determine whether a technical assistance contract would benefit that country and the Michigan State campus. En route, the group stopped in the Philippines, where they met Magsaysay. Arthur Brandstatter, the chairman of Michigan State's police administration department and one of the university's representatives, found the president "delightful" and "very helpful." Magsaysay assigned one of his army colonels to assist the university group while they were in South Vietnam. The MSUG used the Filipinos' knowledge of counterintelligence and jungle warfare for participant training. In 1955, thirty-two police officers, the largest single Vietnamese participant contingent, attended the Philippine Constabulary School in Manila for specialized four- and six-week courses. The MSUG *Final Report* noted that in the Philippines the "conditions and experiences to be studied more closely resemble[d] those in Vietnam."[5]

Ten civil servants comprised the first contingent of Vietnamese participants to visit Michigan State. The group was diverse, ranging from an NIA political scientist, Truong Ngoc Giau, to the director general of budget and foreign aid, Nguyen Quoc Lan. Dr. Charles Killingsworth, a member of the exploratory team that toured Saigon in 1954 and the coordinator of on-campus Vietnam project activities, welcomed the visitors. Arriving in East Lansing during Thanksgiving week 1955, the Vietnamese remained in America for approximately nine months and divided their time between the classroom and fieldwork. They observed government agencies in such places as Washington, D.C., and Tennessee and attended classes in economics, police administration, and public administration at Michigan State.[6]

Ton-That-Thien, a South Vietnamese government official, predated the participants' arrival at Michigan State by one month. An instructor in government, economics, and Vietnamese, Thien prepared MSUG members for service in South

Vietnam. In addition, he eased the cultural transition for Vietnamese coming to the States.[7]

During the university's Christmas vacation, Thien, Michigan State political scientist Norton Long, and Wesley Fishel, the MSUG project leader, took the participants on a seven-day tour of New York and Washington, D.C. In New York, they surveyed slum clearance projects and visited a number of major attractions, including the United Nations, the New York Port Authority, and Columbia University. Tran Phuoc Thanh, the only police administration participant, spent a number of hours at the New York Police Department. Buu Nghi, the former director of Radio Dalat in southeastern Vietnam, toured the facilities of the Columbia Broadcasting System (CBS).[8]

Inclement weather forced the group to cancel its plans to fly to Washington. Traveling instead by rail, the participants arrived in the nation's capital on 4 January 1956, around three in the morning. Once there, they examined various government agencies, including the Bureau of Internal Revenue, and met Senators Charles E. Potter of Michigan and Mike Mansfield of Montana. The Montana Democrat was Fishel's friend and a supporter of South Vietnamese president Ngo Dinh Diem. In addition, the Vietnamese ambassador to the United States, Tran Van Chuong, honored his fellow countrymen with a reception. The foreign visitors agreed that "the trip had been extremely worthwhile," Fishel reported to Michigan State University president John Hannah, "in that it had given them an overall idea" of how government functioned in the United States.[9]

In an August 1956 report, economist Stanley K. Sheinbaum, the MSUG campus coordinator, described the participant program's difficulties. He told the former director in Saigon, political scientist John Dorsey, that the program was "capable of greater success" than the first experience illustrated. "Unfortunately in our own enthusiasm," Sheinbaum observed, the university did the participants "a disservice by doing as much as was possible for them." As a result, the Vietnamese became totally dependent on the campus staff. The participants needed more English-language training before departing Vietnam and during their first months in America. In addition, Sheinbaum asserted that, if possible, the participants should be professionally more homogeneous. A "more highly refined program" could be provided for them if "we can get three to four participants who are interested in the same areas and have similar" government backgrounds.[10]

Sheinbaum suggested that the Vietnamese be asked to complete questionnaires outlining their reasons for coming to the United States and career plans upon going back to Vietnam. The participants who arrive in "East Lansing with specific problems in mind," he noted, "will be the ones who return with the greatest benefits and therefore the most increased usefulness to their country." Moreover, he advocated contacting the returnees and their supervisors for a "follow-up," to find out which aspects of the program had proven effective and what improvements might be made.[11]

Sheinbaum conceded that his own inexperience and "insufficient time to plan and execute" caused many of the first participant group's problems. Part of the curriculum "was not properly programmed" to fit individual needs, he noted. More faculty from other departments should have been placed on the MSUG payroll. For example, someone interested in public information and broadcasting, like Buu Nghi, would have benefited from the "intensified and specialized direction" of a journalism instructor. Sheinbaum's assessment proved correct. The subsequent addition of more staff alleviated a number of the difficulties and provided the participants with more personalized instruction.[12]

On-the-job training for the participants also suffered from inadequate planning. According to Sheinbaum, there was not enough fieldwork and what little existed often did not suit a participant's particular career needs. Part of the reason, he maintained, was a lack of "sufficient coordination" between Michigan State and the agencies in which the Vietnamese were placed. Sheinbaum hoped to solve this problem in the future by enlisting the aid of the Michigan state government. With the state capital located in the city of Lansing, adjacent to the university's campus in East Lansing, "we have a fine opportunity," he commented, "that will probably be taken advantage of" with the next participant group. He concluded by insisting that the MSUG staff had learned from its mistakes and the participant program was "now in a position to be a significant and integral part" of the Vietnam project.[13]

The MSUG continually reassessed and refined the participant program. By the time the second group of Vietnamese arrived in September 1956, the university had modified its language training and fieldwork systems. Subsequent groups experienced even more changes. As time passed, training became increasingly sophisticated. Clustered together professionally in either public or police administration, the Vietnamese took basic courses and received specialized instruction. For example, most police participants who attended Michigan State enrolled in Introduction to Law Enforcement (PLA 110), and, depending on their specific interests, also took classes in crime laboratory, police records management, police patrol, and criminal investigation.[14]

The USOM and the MSUG's Saigon and campus staffs worked with the participants and Vietnamese officials to address South Vietnam's needs. If Michigan

State did not offer a needed course of study, participants went to other institutions, often under USOM auspices. For instance, in police administration, Michigan State did not have certain training specializations that the Vietnamese government desired. Participants who were interested, for example, in riot control, state police operations, traffic law enforcement, radio communications, or immigration were sent by the USOM to places as diverse as the U.S. Treasury Department Law Enforcement School, the Capitol Radio Engineering Institute in Washington, D.C., the Grand Rapids (Michigan) Police Department Recruit School, and Sacramento State College.[15]

Inadequate English-language training continually hampered participant operations. The International Cooperation Administration (ICA), the U.S. government agency through which Michigan State held its Vietnam contract, required that departing participants score a minimum of seventy-five on both a written and an oral examination. Developed by the American Language Center at American University, the test consisted of one hundred questions. The four and one-half months allotted for preparation were typically not enough. As a consequence, several problems occurred. In 1960, the MSUG interviewed eighteen former police participants and found that those who passed the test admitted to having trouble communicating for at least one to three months after arriving in the United States. Unable to meet ICA requirements, the 1959 police participants were forced to remain in Vietnam for an additional four months of instruction.[16]

Time constraints produced most of the language difficulties. Virtually all of the police and public administration participants who went to the United States under MSUG auspices stayed from nine months to a year. The selection procedure in Vietnam, including recruitment, language instruction, medical examination, and American cultural programming, took the same amount of time as the entire overseas training period. The challenge for the MSUG was to enhance the participants' English skills without either lengthening the Saigon processing period or consuming too much training time in the United States. One commonsense solution led several of the participants to be placed with American roommates. This afforded the Vietnamese additional opportunities for using English and fostered increased confidence and self-sufficiency. According to a 1957 report, the Vietnamese women, especially, improved their language skills thanks to "greater integration" with female students residing in the dormitories.[17]

Starting in 1959, the MSUG intensified predeparture English-language instruction from twenty to thirty-five hours a week. Within a year, however, Michigan State had to concede that this was "not a good approach." Instead, "it was an expedient, a shock treatment for a sagging" system.[18] Deliberation over how to resolve the situation persisted into the early 1960s, by which time the participant program and the MSUG project itself were ending. By then, there were no participants in police administration, and only a handful in public administration.[19]

Using local, state, and federal agencies, the MSUG enhanced its fieldwork system to benefit the participant. For example, Nguyen Van Dai, the deputy chief of Banmethuot Province in the central region of South Vietnam, spent a month at the Detroit City Planning Commission and one week each at the Michigan Economic Development Commission and the Lansing City Planning Commission. While in Lansing, he learned the "practical details" associated with the design and zoning of a city. Nguyen Huu Bang, a department of education official, gained experience on both the local and national level. He studied the administration of educational services for two weeks at the Detroit Public Schools and examined the financial features of educational administration for a number of weeks at the U.S. Office of Education.[20]

Although a number of Vietnamese enjoyed on-the-job training, time constraints diminished the value of fieldwork. The time spent at one location varied from one to six weeks and, all too often, the "experiences resemble[d] good-will tours."[21] Participants were barely able to get oriented before departing and rarely saw a project completed. One police participant reported that he witnessed a complete investigation only once. His "remaining observations," the MSUG acknowledged, "were spotty—a smattering of one investigation, one technique, then another—and never of sufficient duration to provide a clear idea of the techniques and procedures involved."[22]

To be effective, the fieldwork system needed restructuring. Since most participants spent a year or less in the United States, they needed to remain in one location and immerse themselves in their particular field of interest. On-the-job training for police participants accomplished nothing substantive because the program was hurried and generalized. As the MSUG conceded in 1960, "[a]lthough all of the participants are somewhat impressed by what they see and are favorably influenced, little has been added to their occupational competence."[23] Public administration participants experienced a similar problem. To cut dollar cost and "valuable staff time," a number of the organizations offering on-the-job training gave participants "packaged" tours. Trainees were not involved in any real projects but instead listened to office employees lecture on their specific "technical specialty."[24]

To strengthen the participant program, the MSUG increased its staff in the late 1950s. Dorsey and other MSUG personnel had at times administered the program in an "auxiliary" manner by splitting their time with other major responsibilities. For example, Dorsey worked with Diem's staff to reorganize the presidency and served for a time as the acting MSUG chief adviser. In November 1957, the first full-time participant director, Howard L. Waltman, arrived in Saigon. Waltman held a master's degree in public administration from Syracuse University and shared Sheinbaum's views on the program. Both men advocated increased English-language preparation for departing Vietnamese and expanded on-the-job-training for participants at state and local government agencies. By 1958, the participant program was better organized, sending public administration participants to such schools as American University to do "specialized course work."[25]

Although the participant program improved under Waltman, the MSUG police advisers in 1959 obtained their own full-time participant coordinator, Victor Strecher, a Michigan State police administration professor. The MSUG did this for consistency and to improve the police program's organization. Prior to this time, the participant programming done in Saigon was often "too generalized" and suffered from a "lack of communication" between Americans and Vietnamese. In one case, a participant's training proved repetitious and unsuited to conditions in South Vietnam. He attended the Grand Rapids Police Department Recruit School and then completed Michigan State's basic police course, in the process covering the same material twice. Moreover, grounded in Michigan statutes and American common law, the information he received was not really pertinent to Vietnam. As Waltman noted, conditions in the United States rarely resembled those in Vietnam. In such cases, any real progress would depend on the transference of "general principles."[26]

In another case, the MSUG sent a participant to the United States for "special investigation and counterespionage" instruction, fully aware that such training was not available. Left in the lurch, USOM stateside personnel assembled an ersatz training program by using "try-on" and "stab in the dark" methods. A summary of this particular participant's remarks indicated that the training he received at the U.S. Treasury Department Law Enforcement School "came the nearest to providing" the requested assistance.[27]

With a public administration background, Waltman, like some other MSUG participant coordinators, was unaware of the different types of police training available in the United States. Ill-equipped to make program decisions, he depended upon Michigan State's law enforcement staff for advice on placing participants. He served more as a liaison between American and Vietnamese police officials. The MSUG asserted that one individual with public safety experience needed to administer the program because "if several police advis[e]rs were involved, there would be a lack of continuity in the programming."[28] Receiving little time to prove the point, Strecher coordinated the training for only one participant group. After 1959, no police participants came to the United States under MSUG auspices. Feeling itself overextended, the university had ended its police administration activities.[29]

Follow-ups conducted with returned participants indicated uneven success. Huynh Van Dao, a 1958 participant, was appointed secretary general of the Ministry of Education. Writing Sheinbaum in 1959, Waltman noted that "Mr. Dao is presently our most highly placed regular participant. He is overjoyed at his promotion and seems immersed in his work." Similarly, Nguyen Thuan, a 1957–58 participant, saw his responsibilities increase upon resuming work at the Directorate of Obligated Expenditures, a branch of the Bureau of Budget and Foreign Aid. Thuan's superior requested that he draft a new finance law for Vietnam. "Thuan has taken the initiative in maintaining contacts with our staff since his return," Waltman observed, "and appears to be quite sympathetic" toward the MSUG's efforts.[30]

Several years later, Waltman wrote an article about the Vietnamese participant program in which he evaluated the experience more negatively. He asserted that the participant's assimilation back into the workforce was often difficult. In many instances, "new knowledge was suspect and the returning trainee was put in a position where he could not use his training. In other cases, rigidities in civil service procedures did not permit the trainee to resume his former position, much less receive a promotion."[31]

South Vietnam's civil service was a patriarchal, tradition-bound mechanism that valued age, formal education, and political loyalty. Vietnam's security agencies shared some of these traits. As a result, using participants to introduce new training methods or procedures proved difficult. Quite often the criteria Vietnam's police officials employed for selecting and placing participants appeared inappropriate. MSUG interviews with former police trainees reflected this. For example, two candidates chosen to study radio communications were better qualified for instruction in either criminal investigation or police administration. Over half of the eighteen people interviewed were selected for training that was inconsistent with their professional background and were reassigned upon returning home. Yet police leaders did not transfer these participants to positions where their training was directly beneficial.[32]

"Personnel turnover" at the sureté's training center and a "lack of written documentation" hindered efforts at understanding the rationale behind police participant selection.[33] Still, some observations can be made. The former chief of the sureté training bureau asserted that proficiency in English was a principal determinant. This certainly accounted for some inconsistencies, but not all. Other factors negatively influenced participant selection. MSUG political scientists Robert Scigliano and Guy Fox insisted that the "Vietnamese government occasionally used" the participant program to "dispose of unwanted personnel by reassigning their jobs while they were abroad or to provide political favorites with free trips to other countries."[34]

There is evidence to support these conclusions. Citing security concerns in the countryside, politically influential Vietnamese province chiefs often refused to send their competent high-level officers for overseas training. Instead, they sent inexperienced young policemen with "intermediate rank" and little real authority to implement change. Police officials transferred many of these participants after they returned to Vietnam. "Without exception," moreover, even before knowing the content of their study program, police candidates wanted "to travel to the United States for training." The MSUG maintained that after selection many of the Vietnamese had "no desire to follow the course" of instruction for which they had been nominated. In such cases, the opportunity to visit another country was the participant's reason for coming to America.[35]

Like their civil service counterparts, police supervisors often viewed returning police participants with "suspicion and envy, and restrain[ed] their efforts to initiate improvements."[36] The principal exceptions were cases in which a participant's superior was also "American-trained." In the summer of 1958 and the spring of 1959, two small groups of high-level Vietnamese police officials visited the United States on two-month observation tours. Among them were Nguyen Van Hay, the deputy to the director general of the sureté; Le Cang Dam, one of the heads of the sureté's passport-visa department; and Nguyen Van Huong, director of training for the sureté. The purpose of the trip was to orient individuals in authority to U.S. law enforcement and government methods. As MSUG police division chief Howard Hoyt noted, Michigan State wanted Vietnamese leaders to be "friendly to American ideas."[37]

The two-month tours involved a great deal of travel in which police leaders visited numerous local, state, and national law enforcement organizations. For example, between July and August 1958, Vietnamese officials visited police departments in Milwaukee, Chicago, and Detroit, as well as in Canada. Additional stops were made in Washington, D.C., at the U.S. Treasury Department, the Federal Bureau of Investigation, and the Central Intelligence Agency. Vietnamese officials typically remained several days in each place, in order to examine police methodology. MSUG member Gilbert Shelby, a former Detroit police officer, noted that the visitors learned a great deal in Chicago, inspecting that department's vice and narcotics division and the investigative and scientific bureaus. He observed that "considerable knowledge of these techniques [was] gained by the visiting officers from Vietnam because they showed a great deal of interest and asked many questions and entered into discussion with the officers."[38]

Following their return to Vietnam, Hay and Dam made a number of instructive comments about the trip. Both valued their experience at the federal law enforcement agencies, and Dam suggested that more time "should have been spent in Washington."[39] Hay recalled that while overall the tour was well planned, in a number of instances the host organization appeared unprepared for visitors. On a personal level, Dam was pleasantly surprised to be treated so well. Hoyt noted that numerous Vietnamese warned Dam that "he would be discriminated against because of his color and that Americans would not be friendly." He was curious "as to why people here [South Vietnam] who had been in America would make such remarks."[40]

In retrospect, the MSUG should have expanded these observational tours, which created goodwill and yielded important information. However, to ease the transition of returnees into the workforce, the trips needed to be integrated into the entire overseas instructional program. In 1960, the MSUG asserted that "used in careful conjunction with longer-term technical training programs for participants, the short-term tours could well pave the way for much more effective post-training utilization of participants."[41]

A more organized program would have alleviated some of the returning participant's problems. Waltman argued that some difficulties might have been averted had the MSUG personnel in Saigon maintained better communication with a participant's superior during training. "Too often," he noted, university advisers did not follow up. They "considered their responsibility for the trainees terminated" once the Vietnamese departed for the United States. In some instances, however, the participants created their own troubles either by acting arrogant or by trying to initiate radical changes too quickly. There were also some unforeseeable situations, such as the reorganization of a bureau and the changing of a participant's supervisor.[42]

In contrast to the police and public administration participant program, all of the NIA's "regular" faculty members, including its leaders, went abroad for training.

The MSUG's close connection to the institute and the primary faculty's small size (sixteen members in 1960) made this feasible. Typically, the professors came to the United States "on four- to nine-month observation and study tours."[43] Michigan State's goal was to replace the NIA's French educational philosophy, which emphasized legal instruction, with an American one stressing public administration.[44]

As Fox and Scigliano noted, these trips, "with a few notable exceptions," were "disappointing." Most of the professors who came to America were older and too set in their ways to profit from the classroom experience. The university had difficulty "locating the proper type and level of course work" for NIA staff. The age difference between them and traditional college students created an "uncomfortable" learning environment. In several cases, Fox and Scigliano observed, institute "personnel seemed to regard" the tours as "pleasure excursions." Yet some NIA faculty did profit from the experience and later assumed responsibility for teaching public administration classes that the MSUG had implemented. In particular, "as a consequence of his trips abroad," Nghiem Dang, the institute's vice rector, "developed a keen understanding of American educational practices and a strong research bent," which culminated in the 1966 publication of *Viet-Nam: Politics and Public Administration*. The book was the first extensive study of Vietnamese public administration produced in English.[45]

To increase the influence of American methodology at the NIA and solve the institute's faculty shortage, in 1958 Michigan State expanded the participant program. The MSUG sent young NIA staff members and talented graduate students abroad for doctorates in public administration and related fields. Further, in an effort to speed up the process, the MSUG recruited several Vietnamese graduate students already studying in the United States. In particular, the university targeted individuals in need of financial assistance. Michigan State was willing to provide these students with funding if they "would commit themselves to teach for a certain number of years" at the NIA.[46] Between 1958 and 1962 the MSUG and the NIA together selected seventeen doctoral candidates, two of them sponsored by the United States Operations Mission (USOM) and fifteen by Michigan State. Most of the students attended American universities, including Michigan State.[47]

The time and energy required to obtain a doctorate hindered the Ph.D. project's success. The participant program did not offer the doctorate until 1958 because Diem's government and the USOM feared that gifted Vietnamese would not return if allowed to leave South Vietnam for extended periods. To complete their training, Vietnamese students often needed to remain in the United States, away from friends and family, for several years. The problems of a normal participant

101

became compounded by the doctoral student's long absence from home and the added pressures of a rigorous study regimen.[48]

The Ph.D. program challenged its participants. On occasion Michigan State was forced to suggest that some of the Vietnamese withdraw from the doctoral program because of poor performance. For example, after almost a year of study, the university informed the NIA's rector, Vu Quoc Thong, that Buu Dich, a political science student at Michigan State, was "not capable of obtaining a Ph.D."[49] Dich was a graduate of the institute and Thong's former assistant there.[50]

Dich's situation was "rather perplexing." Although NIA leaders questioned his capabilities, Michigan State University had accepted him for graduate study. The institute's need for a more educated faculty in public administration justified the gamble. NIA vice rector Dang predicted that Dich would last only one year in America. MSUG and NIA officials agreed to reassess Dich's academic status after two school quarters. If he proved unable to do doctoral work, the institute would recall him to serve in either an administrative or a research position, but not in the classroom.[51]

Michigan State staff evaluations of Dich were decidedly mixed. Political scientist John Fenton notified the MSUG campus coordinator that Dich excelled in his class. "I bring this to your attention because my psychological predisposition was to grade him down after you raised the issue. Then the fact he made an A in PLS 332 is, to me, pretty good evidence that he is one of our better Vietnamese students."[52] In contrast, Dich did poorly in public administration courses, "below the standard expected" of graduate students.[53] Moreover, MSUG officials doubted his work ethic after they could not persuade him to take a regular course load.[54]

Dich balked at taking more classes, saying he had a poor command of spoken English, which hindered his ability to communicate and understand lectures. To remedy the situation, he read *Time* and *Reader's Digest* magazines, attended movies, and translated into English such books as Jean-Jacques Rousseau's *The Social Contract*. In addition, he had an American roommate and made a conscious effort to converse with faculty members. On one occasion, Dich chatted with a teacher "while drinking a cup of coffee in a bar." Although fearful of having made a linguistic mistake, he enjoyed the experience. "Never before had I talked to a professor with so much liberty," he noted, "but I am afraid that this conversation could be a cause of conflict."[55]

In September 1960, some eighteen months after arriving at Michigan State, Dich graduated with a master's degree in political science. The MSUG informed him that the degree was "terminal"; he could not pursue a doctorate. The institute needed public administration instructors, and Dich's poor grades in those courses "outweigh[ed] his success in other areas."[56] Michigan State seemingly had little difficulty rationalizing the decision. MSUG chief adviser Ralph Smuckler maintained that Ph.D. participants "must make the grade academically, and to have a few of them fail would actually add to the prestige" of those returning with the doctorate. Dich subsequently did not receive a regular faculty appointment. Instead, the NIA assigned him to be a research assistant.[57]

Even the most qualified students often struggled. One, Nguyen Duy Xuan, had the advantage of a strong background in English before starting work on his doctorate. He had attended the University of Birmingham in England from 1951 to 1954 and three years later began graduate study in economics at Vanderbilt University. However, by the time he took preliminary examinations for the doctorate in late 1959, his health was declining and Xuan wished to return home. Probably due to stress, he developed a case of ulcers.[58]

Xuan's schooling during the 1957–58 academic year had been financed by the International Cooperation Administration, the U.S. government agency that allocated nonmilitary assistance to foreign countries. In August, the MSUG became his sponsor, selecting him as their first Ph.D. candidate. Having agreed to teach at the NIA after graduation, Xuan received tuition, $240 a month in living expenses, and $150 a year in book allowance. The MSUG evaluation of him emphasized that "[w]e have excercised [sic] extreme caution in selecting Mr. Xuan" as a participant. "His years in England have provided him not only with a facility with English but also with an ability to move in a western world."[59]

By the spring of 1959, Xuan had started to buckle under the pressure of graduate school and exhibited signs of homesickness. Although he passed the doctoral exams that fall, his stomach hurt. In late October, Xuan jokingly remarked that he had already bid "'adieu' to cigarettes, beer, wine, coffee and a number of other good things!"[60] Several weeks later, he entered Vanderbilt Hospital for an appendectomy and treatment for ulcers. Having taken the exams and recuperated, Xuan was determined to go home. Elsie Cunningham, the MSUG campus participant director, observed that Xuan's "desire to return to Vietnam to complete his dissertation has not abated one bit, and in fact, he talks of swimming the Pacific Ocean if necessary."[61]

Xuan's decision worried Michigan State officials for two reasons: they feared, first, that he would not finish his dissertation from Vietnam and, second, that his departure might encourage other participants to leave. Xuan's adviser at Vanderbilt, professor of economics David C. Cole, supported his student's request.

He informed Chief Adviser Smuckler and political scientist Stanley Gabis, Sheinbaum's successor as MSUG campus coordinator, that Vanderbilt permitted foreign students to write their dissertations at home and did not require them to return for oral defenses. Furthermore, Cole argued that the necessary Vietnamese resources were not available in the United States. "Mr. Xuan could not do a thesis in this country on economic conditions in Vietnam that would be satisfactory" to Vanderbilt's economics department.[62] Although acknowledging Cole's point, Gabis asserted that the NIA wanted participants to finish the doctorate before returning and that this was virtually a requirement for joining the faculty.[63]

In a subsequent letter, reiterating his argument, Cole added that Xuan also had overriding personal reasons that could not be ignored. "[O]ne factor that is bearing heavily upon [Xuan's] mind is a forth-coming marriage," Cole noted. "It seems that he has been committed to the eldest of a string of sisters and none of the others can get married until Mr. Xuan skims off the top layer. Thus, you see that your position has earth-shattering sociological implications."[64]

The MSUG relented, and Chief Adviser Smuckler told Cole that although his Saigon staff disapproved, "if an emotional problem exists, we are willing to accept the inevitable."[65] Xuan returned to Saigon in February 1960 and soon after was married. Writing the MSUG East Lansing staff about the ceremony, the groom noted that Cole "was the only 'Ugly American' I had at the party."[66] In spring, Xuan joined the NIA staff. Within a year, he was an assistant professor and head of the research division.[67]

Michigan State believed that Xuan's desire to return to Vietnam indicated that a crisis was developing. Writing Lloyd D. Musolf, the MSUG chief adviser in Saigon, Gabis maintained that while Xuan cited familial concerns, the problem was more serious than homesickness. The "Ph.D. participants simply do not have enough incentive to complete their program," he said. "I find myself grasping for straws." The MSUG should seek "very specific assurances from someone at a rather high level . . . that the Vietnam Ph.D. participants are actively supported and are assured of responsible assignments when they return to Vietnam."[68]

Musolf shared his colleague's anxiety. Contacting Gabis ten days later, Musolf commented that he had met with the secretary of state at the presidency, Nguyen Dinh Thuan, and "emphasized the two points that you had mentioned." Musolf noted that while Thuan would not make guarantees on the professional status of returning participants, he "was very glad to assure me that he would write letters" to each of them. Musolf also spoke with Vice Rector Dang. In a similar manner, Dang would not make "advance commitments . . . as to the rank of returning Ph.D.

participants." In closing, Musolf remarked that although Xuan may have had valid reasons for returning, "I am afraid that the other participants may view the situation as one in which those who can dream up the best excuses for returning can do so. We must break into this line of thinking and improve morale." Musolf assured Gabis that the Saigon staff would do everything it could to facilitate the success of the participants.[69]

The MSUG's fears seemed well placed. During this same period, Tran Ngoc Phat, the participant whom Michigan State faculty members often characterized as their "best candidate," also expressed a desire to return home. Extremely temperamental, Phat continually complained of loneliness and the rigors of graduate study. The MSUG was encouraging and patient with him. On numerous occasions, participant director Cunningham and other Michigan State faculty persuaded him to remain in the doctoral program.

Phat, the son of a retired soldier, was in his early twenties and married. A graduate of the NIA, he possessed an excellent command of English and a background in law and political science, and had served in the General Directorate of Budget and Foreign Aid. Waltman asserted that Phat was "hungry for the degree" and would "work his head off to get it." Consequently, the MSUG was both surprised and troubled when Phat became discontented.[70]

In July 1959, MSUG campus coordinator Sheinbaum sensed that a problem was developing. As Musolf and Gabis illustrated, the participants worried about their job prospects upon returning to Vietnam. In particular, Phat was "very much concerned with prestige and status problems."[71] The doctoral students feared that Vietnamese officials would categorize them with the other participants. Sheinbaum argued that the situation was further aggravated by assigning Buu Dich the status of a doctoral student. Dich had "neither the maturity nor motivation in the academic sense for what is involved," he stated. "There are strong reasons to believe that the other candidates resent being classified with him."[72]

Adamant about the image issue, Phat transferred in the fall semester from Michigan State to Harvard University. Several months later, he telephoned Gabis about some problems he was having and then informed him that he wanted to return to Vietnam. Specifically, he complained about his landlady, about having to sign for textbooks, and about the U.S. government's reduction of his allowance from $10 to $8 a day. Since Phat was doing "very well" academically, Gabis considered the participant's concern over these "minor administrative" difficulties to be "rather strange" and quite disturbing.[73]

105

A flurry of correspondence among the MSUG staff followed Phat's request to go home. After Xuan decided to complete his degree from Vietnam, Michigan State desperately wanted to keep Phat in the United States. The MSUG feared the loss of another promising scholar would severely damage the Ph.D. participant program. During a twenty-day period, Gabis, Musolf, Wesley Fishel, and others wrote at least seven letters reevaluating participant policies and trying to persuade Phat to continue working toward the doctorate. On a personal level, Michigan State faculty member Jason Finkle tried to console Phat by sharing his own graduate school struggles. Finkle recalled that "with continuous financial problems," he felt "eternally frustrated." However, having received the degree, Finkle asserted, "I have never doubted for a moment that it was the wisest choice I have ever made."[74]

In December, Musolf informed Gabis that "both NIA and MSU people have been virtually incredulous at the idea of Phat, whom they regard as a fine and eager student, wanting to return to Vietnam now."[75] Fishel sent Gabis a telling letter in which he pointed out that some of the participants' problems could be traced to Michigan State and Diem's administration. He suggested that Phat perhaps was a "quitter" or, like Dich, "not of top quality," and should never have been sent to the United States for training. "However, it does seem to me that both we [the MSUG] and the [Vietnamese] Government have been rather lax and unsystematic in our planning for this program." Fishel faulted Diem's government for not providing Michigan State with better "talent" and for not showing greater interest in the candidates it sent overseas. Implying that the MSUG's Saigon personnel were partly to blame, he argued that the participants were not "sufficiently well prepared on their arrival" in either the English language or American culture. Furthermore, Fishel suggested that after some eighteen to twenty-one months, the participants should be sent home for a break to reestablish professional and familial ties. Hopefully, he commented, this would combat the "manifest loneliness" felt by some of the Ph.D. candidates who were "working under serious linguistic and psychological handicaps."[76]

Several days after Fishel's letter arrived, Phat himself wrote Gabis. His remarks confirmed some of Fishel's observations, especially those concerning the isolation experienced by participants. "I have found myself physically and mentally so depressed—in part because of homesickness, I guess—, that it is difficult for me to study anymore," Phat remarked. In closing, he emphasized the difficulty of graduate study. Only "privileged and gifted persons can afford a high degree of learning; I have tried and failed. So please . . . accept my humble . . . request for coming back. With what I have learnt I hope to benefit my dear people."[77] By the end of December, the MSUG staff had calmed Phat. As Gabis observed to Musolf, "the immediate crisis with Phat appears to have evaporated, and we can rest easily for the time being." The following fall, Ruben Austin, the assistant dean of the College of Business and Public Service, visited Phat in Boston. Austin reported that he was making satisfactory progress toward the doctorate and now had an American roommate. However, the dean observed that Phat was still high-strung and anxious about his status in Vietnam.[78]

From 1960 to 1962, Phat made steady progress toward completing the doctorate, but repeatedly requested to return home. On one occasion, he told Cunningham that "I JUST CANNOT STUDY ANY MORE . . . and want to go right now back to VN even at the price of humiliating myself."[79] In May 1961, Phat passed his qualifying exams for the doctorate and appeared to be happily working on his dissertation. Having chosen a topic, "Development of Vietnamese Nationalism Up To 1954," he visited the Library of Congress in Washington and conferred with Vietnam specialist Bernard Fall about the availability of Asian resources in the United States. However, by the summer of 1962, Phat was asking to be allowed to complete his work from Vietnam. He noted that "I have advanced in my academic life perhaps, but I cannot live without my family . . . I promise to do anything you want me to, just to be able to get a job at [the] NIA to help my old father and lonely wife and children."[80] Michigan State supported the participant's decision and informed NIA Rector Thong that Phat would probably benefit from access to Saigon library materials.[81]

The MSUG records concerning overseas doctoral students are incomplete because Michigan State's official files go through only 1962, the year the university's Vietnam contract ended. However, from the available data, some observations can be made. The MSUG's doctoral training program proved only partly successful. By 1965, it had produced eight NIA faculty members, most of whom did not earn a doctorate. According to MSUG political scientists Scigliano and Fox, several of the returnees who affiliated themselves with the institute received bachelor's and master's degrees, but only Xuan obtained a doctorate. He graduated from Vanderbilt in 1963 with a Ph.D. in economics. Although the records do not indicate whether Phat returned to the NIA, he never completed his dissertation; he received a master of arts degree in political science in 1962 from Harvard.[82]

Xuan was unique among Ph.D. participants in that he completed his schooling and went home to teach at the NIA and serve as minister of national economy. Two other Vietnamese participants who obtained doctorates chose not to work at the institute, but instead for other government agencies. In another instance, a former participant left the NIA to join the South Vietnamese Army. In several cases, Diem's fear about students leaving South Vietnam appeared warranted. Of the five doctoral candidates remaining in the United States after 1965, Fox and Scigliano asserted, some "apparently have no intention of returning to Vietnam."[83] One of the problems, Xuan noted, was the "relatively low salaries" the institute paid. For a number of participants, the lure of either remaining in the United States or working for a higher-paying, more prestigious Vietnamese government agency proved too strong. Greater "incentives and facilities" were necessary, Xuan argued, "to attract" potential NIA faculty members.[84]

Admittedly, participant training experienced numerous difficulties, and the MSUG was forced to reevaluate its policies a number of times. Michigan State failed to make the program a priority until late 1957, when the first full-time participant director, Howard Waltman, joined the staff. Prior to that, MSUG campus coordinator Sheinbaum was understaffed and worked with a part-time director in Saigon. According to Waltman, university advisers in Saigon were "too preoccupied with immediate problems" to recognize the importance of long-range planning. The MSUG "often viewed" participant training "as an independent program activity," he observed, "rather than a tool available to them in performing their substantive mission."[85]

Waltman's criticism applied to MSUG advisers as well as Vietnamese officials. The program's objective was apparent to both parties: to strengthen South Vietnam's government by training its police and public administration personnel. However, as the 1960 MSUG police participant report noted, somewhere "between the definition of objectives and their accomplishment the clarity ends."[86] Quite often the program lacked sufficient planning and seemed to have been "played by ear."[87] Fishel reiterated this point and also criticized Diem's government for not showing more interest in the participants, especially those pursuing doctorates.

In a 1993 interview, Sheinbaum commented that he had "poured a lot" into the participant program and "felt very good about it." When he returned to Saigon in 1966, he recalled, "I kept seeing" former participants, most of whom "were doing very well."[88] A number of participants like Xuan gained valuable experience and contributed to Vietnam's growth. However, as the MSUG conceded, "a great deal more might have been accomplished" had the participant program been better organized.[89]

NOTES

1. *Final Report of the Michigan State University Advisory Group,* 1962, 36, 46, box 658, folder 6, Michigan State University Vietnam Project Papers, Michigan State University Archives and Historical Collections, East Lansing, Michigan (hereafter cited as Vietnam Project Papers).

2. Ibid., 52–54.

3. Ibid., 40, 60; Michigan State University Participants, 1955–61, box 667, folder 52, Vietnam Project Papers; Robert Scigliano and Guy H. Fox, *Technical Assistance in Vietnam: The Michigan State University Experience* (New York: Praeger, 1965), 36.

4. Michigan State University Participants, 1955–61, *Final Report,* 60; Edward Geary Lansdale, *In the Midst of Wars: An American's Mission to Southeast Asia* (New York: Harper and Row Publishers, 1972), 2, 21–25, 47, 85.

5. *Final Report,* 46; Ralph Turner's Report to the Minister of the Interior, box 680, folder 9, Vietnam Project Papers, p. 26; Howard Hoyt to Arthur Brandstatter, 23 June 1955, box 679, folder 44, Vietnam Project Papers; Arthur Brandstatter, interview with author, 17 July 1992; Scigliano and Fox, *Technical Assistance in Vietnam,* 2.

6. Stanley K. Sheinbaum, "Vietnam—A Study in Freedom," *Michigan State University Magazine* (February 1956), 10, 12; "News Release Department of Information Services," 9 March 1956, box 657, folder 67, Vietnam Project Papers; Michigan State University Participants, 1955–61, Vietnam Project Papers.

7. "News Release Department of Information Services MSU," 6 October 1955, box 657, folder 67, Vietnam Project Papers.

8. Ibid., 30 December 1955, box 657, folder 67; Wesley Fishel to John Hannah, 1 February 1956, box 646, folder 51, Vietnam Project Papers; Stanley Sheinbaum to Edward Weidner, 16 February 1956, box 628, folder 98, Vietnam Project Papers; Michigan State University Participants, 1955–61, Vietnam Project Papers.

9. Fishel to Hannah, 1 February 1956; "News Release Department of Information Services," 30 December 1955, box 657, folder 67, Vietnam Project Papers.

10. Stanley K. Sheinbaum to John T. Dorsey, 15 August 1956, box 667, folder 23, Vietnam Project Papers, pp. 3, 5–9.

11. Ibid., 8, 3, 7.

12. Ibid., 9, 2–3.

13. Ibid., 9, 5.

14. Report on MSUG Police Participant Program, 1960, box 692, folder 14, Vietnam Project Papers, pp. 20, 91; Lawrence J. Baril to Howard Hoyt, 16 December 1958, box 672, folder 3, Vietnam Project Papers.

15. Report on MSUG Police Participant Program, 20, 25, 81–89.

16. Ibid., 29–31, 66–68; Elsie Cunningham to Howard Waltman, 6 June 1958, box 671, folder 57, Vietnam Project Papers.

17. Elsie Cunningham to David Cole, 24 May 1957, box 667, folder 24, Vietnam Project Papers, p. 2; Report on MSUG Police Participant Program, 24; Michigan State University Participants, 1955–61, Vietnam Project Papers.

18. Report on MSUG Police Participant Program, 116.

19. Ibid., 24, 110–11, 116, 123–24; *Final Report*, 60.

20. Cunningham to Cole, 24 May 1957, Vietnam Project Papers, pp. 2–3; Michigan State University Participants, 1955–61, Vietnam Project Papers.

21. Report on MSUG Police Participant Program, Vietnam Program Papers, p. 92.

22. Ibid., 83–84.

23. Ibid., 92.

24. Ibid.; Michigan State University Participants, 1955–61, Vietnam Project Papers; Howard L. Waltman, "Cross-Cultural Training in Public Administration," *Public Administration Review* 21 (summer 1961): 145.

25. *Final Report*, 63; Howard L. Waltman to Stanley K. Sheinbaum, 17 November 1958, box 667, folder 30, Vietnam Project Papers, pp. 1–2; *Public Administration Review* (summer 1961): ii; Report on MSUG Police Participant Program, Vietnam Project Papers, p. 70; First Report of the Michigan State University Vietnam Team in Public Administration, 19 August 1955, box 675, folder 74, Vietnam Project Papers, p. 8.

26. Report on MSUG Police Participant Program, 70–71, 81–84, 89; *Final Report*, 62; Waltman, "Cross-Cultural Training in Public Administration," 146.

27. Report on MSUG Police Participant Program, 88–89.

28. Ibid., 71.

29. Ibid., 70–71; *Final Report*, 60, 62; Ralph Smuckler, interview by author, 13 May 1993; Scigliano and Fox, *Technical Assistance in Vietnam*, 11.

30. Howard Waltman to Stanley Sheinbaum, 6 February 1959, box 667, folder 31, Vietnam Project Papers, p. 1; Nghiem Dang, *Viet-Nam: Politics and Public Administration* (Honolulu: East-West Center Press, 1966), 213.

31. Waltman, "Cross-Cultural Training in Public Administration," 146.

32. Report on MSUG Police Participant Program, 57-61; Waltman, "Cross-Cultural Training in Public Administration," 143.

33. Report on MSUG Police Participant Program, Vietnam Project Papers, pp. 60–61.

34. Scigliano and Fox, *Technical Assistance in Vietnam*, 20; Report on MSUG Police Participant Program, 61, 64.

35. Report on MSUG Police Participant Program, 64–66.

36. Ibid., 42.

37. Howard Hoyt to Coordinator, 31 July 1958, box 672, folder 14, Vietnam Project Papers; Stanley Sheinbaum to Arthur Brandstatter, 12 May 1958, box 672, folder 9, Vietnam Project Papers; Report on MSUG Police Participant Program, 42, 97–99.

38. Report on Police Leaders' Visits, August 1958, box 672, folder 13, Vietnam Project Papers; Hoyt to Coordinator, 31 July 1958, Vietnam Project Papers; Sheinbaum to Brandstatter, 12 May 1958, Vietnam Project Papers.

39. Howard Hoyt, memorandum on Le Cang Dam, 4 November 1958, box 691, folder 43, Vietnam Project Papers.

40. Ibid.; Jack Ryan to Howard Hoyt, 11 September 1958, box 691, folder 43, Vietnam Project Papers.

41. Report on MSUG Police Participant Program, Vietnam Project Papers, pp. 42–43.

42. Waltman, "Cross-Cultural Training in Public Administration," 146.

43. Scigliano and Fox, *Technical Assistance in Vietnam*, 35.

44. Ibid.; *Final Report*, 25.

45. Scigliano and Fox, *Technical Assistance in Vietnam*, 35–36; Dang, *Viet-Nam*, v; Waltman, "Cross-Cultural Training in Public Administration," 145.

46. Chief Advisor to Coordinator, 16 June 1958, box 671, folder 72, Vietnam Project Papers.

47. Scigliano and Fox, *Technical Assistance in Vietnam*, 36; Chief Advisor to Coordinator, 16 June 1958, Vietnam Project Papers.

48. Scigliano and Fox, *Technical Assistance in Vietnam*, 36.

49. Lloyd D. Musolf to Vu Quoc Thong, 22 December 1959, box 664, folder 34, Vietnam Project Papers.

50. Howard L. Waltman to Elsie Cunningham, 25 November 1958, box 667, folder 30, Vietnam Project Papers, p. 3; "Ph.D. Candidates in the United States," box 667, folder 52, Vietnam Project Papers, p. 3.

51. Lloyd D. Musolf to Stanley T. Gabis, 30 September 1959, box 670, folder 40, Vietnam Project Papers; Howard L. Waltman to Elsie Cunningham, 10 December 1958, Vietnam Project Papers.

52. John Fenton to Stanley Gabis, 9 September 1959, box 670, folder 40, Vietnam Project Papers.

53. Stanley Gabis to Howard Waltman, 16 September 1959, box 670, folder 40, Vietnam Project Papers.

54. Elsie Cunningham to Howard Waltman, 12 May 1959, box 670, folder 40, Vietnam Project Papers; Elsie Cunningham to Stanley Sheinbaum, 24 June 1959, Vietnam Project Papers.

55. Buu Dich to Stanley Gabis, 14 June 1959, box 670, folder 39, Vietnam Project Papers; Buu Dich, "Going to the U.S. as a Participant," December 1960, Vietnam Project Papers.

56. Musolf to Gabis, 30 September 1959, Vietnam Project Papers.

57. Ralph Smuckler to Coordinator, 1 October 1959, box 670, folder 40, Vietnam Project Papers; Ruben Austin to Lloyd D. Musolf, 27 September 1960, box 670, folder 40, Vietnam Project Papers; "Buu Dich, 24 October 1960," box 670. folder 39, Vietnam Project Papers; The National Institute of Administration Catalogue, 1961, box 666, folder 2, Vietnam Project Papers, p. xi.

58. Howard L. Waltman to Vu Quoc Thong, 30 January 1959, box 664, folder 34, Vietnam Project Papers; Stanley Gabis to Lloyd D. Musolf, 23 October 1959, box 671, folder 77, Vietnam Project Papers; Edward W. Weidner, ed., *Development Administration in Asia* (Durham, N.C.: Duke University Press, 1970), xviii; Stanley Gabis to Lloyd D. Musolf, 23 December 1959, box 671, folder 79, Vietnam Project Papers, p. 4.

59. "Coordinator's Evaluation of Nguyen Duy Xuan," 7 May 1958, box 671, folder 57, Vietnam Project Papers; Elsie Cunningham to William Roberts, Foreign Student Adviser, Vanderbilt, 26 August 1958, box 671, folder 58, Vietnam Project Papers; Elsie Cunningham to Nguyen Duy Xuan, 6 May 1958, box 671, folder 57, Vietnam Project Papers; Elsie Cunningham to Nguyen Duy Xuan, 30 January 1959, box 671, folder 59, Vietnam Project Papers.

60. Nguyen Duy Xuan to Elsie Cunningham, 21 October 1959, box 671, folder 60, Vietnam Project Papers.

61. Elsie Cunningham to Ralph Smuckler, 7 October 1959, box 671, folder 60, Vietnam Project Papers; Elizabeth C. Campbell to Elsie Cunningham, 4 November 1959, box 671, folder 60, Vietnam Project Papers.

62. David Cole to Ralph Smuckler, 28 October 1959, box 671, folder 60, Vietnam Project Papers.

63. Stanley Gabis to David Cole, 2 October 1959, Vietnam Project Papers; David Cole to Stanley Gabis, 30 September 1959, ibid.; Stanley Gabis to Lloyd D. Musolf, 4 December 1959, box 671, folder 78, Vietnam Project Papers.

64. Cole to Smuckler, 28 October 1959, Vietnam Project Papers.

65. Ralph Smuckler to David Cole, 5 November 1959, box 671, folder 60, Vietnam Project Papers.

66. Nguyen Duy Xuan to Elsie Cunningham, 3 March 1960, box 671, folder 61, Vietnam Project Papers.

67. Nguyen Duy Xuan to Elsie Cunningham, 30 April 1960; Lloyd D. Musolf to Vu Quoc Thong, 1 February 1960, box 664, folder 35, Vietnam Project Papers; National Institute of Administration Catalogue, 1961, Vietnam Project Papers.

68. Gabis to Musolf, 4 December 1959, Vietnam Project Papers; Musolf to Thong, 1 February 1960, Vietnam Project Papers.

69. Lloyd D. Musolf to Stanley Gabis, 14 December 1959, box 671, folder 78, Vietnam Project Papers.

70. Waltman to Cunningham, 25 November 1958, Vietnam Project Papers, p. 2; Tran Ngoc Phat, Certificate of Eligibility for Exchange Visitor Status, 16 November 1960, box 671, folder 12, Vietnam Project Papers.

71. Stanley Gabis to Edward W. Weidner, 15 September 1959, box 671, folder 77, Vietnam Project Papers.

72. Stanley Sheinbaum to Ralph Smuckler, 31 July 1959, box 671, folder 76, Vietnam Project Papers.

73. Gabis to Musolf, 4 December 1959; Gabis to Musolf, 23 December 1959, Vietnam Project Papers; Elsie Cunningham to Tran Ngoc Phat, 24 September 1959, box 671, folder 15, Vietnam Project Papers.

74. Jason Finkle to Tran Ngoc Phat, 18 December 1959, box 671, folder 16, Vietnam Project Papers; Musolf to Gabis, 14 December 1959, Vietnam Project Papers.

75. Musolf to Gabis, 14 December 1959.

76. Wesley Fishel to Stanley Gabis, 5 December 1959, box 667, folder 34, Vietnam Project Papers.

77. Tran Ngoc Phat to Stanley T. Gabis, 7 December 1959, box 671, folder 78, Vietnam Project Papers.

78. Rubin Austin to Lloyd D. Musolf, 5 October 1960, box 671, folder 83, Vietnam Project Papers; *Final Report*, 64.

79. Tran Ngoc Phat to Elsie Cunningham, 1 January 1960, box 671, folder 17, Vietnam Project Papers.

80. Tran Ngoc Phat to James B. Hendry, 20 June 1962, box 671, folder 23, Vietnam Project Papers.

81. Tran Ngoc Phat to Ruben Austin, 9 May 1961, box 671, folder 20, Vietnam Project Papers; Phat to Austin, 14 July 1961, box 671, folder 21, Vietnam Project Papers; Tran Ngoc Phat, "Summer Report," 11 August 1961, box 671, folder 21, Vietnam Project Papers; Ralph Smuckler to Vu Quoc Thong, 6 July 1962, box 671, folder 23, Vietnam Project Papers.

82. Scigliano and Fox, *Technical Assistance in Vietnam*, 36; *Final Report*, 25; Weidner, *Development Administration in Asia*, xviii; Nguyen Duy Xuan, "Technical Assistance to a Public Administration Institute: The Vietnam Case," in ibid., 380; Harvard University Alumni Association, phone conversation with author, 28 February 1994.

83. Scigliano and Fox, *Technical Assistance in Vietnam*, 36.

84. Xuan, "Technical Assistance," 395; Scigliano and Fox, *Technical Assistance in Vietnam*, 36.

85. Waltman, "Cross-Cultural Training in Public Administration," 142.

86. Report on MSUG Police Participant Program, Vietnam Project Papers, p. 65.

87. Ibid., 74.

88. Stanley K. Sheinbaum, interview by author, 18 March 1993.

89. Report on MSUG Police Participant Program, Vietnam Project Papers, p. 74.

CHAPTER 6

"A CRUMBLING BASTION": THE END OF CONSENSUS [1]

By the early 1960s, the government of South Vietnamese president Ngo Dinh Diem was collapsing. Dwight Eisenhower and his successor, John Kennedy, had not persuaded him to enact significant economic and political reforms. As a result, Diem did not enjoy the support of his countrymen and South Vietnam had become financially and militarily dependent on the United States for its survival. Moreover, the regime faced a growing communist insurgency in the countryside. Remnants of the Vietminh, the communist-led revolutionaries who had defeated France in 1954, were growing impatient under Diem's oppressive rule and initiated offensive operations in the south that his forces were incapable of combating. Nation building was failing, causing officials from both countries to doubt Diem's leadership capabilities. He barely survived a coup in 1960 led by dissident South Vietnamese Army colonels. Three years later, the military assassinated Diem. Disillusioned with him, the Kennedy administration encouraged the plot.

For most of the 1960s, the Michigan State University Group (MSUG) project was an object of intense controversy. The controversies went to the heart of the debates on America's Vietnam policies and the role of universities in the cold war. Like U.S. policy makers, the Michigan State community was split in its opinion of Diem. While a number of faculty firmly supported him, others viewed the Vietnamese president as a dictator destined to lose South Vietnam to the communists. Rifts surfaced within the MSUG when several members openly criticized Diem in two 1961 articles. In large part, he declined to renew the university's technical-assistance contract because of this.

Following the MSUG's ouster from Vietnam in 1962, Michigan State faculty debated the propriety of any university involvement in American foreign affairs. Drawing national attention, the conflict reemerged in 1966 with the publication of a story in *Ramparts*, a leftist California-based Catholic magazine. Among other

115

things, *Ramparts* accused the MSUG of acting as a front for Central Intelligence Agency (CIA) operations and of helping to "secure" Diem's dictatorship.[2] Because of his friendship with Diem, MSUG chief adviser Wesley Fishel figured prominently in the exposé and thereafter became a target for the student antiwar movement.

By the spring of 1960, Fishel and other confidants of the South Vietnamese president, such as land reform adviser Wolf Ladejinsky, recognized that their friend was in trouble. Conveying the severity of the situation to Fishel, Ladejinsky observed in early March that assassinations were increasing in the countryside. "The Communists have never been bolder; and . . . while our friend Diem is profoundly disturbed, he shows no inclination (so far) to mend his ways . . ." Ladejinsky concluded ominously: "He'd better court his people if he wishes to remain in the saddle."[3]

Ladejinsky's remarks reflected the temper of many American officials, and Fishel felt compelled to contact Diem the following month. He informed the president that he had been "questioned sharply about the 'dictatorship' in Vietnam" at a recent conference of the Association for Asian Studies, and that while he understood why certain forms of repression were needed, other experts "do not know you or your philosophies as I do, and they tend to be more skeptical of your motivation and of your sincerity of purpose." Fishel advised Diem that he needed information to convince the skeptics "that you continue to fight a war against the Communists even today, and that you deserve to be supported."[4]

Washington was grasping for ways to coax the Vietnamese president to initiate reforms. The dilemma U.S. officials faced was how to get him to do so without withholding aid and thereby hurting South Vietnam. A number of U.S. policymakers, including the ambassador to South Vietnam, Elbridge Durbrow, believed time was growing short and that drastic measures must be taken to prevent the Saigon government from falling. In September, he informed the State Department that "it may become necessary for [the] U.S. Government to begin consideration [of] alternative courses of action and leaders in order to achieve our objective."[5]

Fishel and Ladejinsky's comments appeared prophetic when Diem narrowly subdued a November 1960 coup attempt and Durbrow took a neutral position. Led by three South Vietnamese colonels, an "elite parachute regiment" encircled the presidential palace on the morning of the eleventh and assumed control of the army headquarters, radio station, and airport.[6] Diem, and his brother and sister-in-law, Ngo Dinh Nhu and Madame Nhu, retreated to the wine cellar as the Vietnamese president's personal guard engaged the revolutionaries. Although they could have easily captured Diem, the coup leaders chose not to. "[M]otivated by personal and patriotic frustrations," one scholar has written, "[they] sought only to compel Diem to agree to reforms and not to force him out."[7] On the surface, Diem appeared to negotiate with the colonels in good faith and promised to make significant changes, including the formation of a new government. In private, he used the time to radio loyal army troops outside of Saigon. These forces entered the capital on the twelfth and ended the coup.[8]

MSUG reports of the event are detailed, and subsequent correspondence shows Michigan State divided in its assessment of Diem and the university's role in South Vietnam. MSUG Police Division chief Ralph Turner and his family lived three blocks from the presidential palace and had to evacuate because of the proximity of the fighting. On the day of the coup, a neighbor informed Turner that "troops were setting up a six inch mortar" next to his house and "they might start shelling the [p]alace" within the hour. The Turners joined a number of other Michigan State families staying with MSUG police adviser Victor Strecher, whose home was "quite a ways from the [p]alace." In all, twenty-six adults and children "s[a]t out [the] revolution" there. "[H]aving been through a revolution or two during his South American experience," another MSUG police adviser, "Tommy" Adkins, "thoughtfully brought along a supply of scotch," Turner noted. "We had to send out for beer a few times, and were continually running out of soda and ice cubes; otherwise, we managed quite well." The children also adjusted to the situation by creating a game they called "Palace." "Every time they heard gunfire," Turner observed, "they would holler 'Palace!' and dive under a bed or sofa."[9]

Turner returned to his home on the thirteenth and found everything intact. After unpacking, he toured the city, discovering the Saigon streets as crowded "as ever; however[,] there was a hushed and sober atmosphere everywhere." He concluded that this was probably due to several factors: the failure of the revolt, the "uncertainty as to what the future held for many," and "the presence of pools of blood" around the palace. Diem's response to the revolt was severe, and "at least four hundred civilians who had joined the paratroopers in their march on the presidential" grounds had died in the fighting.[10] Local feeling about the coup impressed Turner as mixed. "Many [Vietnamese] were pleased and happy that President Diem was still in control, others unquestionably were discouraged, and a certain few were fearful." The "long-range impact" on the MSUG was "still very cloudy," he noted, as American officials waited for indications of political reform from Diem's government. However, "[a]s a result, all of us have a little better understanding of the struggle against Communism and the meaning of Democracy."[11]

Turner's remark reflected a growing sense of concern and disillusionment on the part of the MSUG and home campus staff. MSUG chief adviser Lloyd D. Musolf also believed that a significant segment of Saigon's population appeared happy when the revolutionaries attempted to assume control. Musolf predicted to Fishel that if Diem became "more repressive and . . . no really effective actions are taken to move the country forward on the political and military front, the President is likely to be in for a more serious rebellion in the future."[12]

Only days after the coup, Fishel and Michigan State president John Hannah wrote Diem letters of encouragement. Fishel reassured the Vietnamese president that he still had influential friends in the United States, noting that Hannah and the new Senate Majority Leader, Mike Mansfield, were worried about him. The day of the coup, John Kennedy had urged Mansfield to accept the post of majority leader. "Senator Mansfield," Fishel asserted, "phoned me several times . . . to discuss the situation as did . . . President Hannah, of MSU." Fishel asserted that Hannah "has been a staunch defender of yours in official circles," and is an "unusually well informed man" who "has been Vice President [Richard] Nixon's principal advisor on Foreign Aid questions during the recent [presidential] campaign." Moreover, Fishel professed that Hannah asked him "to go to Vietnam at once," and before departing for Washington, D.C. "had taken the unusual step of writing directly to you."[13] In a subsequent reply, Diem thanked Hannah for his concern, informing him that "[y]our last letter . . . touched me deeply." However, he requested that Fishel remain home because the professor would be more valuable "on the American front line," because the "foreign press" was treating his government unfairly.[14] Immediately after the rebellion, various U.S. journalists became more critical of Diem and started characterizing him as "high-handed" and "authoritarian."[15]

In the past Fishel had written articles defending his friend, and he was willing to do so again. In fact, he had already sent a letter to the *New York Times* asserting that Diem's achievement, the establishment of a viable anticommunist state, was too often overlooked. Although conceding that "Vietnam today still has serious problems and is not a parliamentary democracy on the Western order," he asked whether "such a development [could] reasonably be expected" in just five years in a nation emerging "from nearly a century of colonialism and eight years of bloody civil war." In their attachment to democratic principles, he said, Americans must not be "blinded to the practical limitations imposed by reality."[16]

Numerous faculty in both East Lansing and Saigon sharply disagreed. For example, only eleven days after the coup, Fishel moderated a campus debate between a former MSUG member, political scientist Ralph Smuckler, and a Michigan State economist, Walter Adams. The topic was universities and overseas technical assistance.[17] Along with Michigan State historian John A. Garraty, Adams had just published a critique of American university programs in Europe and Turkey entitled, *Is the World Our Campus?* The Carnegie Endowment had sponsored the research trip for the book during the 1957–58 academic year.[18] "On the basis of our own findings," Adams later recalled, "we became increasingly disillusioned with the effectiveness" of these types of endeavors. "This gave me further perspective on our own efforts in Vietnam, and I became . . . an outspoken critic" of the MSUG project "on the campus."[19]

Ruben Austin, an MSUG coordinator and assistant dean of the College of Business and Public Service at Michigan State, attended part of the debate. He observed that "Walt presented a dramatic case," and that the "whole thing seemed to be centered around VietNam." Had a crowd survey been conducted, Austin believed that Adams would have been the clear winner. "In a most evangelistic fashion, he accused those officially attached to the [Vietnam] [p]roject of supporting" Diem's dictatorship for reasons of personal gain. According to Austin, Adams argued that had the coup succeeded, Michigan State would have quickly switched allegiance to the rebels in order to salvage the MSUG project, "which gives the members diplomatic immunity, a myriad of social activities, cocktail parties, diplomatic automobile plates, etc."[20]

Although he did not discuss Smuckler's defense of the Vietnam program, Austin relayed the story to MSUG chief adviser Musolf. He did so, he said, to warn him of the "bitterness engendered in some sectors" of the campus "against the VietNam [p]roject" and "against all [u]niversity projects." Austin justified the MSUG's work by arguing that Vietnam received long-range benefits from the "guidance of true intellectuals." In addition, he urged Musolf to use "discretion" in politically sensitive situations and not assume a "gadfly position," which served no purpose. Austin advocated a middle-of-the-road approach, arguing that Michigan State could neither be "pure academicians while in VietNam" nor disregard American democratic principles. The campus debate reflected the divisiveness already caused by Vietnam and previewed the turmoil that would later engulf many universities.[21]

Problems first surfaced between Diem and Michigan State in late 1960, when MSUG members back home from South Vietnam began writing articles moderately critical of the Vietnamese government. Among the first were two Michigan State professors, political scientist Robert Scigliano and economist James B. Hendry, who published pieces in the December issue of *Pacific Affairs*, a scholarly journal devoted to the history and contemporary concerns of eastern and southern Asia. Although neither article sought to discredit Diem, both offended him and started a process that led to MSUG's demise.

Though he advocated more freedom to express "opposition viewpoints" in South Vietnam, Scigliano also acknowledged that the threat of communist attack there necessitated certain restrictions on "political liberty."[22] Hendry lobbied for the creation of "short range, high impact" aid programs for brightening the "daily lives" of South Vietnam's farmers.[23] Several months after the articles' publication, Musolf confided to Austin that "President Diem was resentful of Bob Scigliano's article . . . and also took exception to Jim Hendry's notes in the same" journal. Diem did not elaborate on why the pieces offended him, but he noted that they reflected an "ignorance of 'how we do things here.'"[24]

Diem became increasingly intolerant of criticism. Eventually he terminated the MSUG contract, in part because of two articles written by three Michigan State professors who had worked in Vietnam. Appearing in 1961 in the *New Republic*, both essays denounced the South Vietnamese government. Their publication and the MSUG's subsequent ouster prompted vigorous discussion among East Lansing faculty. Editorials appeared in several newspapers, including the university's *State News* and the *Lansing State Journal*.

The first of these two articles was a collaboration by Adrian Jaffe, a visiting professor of English at the University of Saigon, and Milton C. Taylor, a MSUG economist.[25] The two close friends wrote the piece at the urging of fellow economist and confidant Walter Adams. Jaffe and Taylor were an unlikely team. Adams has described the "delightful" Jaffe as "the ultimate satirist and cynic." Taylor, on the other hand, was "a devout Catholic," who went to Vietnam to "help a regime loyal to the West, a regime run by Catholics, . . . that received refugees" from the communist-led North. Taylor returned from Vietnam very disenchanted and together with Jaffe constantly complained about the circumstances there and the MSUG project. "I was getting tired of listening to all that talk," Adams recalled. "I said, 'I don't want to hear you guys continuing this babble at the luncheon table. If you have something to say, publish it! . . . [S]end an article to the *New Republic*. If they reject it, then you can come back and complain.'"[26]

In their essay, Jaffe and Taylor argued that Diem had alienated the Vietnamese people by using oppressive methods (secret police, informants, and concentration camps) against communist and noncommunist political opposition alike.[27] "When the population sees little difference between Diem's autocratic control and Communism, there is little will to defend the government," they asserted.

"Communism may have no positive appeal, but there is also no militant urge to resist the guerrillas."[28] The writers also criticized other MSUG members for refusing to speak out against the South Vietnamese president, alleging that many of the staff did not wish to give up the prestige and benefits of overseas service.[29]

The second article, authored by another MSUG economist, Frank C. Child, echoed many of the complaints about Diem's "police state" methods but also discussed the failed coup. According to Adams, Child was "not a flag waver," but a "very moderate man." After the Jaffe-Taylor publication, he apparently felt the need "to bare his soul."[30] Having witnessed the November insurrection, Child judged that another one was probable and he "strongly request[ed] permission to go home" three months before his MSUG service was to end.[31] Although concerned over the "uneasy security situation," he did not necessarily oppose a military takeover. In reality, Child believed that the military might provide a viable "alternative" to Diem's government. "A military coup," he asserted, might be "the only means by which [effective] leadership could be brought to the fore" and prevent South Vietnam from becoming communist.[32]

Outraged by the articles, Diem notified Michigan State that its contract would not be renewed unless the university could guarantee that its faculty would not publish criticism of his government. Diem informed MSUG chief adviser Guy Fox that the authors "would have been tried . . . for fomenting an insurrection," had they written the pieces while still in Vietnam.[33] Hoping to continue their work at the National Institute of Administration, Michigan State officials tried to placate Diem.[34] They advised him that censoring former project members violated their academic freedom and was impossible. They assured him, however, that future staff would be chosen carefully and individuals likely to write sensationalized articles would not be employed. Diem remained unmoved.[35]

From his perspective, Michigan State probably had outlived its usefulness. Although the university had trained the municipal police and sureté in basic police tactics, its relationship with the civil guard had proven problematic. The MSUG tried to make the guard a civil agency operating on the village level and equipped with simple weaponry. Yet Diem and U.S. Army advisers had envisioned it as a paramilitary unit capable of exercising national police duties and providing support for the South Vietnamese Army. This conflict resulted in bureaucratic infighting and unpreparedness when communist insurgency threatened the South in 1959. Consequently, Diem worried little about Michigan State's departure in June 1962.[36]

Although disenchanted with Diem's dictatorial policies, Fishel visited South Vietnam in 1962 in an attempt to ameliorate the problems between the university and his friend. He wanted Diem to retain Michigan State's services and to soften his regime's antidemocratic methods. Specifically, Fishel was concerned about the growing concentration of power in the hands of Diem's family. "For the first time in seven and one-half years," he wrote Hannah, "I have become a pessimist about the fate of South Vietnam." Referring to Diem's brother and sister-in-law, Ngo Dinh Nhu and Madame Nhu, he asserted that the Vietnamese president was surrounded increasingly by "evil influences." Nhu's policies had hindered the regime for the last six years and "failed miserably to win the people to the side of the government." Madame Nhu, Fishel added, was "as brilliant, vivacious, bitchy, and brutal in her Borgia-like fashion as ever—and . . . alienating substantial segments of the population."[37] If the situation remained unchanged, Fishel confided to Hannah, Diem would not stay in power. Valuing his colleague's opinion, Hannah forwarded the letter to President Kennedy.[38] Thankful for the information, the president's national security adviser, McGeorge Bundy, told the Michigan State president that "Fishel['s] report" was being circulated among those staff "following the situation in Vietnam."[39]

In East Lansing, termination of the project provoked anger among some faculty and administrators, resulting in a number of editorials. Taylor and Jaffe were at the center of the controversy. In a recent interview, Taylor—a self-proclaimed radical—maintained that "I still use Vietnam as a litmus test for where were you when the chips were down? Where was [Bill] Clinton when the chips were down? Well, Clinton was . . . against the war," and "[t]hat [is] good enough for me."[40] About one month after Diem's decision to discontinue the MSUG, Taylor and Jaffe published another article in the *New Republic*, attacking university administrators for accepting government contracts too readily. "What is alarming about university operations abroad," they asserted, "is that the schools have been caught up in endeavors which are often irreconcilable with serious scholarship and which have caused deterioration in the ethical and professional standards of many participating faculty members."[41] Taylor and Jaffe's remarks went to the heart of the conflict over academic participation in foreign affairs. During the mid-to-late 1960s, the issue became increasingly controversial.

Although Taylor and Jaffe had some campus support, there were also a number of vocal critics. One, MSUG economist John M. Hunter, recalled being "aggravated by what was published," because it "wasn't based much on fact."[42] Moreover, he characterized Jaffe and Taylor as "hopelessly naive and unrealistic [in their] view of the world."[43] Stanley E. Bryan, a professor of management, chided the authors for "making sweeping generalizations" about overseas aid projects.[44]

Although President Hannah took no punitive action against Jaffe and Taylor, he did express irritation over the matter. "When Adrian . . . and I got the group kicked out of Saigon," Taylor recalled, "I was called on the carpet." Reportedly Hannah scolded him for having "lost" Michigan State a large "amount of money" and stated that "frankly, Professor Taylor, you're not worth it!"[45]

Like Michigan State, the U.S. government was split in its assessment of Diem. A number of U.S. officials agreed with Jaffe and Taylor, and by the summer of 1963 the average American also was concerned. At this time, Kennedy was increasingly prodding Diem toward democratic reforms. In June, Jaffe and Taylor's argument was brought home by a 73-year-old Buddhist monk named Quang Duc. Protesting Diem's repressive measures, he committed suicide in the middle of a Saigon intersection by setting fire to himself. According to historian David W. Levy, the "horrifying pictures of monks burning themselves to death" and Diem's subsequent reprisals against the Buddhists triggered the first series of anti-Vietnam protests in the United States. Diem's assassination in early November by dissident South Vietnamese generals slowed the demonstrations temporarily. Following his death, however, America backed a number of Vietnamese leaders who also failed to create a workable government, and by 1965 U.S. combat troops became necessary to sustain South Vietnam. This development revitalized war protesters.[46]

By 1966, as the national debate on Vietnam heated up, Michigan State found itself embroiled in yet another controversy that went to the core of the debate about American involvement in Vietnam and the role of universities in the cold war. Building on the Jaffe-Taylor articles, and collaborating with former MSUG member Stanley K. Sheinbaum, *Ramparts* magazine published an exposé of Michigan State's Vietnam project. The most serious charges were that the university had provided cover for CIA activities in Vietnam, that MSUG members had helped entrench Diem's dictatorship by training and equipping his police forces, and that they had remained quiet about his oppressive rule. The implication was that the professors had done so because they were "automatic cold warriors" and did not want to lose the perquisites of overseas service.[47]

Sheinbaum had left Michigan State in 1959 for various reasons. After arriving at the university in the mid-1950s, he taught economics and served as the MSUG campus coordinator. "They didn't fire me but they left me no alternative but to get the hell out," he recently remarked.[48] He was increasingly at odds with the university. The MSUG's CIA connection disturbed him, and he had failed to complete his dissertation.[49] The thesis was "four-fifths done but I hated it," Sheinbaum said. The topic, "The French Balance of Payments in the Nineteenth Century," was "terribly dull," and the MSUG had become "a full-time job." The final straw came when the administration passed him over for a merit pay increase. Having worked so hard on the Vietnam project, he asserted, it really angered him "not to get" that raise.[50]

Sheinbaum and journalist Robert Scheer quickly moved to the forefront of the Vietnam antiwar movement. The two had met in 1963 while Sheinbaum worked at the Center for the Study of Democratic Institutions in Santa Barbara, California, one of the nation's early liberal "think tanks."[51] Sheinbaum accepted a position there after meeting the director of the facility, Robert Maynard Hutchins. The former president of the University of Chicago, Hutchins was one of the nation's leading educators. Sheinbaum recalled that, in retrospect, "the most important chapter" in his life was spent with Hutchins.[52]

During this period, Sheinbaum and Scheer began discussing the MSUG pro-ject. In 1965, the center published a pamphlet by Scheer, "How the United States Got Involved in Vietnam." It accused Fishel and the MSUG of working with the CIA. Scheer quoted Fishel as saying that after assisting General J. Lawton Collins, Dwight Eisenhower's special ambassador to South Vietnam, "I surfaced—to use a C.I.A. term—to become head of the M.S.U. program."[53] Fishel denied that he was an agent and on a number of occasions even wrote Edward Lansdale to joke about the matter. Lansdale was a U.S. Air Force intelligence expert working for the CIA. The agency's director, Allen Dulles, sent him to assist Diem. Lansdale's escapades were legendary and "the real-life inspirations for Graham Greene's *The Quiet American* and the character of Colonel Hillandale" in *The Ugly American*.[54] Lansdale and Fishel obviously knew each other and were both close associates of the Vietnamese president. Moreover, Fishel had a military intelligence background and served as an informant for the State Department during the Diem regime's early days. Although Michigan State records do not indicate that the CIA employed Fishel, he could have easily worked for the agency in either a formal or an informal capacity.[55]

In 1965, several negative publications appeared about the MSUG and Fishel, most notably Scheer's booklet and *Background to Betrayal: The Tragedy of Vietnam* by Hilaire du Berrier, a right-wing, American freelance writer.[56] In bizarre fashion, du Berrier accused Fishel and other members of the American Friends of Vietnam of conspiring "to sell out South Vietnam to the Communists by supporting Diem."[57] As the following passage indicates, du Berrier's argument verged on the outlandish and reflected a strong bias. "Wesley Fishel himself arrived in Washington to take a hand. Short, swarthy, well-built and with the cat-like tread

124

of a boxer, Fishel had all the worst characteristics of the genus liberal currently gripping American education. Where he came from, who he was, no one seemed to know."[58]

Du Berrier's conclusions generally have been viewed as ill-founded. Except for some editorials and newspaper articles, neither his nor Scheer's work seemed to spark much public debate. This concerned both Sheinbaum and Scheer.[59]

To shed more light on Michigan State activities in Vietnam, they joined dovish U.S. senator Wayne Morse of Oregon and twenty-seven other speakers in May 1965 at one of the first antiwar teach-ins. Held at the University of Oregon, the twelve-hour program drew a crowd estimated at three thousand who "jammed" into the school's student union. One *New York Times* reporter described the event as "a marathon protest" against American policies in Vietnam. "[A]fter 400 sandwiches, 60 gallons of coffee, 30 speakers, nine 'seminars,' three folk singers, two poetry recitations and an edgy interlude of drunken jeering and brief violence[,] . . . the evening- till-morning demonstration stumbled to a weary finish."[60]

Morse preceded him, Sheinbaum recalled, and "made all the principal points I wanted to make." However, the senator then "launche[d] into an anticommunist tirade." This "cold war mindset" disturbed Sheinbaum because he believed it was a major cause of U.S. intervention in Vietnam. When he took the podium, Sheinbaum felt great emotion. "It was a very dramatic moment for me," he stated. "I was just in a fury with Wayne Morse." As a result, "I passed out [momentarily while] holding onto the lectern." However, Sheinbaum contended he never fell and was able to discuss, among other things, Michigan State's CIA involvement.[61] The teach-in and subsequent *New York Times* article about it prompted little public response. In fact, the *Times* reporter referred to the MSUG erroneously as the "University of Michigan technical-aid project in Vietnam."[62]

Hoping to reach a wider audience, Scheer and Sheinbaum decided to write the *Ramparts* article, which created a great deal of publicity for both the authors and Michigan State. The piece "labeled me . . . a radical," Sheinbaum recalled, and most of the university "cut off all contact." According to Sheinbaum, his former colleagues considered him a "traitor." He compared his experience to the alienation actress Jane Fonda encountered after her trip to Hanoi. In contrast, the publication also made him "a hot product." He received numerous invitations to appear on talk shows and speak at teach-ins.[63]

"I even ran for the United States Congress" as a result of the notoriety, he remarked.[64] In 1964, Sheinbaum had married Betty Warner, the daughter of movie mogul Jack Warner. On the strength of the *Ramparts* article and "with Betty at his

125

side," he sought the 1966 and 1968 Democratic congressional nominations.[65] His anti-Vietnam stance angered Democrats in the Santa Barbara area because it went against the position of the party's leader, Lyndon B. Johnson. Although losing both times, Sheinbaum felt that his efforts had at least worried Johnson. Referring to the 1966 election, he took delight in saying that "I know from the woman who happened to be sleeping with him at the time that Lyndon Johnson stayed up all night," listening to returns.[66]

Although the *Ramparts* story had some basis in truth, the magazine distorted numerous facts and dramatized others. Founded in 1962 as a medium for socially conscious California Catholics, early editions tackled such issues as racism. The magazine, however, could not make money with this format and turned radical in 1964 under the direction of Warren Hinckle, a young journalist with a public relations background. He wanted to discuss shocking topics in a stylish manner, using flashy covers and exciting copy—something akin to "intellectual muckraking." Termed "Hinckling" by the staff, *Ramparts* often sensationalized stories that had been previously published in an inconspicuous journal or book. As *Time* observed in January 1967, "[m]any of *Ramparts*' 'bombs' have been lying around undetonated" for a while.[67]

The exposé on Michigan State drew heavily on a book written in 1965 about the Vietnam project by former MSUG members Scigliano and Fox. The publication suffered from a colorless text and title, *Technical Assistance in Vietnam: The Michigan State University Experience*, but it did acknowledge the presence of the CIA in the MSUG. *Ramparts* enlivened the copy, alleging that Michigan State professors operated on a "hear-no-CIA, see-no-CIA basis" and that the agents were actively involved in spying.[68] The article also insinuated that certain MSUG members remained quiet about Diem's dictatorship because they wished to stay in Vietnam and enjoy Saigon's "exotic and free-wheeling life[style]." Fishel was characterized as "being the closest thing to a proconsul that Saigon had," entertaining "frequently and lavishly in his opulent villa."[69] Once again, a number of these charges had already been leveled against the MSUG in 1961 by Michigan State professors Jaffe and Taylor. The *Ramparts* piece garnered greater attention because of the emerging antiwar effort and Hinckle's flamboyant handling of the subject matter. The cover featured a "rather well-endowed" color caricature of South Vietnam's first lady, Madame Nhu, in a Michigan State cheerleader's outfit with the headline "The University on the Make."[70]

Michigan State's response to the *Ramparts* article was inconsistent. President Hannah's assistant, James H. Denison, denied that the university "knowingly hire[d] any CIA men." Moreover, "when we found out about their role," he said, "we dropped them."[71] In contrast, Fishel asserted that university officials were aware of the CIA presence but that the agents engaged in "no cloak-and-dagger work."[72] Although acknowledging that Michigan State trained Vietnamese police-men, Hannah contested the allegation that the university equipped them. He argued that MSUG personnel "advised the [U.S.] aid mission on such purchases, and . . . saw to it that the funds were efficiently spent and the equipment was well used."[73] Hannah and Fishel both refuted charges that the MSUG lived lavishly in Vietnam. Moreover, Hannah observed that several faculty did not remain quiet about Diem's abuses, but publicly denounced him. Nevertheless, Jaffe and Taylor, two of the Vietnamese president's detractors, conceded that MSUG members had lived in a luxurious fashion.[74]

Although CIA records concerning the matter remain classified, MSUG files support Fishel's contention that the agents were not spies. Michigan State employed them to teach the Vietnamese civil police countersubversive tactics. The university did not have qualified personnel to provide this type of instruction, and the advent of communist guerrilla activity necessitated it.[75]

The university modernized South Vietnam's police forces and trained them in basic police methods, but it could not specify or control how the government uti-lized that knowledge. Michigan State was not a policy maker in Vietnam and could not impose American standards of democracy. For example, after the MSUG modernized the Vietnamese fingerprint system, they were unable to prevent Diem's regime from using it in an antidemocratic fashion against political oppo-nents.

Whether some faculty muted criticism of Diem's regime because of the overseas perquisites is debatable. However, there were undeniable advantages to being sta-tioned in South Vietnam. The U.S. government designated the country a "hard-ship" assignment, with pay incentives and American commissary privileges. Michigan State professors could almost "double their normal salaries," as well as purchase low-cost grocery items and liquor.[76] The MSUG chief adviser lived in a spacious home "with a living room large enough for receptions of 200, 20[-]foot ceilings, and three servants."[77]

The nightlife was also stimulating. At times Michigan State hosted large recep-tions and invited such dignitaries as the vice president of South Vietnam, Nguyen Ngoc Tho, Ambassador Frederick Nolting, and CIA official William Colby. On one occasion, the MSUG bought scotch, gin, bourbon, tonic, and ten pounds of ham, totaling about $300.00. Lillian Smuckler, the wife of a MSUG member,

noted that "[s]ometimes in one evening we went to three cocktail parties or recep-
tions and then to an 8:30 dinner party."[78]

Similarly, Taylor asserted that American behavior could be offensive to the
Vietnamese. He arrived in Saigon just after William J. Lederer and Eugene Burdick
had published *The Ugly American* (1958), which explored the negative cultural
impact of U.S. nation-building efforts on Third World countries. Taylor maintained that there were numerous "ugly Americans" in Saigon. "Some people were
out every night. It was a place where the liquor ran very free. I never heard anybody order less than a double." Moreover, he recalled once having heard the comment that the only Vietnamese at an American Embassy party were "standing
behind a bar serving drinks."[79]

Not all university staff lived in large houses, however, and life in Vietnam had
its difficulties. The oppressive heat caused people to change "clothes several times
a day" and to take early afternoon "siestas."[80] Mold was a continual problem; a pair
of shoes could be damaged "over-night."[81] Economist Hunter's situation was typi-
cal of most MSUG families. His household had no washing machine and only the
smallest refrigerator. However, he employed five servants for $100.00 a month and
thought it was money well spent. All drinking water had to be boiled and most of
the MSUG still "were hospitalized or treated for amebic dysentery and/or hepati-
tis."[82] According to Hannah, at least one person, radio engineer Royce Williams,
died as a "result of distressing living conditions, and the lack of appropriate medi-
cine."[83] MSUG psychologist Fred Wickert, who worked with the Vietnamese
mountain tribes, repeatedly contracted dysentery and had to have his intestines
operated on in the United States.[84]

On 22 April 1966, Hannah held a press conference attended by both national
and local news agencies, including the *New York Times*, Associated Press,
Newsweek, and the *Detroit Free Press*.[85] He refuted the principal charges in
Ramparts and questioned the reasons for the attack. Implying that the university
was being used as a political "whipping boy," he pointed out that two of the writers were "running for Congress in California." Moreover, he hinted that revenge
might also be a motive because Sheinbaum had departed Michigan State "in a very
unhappy mood."[86] Several weeks later, Fishel reiterated Hannah's argument,
asserting that Sheinbaum, contributing author Robert Scheer, and one of the edi-
tors at *Ramparts*, Edward Keating, were "campaigning on a 'Get the U.S. Out of
Viet Nam' platform," an issue that was "'big' in Berkeley" at the time. What they
had done, he concluded, was "to twist facts and confuse myth with reality for their
own political ends."[87]

Hannah and Fishel were the focus of the *Ramparts* controversy. In the wake of the publication, both national and local politicians expressed interest in Michigan State's Vietnam involvement. Hannah was called on continually to defend the project and appeared before the state legislature. Two high-profile critics of U.S. policy in Vietnam, J. William Fulbright, the chairman of the Senate Foreign Relations Committee, and Wayne Morse, another member of that group, expressed dismay. Morse conceded that he was worried by "the extent to which academic research and opinions about foreign policy are polluted by government sponsorship."[88] Disturbed by the statement, Hannah later informed the Oregon senator that the *Ramparts* piece was a "distortion of both the University's role in Vietnam and our relationship to government agencies including the CIA."[89]

In May 1966, Hannah, Fishel, Sheinbaum, and Warren Hinckle, an editor at *Ramparts* and contributing author to the much-publicized Michigan State article, appeared before the Michigan House of Representatives's Ways and Means Subcommittee. An ardent anticommunist, Hannah refused to apologize for MSUG participation in Vietnam and restated his position from the 22 April press conference. Fishel also denied a number of the magazine's charges, including those concerning the "alleged opulent living conditions" in Saigon.[90] Although Sheinbaum confessed that a few of the "facts in the story" were not true, he and Hinckle stood by the article. The chairman of the subcommittee concluded the proceedings by recommending that the legislature adopt rules for future university assistance projects.[91]

The *Ramparts* exposé was particularly harsh on Fishel, and by 1966, he was in the middle of a widening national debate on American policy in Vietnam. Students and professors were among the principal protesters. In 1965, President Johnson sent the first American combat troops to Vietnam and the teach-in had "achieved a vogue on campuses across" the country. Unlike many of his colleagues, Fishel aligned himself with the administration in support of the war in Vietnam.[92]

After the MSUG project ended in 1962, Fishel had remained interested in Vietnamese affairs, returning there numerous times. In 1964 he became a consultant to the U.S. assistant secretary of state for Far Eastern affairs. From 1964 to 1966, he also served as the chairman of the American Friends of Vietnam (AFVN), an organization created in 1955 to promote Ngo Dinh Diem in the United States and whose stated purpose was the "support of a free and democratic Republic of Vietnam."[93] Several of the AFVN's members were also personal friends of Diem. In particular, Leo Cherne and Joseph Buttinger, leaders of the International Rescue Committee, a private relief organization, were especially

129

close to him. Believing that Diem's antidemocratic policies would not stop communism, Fishel and his associates reluctantly broke with Diem in 1963, but only after failing to persuade him to initiate reforms.[94]

As head of the AFVN, Fishel assisted President Johnson in combatting the student antiwar movement. The White House secured private funding for the group to "establish a national prowar speakers' bureau and information center."[95] The AFVN also employed a national field coordinator to direct activities and to communicate with campus organizations. All those contributing to the AFVN were close friends of the president: Sidney Weinberg, a financier, and Arthur Krim, an executive at United Artists Corporation, helped finance the 1964 Democratic campaign, while Edwin Weisl Sr., a New York lawyer, had been a Johnson supporter since the late 1930s.[96]

One of the AFVN's first speaking engagements featured Vice President Hubert Humphrey. The event occurred in June 1965 at Michigan State, where Fishel had been sparring with various faculty doves, such as Thomas Greer, chairman of the humanities department. The atmosphere of the campus debates was increasingly confrontational and filled with hecklers. In one instance, about 30 individuals out of a crowd of 450 gave Greer "a standing ovation." Fishel responded by taunting the antiwar contingent. "After that I'm not sure whether to address you as members of the Madmen's Society, or Future Beasts of America," he quipped.[97] Although Humphrey's visit was designed to drum up support for administration policies and not to stage a debate, a small incident took place. Following his speech, Greer presented Humphrey with a "peace petition" from several hundred university faculty. The professor was cordial, informing the vice president that the signees did not fault him for Johnson's "wrong-headed" position on Vietnam. According to historian Kenneth J. Heineman, "Humphrey crushed the petition between his trembling hands and sputtered that he had been a foe of Communist conspirators long before Johnson had become president."[98] For its part, the White House characterized the students as "friendly and receptive," and considered the visit a success.[99]

To assist the Johnson administration, Fishel also wrote editorials and the AFVN produced a periodical, *Vietnam Perspectives*. In December 1965, for example, Fishel sent a letter to the Providence (R.I.) *Journal* criticizing the tactics of antiwar activists. He argued that "draft card burning, noisy demonstrations and so-called 'teach-ins' which have the character of a football rally" were unproductive. He continued: "[neither is it] honorable, much less truthful, to brand the President and his supporters as murderers of innocent people, butchers, or [f]ascists."[100] The first copy of *Vietnam Perspectives* appeared in the fall of 1965. Frank Trager, a professor of international affairs at New York University and the treasurer of the AFVN, described it as "an intended answer to *Viet Nam Report* put out by the '[t]each-in' crowd."[101] Johnson's staff liked the finished product and arranged to distribute five thousand copies.[102]

In early 1966, the White House and the AFVN started drifting apart. Suffering from "monetary and organizational troubles," the group was unable to raise funds on its own. In addition, some leaders were concerned about Johnson's management of the war. Opposed to bombing North Vietnam, Buttinger resigned in 1965. The following spring Fishel relinquished the chairmanship and in 1967 left the AFVN, citing professional and family responsibilities. He was also disillusioned with U.S. strategy in Vietnam.[103]

Although still respected in official circles, Fishel was increasingly harassed by student activists. The *Ramparts* story "discredited" Hannah and Fishel and severely weakened the prowar forces at Michigan State. According to Heineman, several faculty supporters of U.S. policy in Vietnam, including economist and former CIA analyst Chitra Smith, "defected to the peace movement."[104] Led by numerous National Merit Scholars, the antiwar faction "went on the offensive."[105] Established as a chapter at Michigan State in 1963, Students for a Democratic Society (SDS), one of the leading antiwar groups, became active in the mid to late 1960s. *The Paper*, the "first campus-based underground newspaper" in the United States, appeared. Full of biting satire, it even developed a comic strip about Hannah titled "Land Grant Man."[106]

Fishel also suffered a number of indignities. Commenting on the *Ramparts* fallout, he told journalist Robert Shaplen, "I am as well roasted as a French chestnut."[107] In late April 1966, approximately forty SDS members, including the "Freedom Singers," demonstrated in front of the university's Center for International Programs, a building constructed with MSUG project funding. The protestors carried placards bearing such slogans as "Bodies by Fishel," "Put Silver Wings on Fishel's Chest," and "CIA Go Home."[108] Moreover, the Freedom Singers performed a song composed to the tune of Johnny Rivers's "Secret Agent Man." Part of the parody went:

> Super-Fishel man, Super-Fishel man,
> Where Wesley takes his field-trips
> Not even Bond would go.
> Saigon's first regime was his creation,

We wondered where he went that spring vacation,
Super-Fishel man, Super-Fishel man,
We haven't lost a teacher,
We've gained an agent man.[109]

Controversy followed Fishel. At the personal request of the Southern Illinois University (SIU) president, Delyte W. Morris, Michigan State released him for one year (1969-70) to serve as a visiting professor. Specifically, he helped establish the Center for Vietnamese Studies at the school. The Agency for International Development (AID), a U.S. foreign assistance bureau, granted SIU $1 million to gather data and train individuals to serve Vietnam "in social and economic areas."[110] Fishel's friend and former boss, John Hannah, approved the center's funding. In 1969 he resigned from Michigan State, and President Richard Nixon appointed him head of AID.[111]

Within four months, Fishel was again embroiled in conflict. A number of SIU faculty and students began implying that the center might be engaged in CIA activity. Anticenter bumper stickers surfaced on campus asserting that "MSU + CIA = SIU."[112] Student activists "decided that I was villain number one, their most evil man," Fishel later recalled in an interview.[113] Six individuals even convicted him of "war crimes" in a mock trial in the university's cafeteria. The proceedings ended with a stand-in for Fishel being pummeled with "pies, cakes, and whipped cream."[114] Yet he also had defenders. One organization, Concerned Students for Academic Freedom and Responsibility, wrote editorials on his behalf, arguing that Fishel had unfairly "been singled out with utter disregard for the truth."[115] In part, his defenders were correct. To many demonstrators, Fishel noted, "I was nothing but a name that they had read about in *Ramparts*."[116]

His work at SIU complete, Fishel took a year's sabbatical to do research in Hawaii and then returned to East Lansing in the fall of 1971. Although he had been quoted in the *New York Times* as "being against the war," SDS opinion of him remained unchanged.[117] Walter Adams, Hannah's replacement as interim president, recalled that the antiwar activists "personalized" their movement and "disrupted" Fishel's classes.[118] SDS demanded his dismissal and called for all interested students to "help shut [him] down."[119] The university employed plain-clothes policemen to assist graduate assistants in keeping order and verifying the names of enrolled students. About thirty demonstrators who tried to gain admittance to Fishel's classroom were stopped at the door. At one juncture, however, two people entered from the rear of the room and chanted "murderer, murderer," while others outside yelled "[r]acist butcher, out of [s]tate!" When one student waved a Viet Cong flag at Fishel, the professor informed him that he was "welcome to hold on to his 'security blanket.'"[120] SDS even distributed "wanted" posters, which referred to Fishel as "THE [JOSEPH] GOEBBELS, THE [ADOLF] EICHMANN, OF VIETNAM."[121]

Once Fishel "could no longer deliver the bacon," the administration mistreated him also, Adams asserted. The university had profited financially from Fishel's friendship with Diem, but the MSUG program was over. Fishel had become "a problem rather than an asset." Thereafter his salary increases "were very modest."[122]

In April 1977, Fishel died at the age of fifty-seven. In a 1993 interview, Sheinbaum commented that "I have been accused of having accelerated his death, which really irritates the hell out of me." The New York Times noted that friends believed Fishel "had been denied advancement because of the [Ramparts] controversy."[123] Fellow political scientist and former MSUG member Ralph Smuckler maintained that Fishel was "physically broken" by constantly having "to defend" his actions in Vietnam. "I don't think a doctor would relate his illness later to that situation," he observed, "but I think it certainly could not have done it any good."[124] In contrast, by this time Sheinbaum was a major figure in the national Democratic Party and had directed the fund-raising drive to finance the defense of former Pentagon official Daniel Ellsberg. Charged with "espionage, conspiracy and misuse of [g]overnment property," Ellsberg was on trial for releasing the Pentagon Papers, a classified Department of Defense study of U.S. policy in Vietnam.[125]

Hannah found the post of head of AID tailor-made for him.[126] Milton Taylor once characterized him as an "America firster" and a "brick and mortar man." Taylor's comments are insightful on a number of levels. Hannah, an ardent anticommunist, was the representative man of the cold war era, "a Republican during a very Republican administration."[127] His agenda was twofold: first, stop communism; and second, expand Michigan State in order to provide everyone with an opportunity to attend college. In Hannah's mind, the goals were compatible. Projects such as the MSUG provided the university increased government revenue as it assisted nation building.[128]

Like Hannah, most Americans believed the "menacing cloud of [c]ommunism" threatened to engulf the world and had to be contained.[129] Third World countries such as Vietnam were at the flash point of the United States' fight against communism. Instead of using U.S. combat forces to counter the perceived threat, Eisenhower's administration utilized nation building and the CIA. Essentially, Michigan State's experience was not unusual. For instance, Eisenhower had used covert operations against other Third World communist movements, such as in

133

Iran (1953) and in Guatemala (1954). In view of the importance that U.S. policy makers placed on Southeast Asia, the agency's presence in Vietnam should have been anticipated. As Eisenhower biographer Stephen E. Ambrose noted, the "size and scope of the CIA's activities increased dramatically during the 1950s."[130] Although Hannah denied allegations of CIA involvement, he must have been aware of the agency's presence and probably saw nothing wrong with it. He was not alone. After the Second World War, officials at a number of universities, including Harvard and Yale, worked with intelligence agents on government projects and exposed suspected subversives on campus.[131]

The cold war consensus of the 1950s fell apart in the next decade. During that period, Michigan State divided over Vietnam and began grappling with many of the issues that later split the nation. Fishel, Hannah, and Sheinbaum were important figures in the emerging debate. The controversy the university experienced over its project termination in 1962 and the *Ramparts* exposé in 1966 were at the center of the argument on Vietnam. Afterward, higher education reexamined the propriety of its role in foreign affairs and, together with a large segment of the United States, the validity of American involvement in Vietnam.

NOTES

1. "A Crumbling Bastion: Flattery and Lies Won't Save Vietnam" is the title of an article written by Michigan State professors Adrian Jaffe and Milton C. Taylor and published in the *New Republic* 144 (June 1961): 17–20. The piece angered Vietnamese president Ngo Dinh Diem and was one reason the MSUG project was terminated.

2. Warren Hinckle et al., "The University on the Make," *Ramparts* 4 (April 1966): 11–22.

3. Wolf Ladejinsky to Wesley Fishel, 1 March 1960, box 28, Wesley Fishel Papers, Michigan State University Archives and Historical Collections, East Lansing, Michigan (hereafter cited as Fishel Papers).

4. Wesley Fishel to Ngo Dinh Diem, 30 April 1960, box 1184, Fishel Papers.

5. Elbridge Durbrow to the Department of State, 16 September 1960, reprinted in John P. Glannon, ed., *Foreign Relations of the United States, 1958–60, vol. I Vietnam* (Washington, D.C.: U.S. Government Printing Office, 1986), 579; David Anderson, *Trapped by Success: The Eisenhower Administration and Vietnam, 1953–1961* (New York: Columbia University Press, 1991), 188–89.

6. George McT. Kahin, *Intervention: How America Became Involved in Vietnam* (New York: Knopf, 1986), 124.

7. Anderson, *Trapped by Success*, 192.

8. Ibid., 192–93; Kahin, *Intervention*, 124–25.

9. Ralph Turner, "Impressions of Events which Occurred November 11–13, 1960, in Saigon, Vietnam," box 680, folder 7, Michigan State University Vietnam Project Papers, Michigan State University Archives and Historical Collections, East Lansing, Michigan (hereafter

cited as Vietnam Project Papers); Ralph Turner, "A Log (Rumors and All) of the Events of November 11– 13, 1960," box 691, folder 38, Vietnam Project Papers.

10. James Aronson, *The Press and the Cold War* (Indianapolis and New York: Bobbs-Merrill Co., 1970), 189.

11. Turner, "Impressions of Events," Vietnam Project Papers.

12. Lloyd D. Musolf to Wesley Fishel, 14 November 1960, box 17, Fishel Papers.

13. Wesley Fishel to Ngo Dinh Diem, 19 November 1960, box 1184, Fishel Papers.

14. Ngo Dinh Diem to John Hannah, 15 December 1960, box 1184, Fishel Papers.

15. Aronson, *The Press and the Cold War*, 189; Charles DeBenedetti and Charles Chatfield (assisting author), *An American Ordeal: The Antiwar Movement of the Vietnam Era* (Syracuse, N.Y.: Syracuse University Press, 1990), 82; Gregory A. Olson, *Mansfield and Vietnam: A Study in Rhetorical Adaptation* (East Lansing: Michigan State University Press, 1995), 87–88; *Life*, 28 November 1960, 30; *U.S. News and World Report*, 28 November 1960, 84.

16. Wesley Fishel, letter to the editor of the *New York Times*, 22 November 1960, box 11, Fishel Papers.

17. Ruben V. Austin to Lloyd D. Musolf, 23 November 1960, box 677, folder 26, Vietnam Project Papers.

18. Walter Adams and John A. Garraty, *Is the World Our Campus?* (East Lansing: Michigan State University Press, 1960), ix.

19. Walter Adams, interview by author, 10 August 1993.

20. Austin to Musolf, 23 November 1960, Vietnam Project Papers; *Final Report of the Michigan State University Advisory Group*, 1962, box 658, folder 6, Vietnam Project Papers, 64.

21. Austin to Musolf, 23 November 1960.

22. Robert Scigliano, "Political Parties in South Vietnam Under the Republic," *Pacific Affairs* 33 (December 1960): 345–46.

23. James B. Hendry, "American Aid in Vietnam: The View from a Village," *Pacific Affairs* 33 (December 1960): 391.

24. Lloyd D. Musolf to Ruben V. Austin, 10 March 1961, box 677, folder 27, Vietnam Project Papers.

25. Jaffe and Taylor, "A Crumbling Bastion," 17.

26. Adams, interview.

27. Jaffe and Taylor, "A Crumbling Bastion," 17.

28. Ibid., 19.

29. Ibid.

30. Adams, interview.

31. Lloyd D. Musolf to Ruben V. Austin, 26 November 1960, box 677, folder 26, Vietnam Project Papers.

32. Frank C. Child, "Vietnam—The Eleventh Hour," *New Republic* 145 (4 December 1961): 14–16.

33. Guy Fox to James B. Hendry, 19 February 1962, box 656, folder 72, Vietnam Project Papers.

34. The National Institute of Administration was the civil servant training school the MSUG helped establish in Vietnam.

35. *New York Times*, 20 February 1962, box 4, Fishel Papers; Robert Scigliano and Guy H. Fox, *Technical Assistance in Vietnam: The Michigan State University Experience* (New York: Praeger, 1965), 53.

36. Scigliano and Fox, *Technical Assistance in Vietnam*, 11–12; Ronald H. Spector, *The United States Army in Vietnam: Advice and Support: The Early Years, 1941–1960* (Washington, D.C.: GPO, 1983), 375–78.

37. Wesley Fishel to John Hannah, 17 February 1962, box 42, folder 56, John A. Hannah Papers, Michigan State University Archives and Historical Collections, East Lansing, Michigan (hereafter cited as Hannah Papers).

38. John Hannah to John F. Kennedy, 26 February 1962, box 42, folder 56, Hannah Papers.

39. McGeorge Bundy to John Hannah, 26 March 1962, box 24, Fishel Papers.

40. Milton Taylor, interview by author, 11 May 1993.

41. Milton C. Taylor and Adrian Jaffe, "The Professor-Diplomat: Ann Arbor and Cambridge Were Never Like This," *New Republic* 146 (5 March 1962): 28–30.

42. John M. Hunter, interview by author, 22 July 1992.

43. Michigan State University *State News*, 2 April 1962.

44. Ibid., 6 April 1962. At the time, Bryan was a member of the Michigan State University Brazil Project, which helped establish a school of business administration in the city of Sao Paulo.

45. Taylor, interview; Michigan State University *State News*, 23 February, 12 March 1962; *Lansing State Journal*, 25 February 1962; Paul L. Dressel, *College to University: The Hannah Years at Michigan State, 1935–1969* (East Lansing: Michigan State University Publications, 1987), 277.

46. David W. Levy, *The Debate Over Vietnam* (Baltimore: Johns Hopkins University Press, 1991), 125; George C. Herring, *America's Longest War: The United States and Vietnam, 1950–1975*, 2d ed. (New York: Alfred A. Knopf, 1986), 94–96; Neil Sheehan, *A Bright Shining Lie: John Paul Vann and America in Vietnam* (New York: Random House, 1988), 334–35.

47. *Ramparts*, April 1966, 11–22; Anderson, *Trapped by Success*, 144.

48. Stanley Sheinbaum, interview by author, 18 March 1993.

49. Hunter, interview.

50. Sheinbaum, interview.

51. Robert Scheer, "Prince of the City," *L.A. Style* 8 (March 1993): 24–26.

52. Sheinbaum, interview; "Statement by Stanley K. Sheinbaum to the Los Angeles City Council Confirmation Hearing Reappointment to the Police Commission," 3 April 1991, copy in possession of Ralph Turner, East Lansing, Michigan; *New York Times*, 9 May 1965.

53. Robert Scheer, *How the United States Got Involved in Vietnam* (Santa Barbara, Calif.: Center for the Study of Democratic Institutions, 1965), 34; *Detroit News*, 28 November 1965.

54. Anderson, *Trapped by Success*, 76.

55. Ibid., 75–76, 145–46; J. Lawton Collins to John Hannah, 11 March 1955, box 42, folder 50, Hannah Papers; Wesley Fishel to Weidner, 20 September 1954, box 628, folder 101, Vietnam Project Papers; William Colby with James McCargar, *Lost Victory: A Firsthand Account of America's Sixteen-Year Involvement in Vietnam* (Chicago: Contemporary Books, 1989), 27, 395; Sheinbaum, interview; Scheer, "Prince of the City," 24.

56. Hilaire du Berrier, *Background to Betrayal: The Tragedy of Vietnam* (Boston and Los Angeles: Western Islands Publishers, 1965), 298–306. Also of note is Martin Nicolaus's "The Professor, The Policeman and the Peasant." Published in the February and March 1966 issues of *Viet-Report*, it builds on Scheer's work and that of Scigliano and Fox.

57. Joseph Buttinger, *Vietnam: A Dragon Embattled, vol. 2, Vietnam at War* (New York: Frederick A. Praeger, 1967), 1260.

58. du Berrier, *Background to Betrayal*, 103.
59. *St. Louis Post-Dispatch*, 10 October 1965; *Oregonian* (Portland), 1 November 1965; *Detroit News*, 28 November 1965; Sheinbaum, interview; Buttinger, *Vietnam*, 1109n, 1260.
60. *New York Times*, 9 May 1965.
61. Sheinbaum, interview.
62. *New York Times*, 9 May 1965.
63. Sheinbaum, interview.
64. Ibid.
65. Cass Warner Sperling and Cork Millner with Jack Warner Jr., *Hollywood Be Thy Name: The Warner Brothers Story* (Rocklin, Calif.: Prima Publishing, 1994), 342.
66. Sheinbaum, interview.
67. Carlene Marie Bagnall Blanchard, "Ramparts Magazine: Social Change in the Sixties" (Ph.D. diss., University of Michigan, 1969), 1, 12–13, 15–16, 18, 24, 27.
68. *Ramparts* 4 (April 1966): 17–18.
69. Ibid., 17.
70. Susan Cecilia Stasiowski, "A History and Evaluation of *Ramparts* Magazine, 1962–1969" (master's thesis, San Jose State College, 1972), 107; Jaffe and Taylor, "A Crumbling Bastion," 19; Scigliano and Fox, *Technical Assistance in Vietnam*, 11, 21, 60.
71. *National Observer*, 18 April 1966, box 55, folder 49, Hannah Papers.
72. Ibid.
73. Statement by John A. Hannah, President Michigan State University, 22 April 1966, box 55, folder 50, Hannah Papers, p. 7.
74. *Detroit News*, 17 May 1966; Jaffe and Taylor, "A Crumbling Bastion," 19; Statement by John A. Hannah, 22 April 1966, 9.
75. *National Observer*, 18 April 1966, box 55, folder 49, Hannah Papers; Anderson, *Trapped by Success*, 144.
76. *Ramparts*, April 1966, 17.
77. *Milwaukee Journal*, 13 January 1957.
78. Ibid.; Request of Reimbursement, 5 October 1961, box 643, folder 106, Vietnam Project Papers; Request of Reimbursement, 9 May 1958, box 643, folder 101, Vietnam Project Papers.
79. Taylor, interview.
80. *Milwaukee Journal*, 13 January 1957.
81. Ibid.
82. Statement by John A. Hannah, 22 April 1966, Hannah Papers, p. 8.
83. Ibid.
84. Hunter, interview; Fred Wickert, interview by author, 20 July 1992; Royce Williams's Obituary, box 648, folder 91, Vietnam Project Papers.
85. Memorandum from James Denison to John Hannah, 22 April 1966, box 55, folder 50, Hannah Papers.
86. Statement by John A. Hannah, 22 April 1966, Hannah Papers, p. 11.
87. North American Newspaper Alliance, 7/8 May 1966, box 4, folder 2, Gilbert Jonas Papers, Michigan State University Archives and Historical Collections, East Lansing, Michigan (hereafter cited as Gilbert Jonas Papers).
88. *Detroit News*, 6 May 1966.

89. John Hannah to Wayne Morse, 19 July 1966, box 55, folder 50, Hannah Papers; *Ann Arbor News*, 22 April 1966; *Lansing State Journal*, 3, 4, May 1966.

90. *Detroit News*, 17 May 1966.

91. Michigan State University *State News*, 17 May 1966; *Detroit News*, 16 May 1966.

92. Levy, *Debate Over Vietnam*, 126–27.

93. Wesley Fishel to Gilbert Jonas, 4 September 1965, box 3, folder 30, Gilbert Jonas Papers.

94. Charles A. Joiner to Wesley Fishel, 4 August 1964, box 9, folder 8, Fishel Papers; *Cleveland Plain Dealer*, 14 November 1971, Michigan State University Special Collections; Louis A. Wiesner, *Victims and Survivors, Displaced Persons and other War Victims in Viet-Nam, 1954–1975* (Westport, Conn.: Greenwood Press, 1988), 9–12; Anderson, *Trapped by Success*, 158; Joseph G. Morgan, "The Vietnam Lobby: The American Friends of Vietnam, 1955–1975" (Ph.D. diss., Georgetown University, 1992), 62, 76, 84, 379, 403; Buttinger, *Vietnam*, 2:1133, 1157; *Detroit Free Press Magazine*, 11 June 1972.

95. Kenneth J. Heineman, *Campus Wars: The Peace Movement at American State Universities in the Vietnam Era* (New York: New York University Press, 1993), 132.

96. Morgan, "Vietnam Lobby," 371–72, 383–86.

97. Michigan State University *State News*, 5 May 1965, Student Activities File, Michigan State University Archives and Historical Collections; Heineman, *Campus Wars*, 132.

98. Heineman, *Campus Wars*, 51.

99. Ibid., 49; Morgan, "Vietnam Lobby," 373–74.

100. Wesley Fishel to the editor of the *Providence Journal*, 16 December 1965, box 11, folder 15, Fishel Papers.

101. Morgan, "Vietnam Lobby," 386.

102. Ibid., 374–77, 386–87.

103. Ibid., 379, 395, 403; *Detroit Free Press Magazine*, 11 June 1972.

104. Heineman, *Campus Wars*, 49.

105. Ibid., 95; *Lansing State Journal*, 14 June 1966.

106. Heineman, *Campus Wars*, 6, 54, 89–90, 140.

107. Wesley Fishel to Robert Shaplen, 24 April 1966, box 11, folder 16, Fishel Papers.

108. Michigan State University *State News*, 25 April 1966.

109. Heineman, *Campus Wars*, 137–38; Michigan State University *State News*, 25 April 1966; Walter Adams, *The Test* (New York: Macmillan Company, 1971), 173–74; Hinckle et al., "University on the Make," 14.

110. Southern Illinois University *Daily Egyptian*, 6 February 1970.

111. Douglas Allen and Ngo Vinh Long, *Coming to Terms: Indochina, the United States, and the War* (Boulder, Colo.: Westview Press, 1991), 221; Heineman, *Campus Wars*, 21.

112. Allen and Long, *Coming to Terms*, 221.

113. Quoted in Gloria Emerson, *Winners and Losers: Battles, Retreats, Gains, Losses and Ruins from a Long War* (New York: Random House, 1976), 303.

114. *Lansing State Journal*, 30 January 1970.

115. John P. McCormick to the editor of the *New York Times*, 23 February 1970, box 1184, Fishel Papers; John P. McCormick to the editor of the *Daily Egyptian*, 24 February 1970, Fishel Papers; Delyte W. Morris to Howard R. Neville, 16 June 1969, box 3, folder 2, Fishel Papers; *Daily Egyptian*, 6 November 1969, box 2, Fishel Papers; Richard Niehoff, *John A. Hannah:*

Versatile Administrator and Distinguished Public Servant (Lanham, Md.: University Press of America, 1989), 133.

116. Quoted in Emerson, *Winners and Losers*, 306; Allen and Long, *Coming to Terms*, 221.

117. Michigan State University *State News*, 15 October 1971.

118. Adams, interview.

119. Michigan State University *State News*, 24 September 1971.

120. Ibid., 27 September 1971.

121. "Wanted Poster," Fishel Papers; *Lansing State Journal*, 30 January 1970. Joseph Goebbels was Nazi Germany's minister for public enlightenment and propaganda. Adolf Eichmann was chief of Hitler's Gestapo.

122. Adams, interview.

123. *New York Times* Biographical Service, April 1977, 526.

124. Ralph Smuckler, interview by author, 13 May 1993.

125. Herring, *America's Longest War*, 242; *New York Times*, 2 August 1972.

126. Niehoff, *John A. Hannah*, 133.

127. Taylor, interview.

128. Michael Klare, "The Military Research Network—America's Fourth Armed Service," North American Congress on Latin America, 1970, Michigan State University Special Collections, Watchdog Collection, East Lansing, Michigan, p. 2; Heineman, *Campus Wars*, 22.

129. Heineman, *Campus Wars*, 22.

130. Stephen E. Ambrose, *Eisenhower: The President*, vol. 2 (New York: Simon and Schuster, 1984), 111.

131. Stephen E. Ambrose with Richard H. Immerman, *Ike's Spies: Eisenhower and the Espionage Establishment* (Garden City, N.Y.: Doubleday, 1981), 194–246; Sigmund Diamond, *Compromised Campus: The Collaboration of Universities with the Intelligence Community, 1945-1955* (New York and Oxford: Oxford University Press, 1992), 20–21, 48–49, 50–53.

CONCLUSION

"To my good friend, Wesley R. Fishel, who helped in building a free Vietnam. I will not forget," read the photograph's inscription.[1] The picture was of South Vietnamese president Ngo Dinh Diem. He and Fishel formed a close bond that had fateful consequences, both for the two men and for their countries. "I had a kind of rapport with Diem," Fishel later observed, that American officials "envied and which they could not duplicate."[2] After meeting in 1950, the two men embarked on a thirteen-year odyssey that led to Diem's death, United States involvement in its longest war, and Fishel's disgrace.

Diem, Fishel, and Dwight Eisenhower became partners in a disastrous effort to establish an anticommunist South Vietnam. Having suppressed other communist-led movements in developing countries, Eisenhower ignored the warnings of American security advisers that Vietnam was an unstable nation emerging from colonial rule and an unsuitable place to take a stand against communism. In October 1954, Secretary of Defense Charles E. Wilson warned that he could "see nothing but grief in store for us if we remained in that area."[3]

Nevertheless, nation building glossed over the complexities of Vietnam and began with a burst of enthusiasm. Wilson's former lieutenant, Assistant Secretary of Defense John Hannah, supported Fishel and happily joined in the venture. Resigning only three months before Wilson's prophetic remarks, Hannah resumed his responsibilities as Michigan State's president. Soon after, he expedited federal approval of the Michigan State University Group (MSUG), a technical-assistance program established under the auspices of Eisenhower's nation-building effort in South Vietnam.[4]

Nation building failed miserably and resulted in Diem's death and the introduction of American combat forces in Vietnam. Although he had solicited U.S. help, Diem became the most troublesome obstacle to nation building. Reluctant

141

to alter existing governmental and military structures, he and the South Vietnamese bureaucracy resisted change. His supporters, many of them Catholics like himself, constituted a minority in South Vietnam and sought to perpetuate themselves in positions of power. Diem, for his part, trusted few individuals outside his family and based most military and government appointments on political loyalty, not talent. As historian Ronald Spector has observed, "rampant politicization in the higher ranks of the officer corps had enabled incompetent but politically reliable officers to attain and retain positions of responsibility and high command."[5] Diem tried to influence every decision himself, even the minor ones involving the daily operations of the government and military. Despite the suggestions of Fishel and other U.S. advisers, Diem refused to initiate economic, political, and structural reforms. As a result, he alienated the non-Catholic population. Moreover, South Vietnam never developed a self-sustaining economy and became financially and militarily dependent on the United States.

U.S. advisers were not without fault, and nation building suffered from a number of miscalculations. "The Americans always thought they discovered fire and they discovered the wheel in Vietnam," declared MSUG anthropologist Gerald Hickey.[6] U.S. officials placed too much confidence in the benefits of the American democratic system. Diem was right to resist certain suggestions. South Vietnam was not the Midwest, and in some instances, U.S. concepts clashed with the political realities of a Third World nation facing a growing communist insurgency. For example, the MSUG's decision to try and mold the Civil Guard into an agency resembling the Michigan State Police was misguided.

In contrast, American officials also allowed Diem too much latitude. Afraid of weakening South Vietnam, Eisenhower's administration did not utilize what appeared to be its only available leverage: withholding aid. Many U.S. policy makers, including Fishel, did not believe a replacement for Diem existed, and the autocrat used this situation to his advantage. Diem only appeared conciliatory after dissident South Vietnamese generals had already decided to overthrow his regime. "[A]s early as March of 1962," Fishel recalled, "I had predicted the downfall of the Diem government. I said to Diem himself that I thought his government had about 18 months to last."[7] Within a year, Fishel had reluctantly broken with his friend, but only after becoming convinced Diem had to be removed to prevent the country from going communist. American officials were so frustrated with Diem that they encouraged the November 1963 coup. Fishel was correct about the lack of choices for a viable successor. Following Diem's assassination, the United States sponsored a succession of leaders who also failed to create a workable government, and by 1965 U.S. combat forces became necessary to sustain South Vietnam.[8]

Michigan State's eagerness to become involved in nation building reflected a postwar "can-do" hubris that clouded the judgment of U.S. academicians and policy makers alike.[9] America's enhanced economic and military position after the Second World War led officials to overestimate its capabilities and become involved in inappropriate endeavors. "I had never visited Indochina, nor did I understand or appreciate its history, language, culture, or values," former secretary of defense Robert S. McNamara recently admitted. "The same must be said, to varying degrees, about . . . many others. When it came to Vietnam, we found ourselves setting policy for a region that was terra incognita."[10] Based on their connection with Diem and a few trips to Indochina, men such as Fishel and Senator Mike Mansfield qualified as experts on Vietnam.[11]

Fishel was part of a new breed of intellectual surfacing after the Second World War. The philosopher and historian Garry Wills appropriately dubbed them "Bogart professors," the get-tough, take-action liberal academics of the cold war. Similar to actor Humphrey Bogart's character in the popular movie *Casablanca*, they were idealists with an edge, individuals with a job to do: stop the communist menace at whatever cost. They would "present themselves as the realists," Wills noted, "men acquainted with the hard facts of power." Like Fishel, many had been intelligence officers during the world war and afterward returned to campus to give the ivory-tower types a "tough-minded going over."[12] Fishel clearly relished this macho persona, a fact that is illustrated by his rendering of an antiwar demonstration that occurred outside his office: "I was under fire a good deal of the time [during the war] and, . . . You don't think about the fact that you're in danger . . . I was trying to protect my files and . . . the women who worked for me," he said. "They were very brave, but only, I suppose, because I didn't seem to be alarmed."[13]

Fishel became so heavily involved in Vietnamese affairs in part because his boss, President Hannah, encouraged him to do so. Both were ambitious men and enjoyed moving in powerful circles. Hannah, in particular, had strong ties to the federal government. "I had one foot in Washington [D.C.]," he noted in a 1985 interview.[14] Hannah prided himself on the fact that Michigan State was among the first land-grant colleges, and regularly offered its services to governmental and private agencies. He once asserted "that higher education can be put to use for mankind's benefit, that professors can be practical, that they can make contributions" in numerous areas.[15] Although not a great intellect, Hannah possessed vision and talents of persuasion. During the postwar period, the East Lansing campus blossomed under his

143

direction, creating a rivalry with neighboring Ann Arbor, home of the University of Michigan. Graduates from the latter still take pleasure in referring to Michigan State as "Moo U" because of its agricultural beginnings. Much to their chagrin, however, Hannah built Michigan State into a major research institution using local, state, federal, and private financing. By 1969, Hannah's last year at the helm, the school had eighty-five academic departments, the annual budget exceeded $100 million, and it could boast of having more National Merit Scholars (684) than Harvard University (503).[16] Over a twenty-year period, 1951–71, Michigan State took part in thirty-five overseas technical-assistance projects. Funds derived from these ventures were often channeled back into the school's physical plant and academic programs. Michigan State's Center for International Studies, for example, was built from part of the $25 million that the university made on the MSUG.[17]

Hannah enthusiastically endorsed the MSUG because it combined his love of institution building and dislike of communism. "I am sure that the world today is a better world than it would have been," Hannah affirmed in 1960, "had there been no programs of university assistance in the developing areas."[18]

The nation-building endeavor in Vietnam, however, backfired on the United States and Michigan State. Much of the American missionary zeal for foreign aid diminished, in part, because of protracted U.S. involvement in the Vietnam War. To some degree, Michigan State continued to accept overseas technical-assistance contracts and even hosted a conference on the topic in the late 1980s. However, the university avoided politically sensitive, massive projects like the MSUG. Instead, Michigan State worked primarily in agricultural development. Fishel's friend and former MSUG chief adviser Ralph Smuckler later noted, "I think the university learned a lot . . . about the kinds of things you get into and you don't get into."[19]

As a result of the *Ramparts* exposé on the MSUG, Fishel was singled out by antiwar demonstrators and suffered more than other Michigan State faculty. In 1955, the first year of the Vietnam contract, he was voted "Teacher of the Year" by Excalibur, Michigan State's senior men's society. Just over a decade later, students disrupted his classes and referred to him as a butcher. One activist at Southern Illinois University called him a "complete bastard," Fishel recalled, "a warmaker who must be driven from the campus." Fishel appeared to enjoy the notoriety. "He regretted nothing he had done," observed *New York Times* journalist Gloria Emerson after conducting a 1971 interview with him. "[I]t was clear, however, that he felt many other people should regret their actions." According to Emerson, Fishel did not believe Stanley Sheinbaum, a MSUG member who coauthored the *Ramparts* piece, was sincere about his antiwar stance. Fishel argued that Sheinbaum wrote it because he "simply burned to get even" with the university for forcing him out of academia. "And I was simply," Fishel said, "sort of accidentally his victim . . . the happy symbol of everything that was evil."[20]

Emerson's observation about Fishel was correct. He stood by Diem until virtually the end of the Vietnamese president's life, and initially supported Lyndon Johnson's stance on Vietnam, working with the White House in 1964 and 1965 to combat student protest. Fishel enjoyed his moment in the spotlight and shrugged off the suggestion that the antiwar movement hampered his career. It "hurt only in a salary sense," he declared. "I am not one of the university's highest-paid professors, even if I am one of its best-known and perhaps respected ones. This simply reflects the fact that for . . . years I was highly unpopular and I was busy in the public arena."[21]

Fishel's basic view that America could have succeeded in Vietnam had it found "the middle road of non-Communist national leadership" never changed.[22] Naively, he continued to maintain that the communists did not have broad-based support in the South and speculated about a viable alternative to them. "People ma[d]e him out to be a dark plotter," MSUG member Hickey later said of Fishel, "but I don't think he was a schemer. Poor Wesley was really a bit bumbling in many ways, and his sins were sins of omission more than anything else."[23] In a sense, Fishel resembled Alden Pyle, the protagonist in Graham Greene's *The Quiet American* (1955), a novel about the demise of French power in Vietnam and early U.S. nation-building initiatives there. Pyle, a young, inexperienced Bostonian working for the American Economic Mission, searched for a "Third Force . . . free from Communism and the taint of colonialism," what Fishel hoped Diem would be. In the process, Pyle became involved in covert activities resulting in his death and the deaths of numerous innocents.[24]

Youthful, ambitious, and overly idealistic, Fishel and Pyle were symbols of what was wrong with U.S. foreign policy following the Second World War. Embracing the role of cold warrior too quickly, they, like other policy makers, overestimated America's ability to change Vietnam, made mistakes, and as a result, suffered the consequences. Vietnam had a much stronger impact on Michigan State than the reverse. Adhering to the prevailing cold war rationale, the university became involved in endeavors that had little to do with academics, such as cooperating with Central Intelligence Agency personnel to train South Vietnamese police in counterintelligence tactics. Discussing the propriety of higher-education's involvement in foreign affairs, Hannah himself later observed that "we reached a point where we had to be damn careful . . . but we weren't so smart" and "g[o]t hurt a time or two."[25] These types of activities ultimately proved detrimental to Michigan State's campus and had a profoundly negative impact on the public's perception of the university's role in foreign policy. The "credibility gap" between the American people and its policy makers emerged at this time, and the result was a frank repudiation of American actions in Vietnam.

NOTES

1. *Cleveland Plain Dealer*, 14 November 1971.

2. Quoted in Gloria Emerson, *Winners and Losers: Battles, Retreats, Gains, Losses and Ruins from a Long War* (New York: Random House, 1976), 305.

3. Quoted in George C. Herring, *America's Longest War: The United States and Vietnam, 1950–1975*, 3d ed. (New York: McGraw-Hill, 1996), 51.

4. *New York Times*, 30 July 1954; Ralph Smuckler, interview by author, 13 May 1993.

5. Ronald H. Spector, *Advice and Support: The Early Years of the U.S. Army in Vietnam, 1941–1960* (New York: Free Press, 1985), 378.

6. Emerson, *Winners and Losers*, 283.

7. *Cleveland Plain Dealer*, 14 November 1971.

8. David L. Anderson, *Trapped by Success: The Eisenhower Administration and Vietnam, 1953–1961* (New York: Columbia University Press, 1991), 209.

9. George C. Kahin, *Intervention: How America Became Involved in Vietnam* (New York: Knopf, 1986), 69–70.

10. Robert S. McNamara with Brian VanDemark, *In Retrospect: The Tragedy and Lessons of Vietnam* (New York: Times Books, 1995), 32.

11. Gregory A. Olson, *Mansfield and Vietnam: A Study in Rhetorical Adaptation* (East Lansing: Michigan State University Press, 1995), 23.

12. Garry Wills, *Nixon Agonistes: The Crisis of the Self-Made Man* (Boston: Houghton Mifflin Company, 1970), 572.

13. Quoted in Emerson, *Winners and Losers*, 304.

14. John Hannah, interview with David Anderson, 14 June 1985.

15. Paul L. Dressel, *College to University: The Hannah Years at Michigan State, 1935–1969* (East Lansing: Michigan State University Publications, 1987), 292.

16. *Time*, 21 March 1969, 42; Michael E. Unsworth, "War on Campus: Michigan State," *Vietnam* (August 1995), 27.

17. Dressel, *College to University*, 293; Kenneth J. Heineman, *Campus Wars: The Peace Movement at American State Universities in the Vietnam Era* (New York: New York University Press, 1993), 137; Milton C. Taylor and Adrian Jaffe, "The Professor-Diplomat: Ann Arbor and Cambridge Were Never Like This," *New Republic* 146 (5 March 1962): 28; Guy Fox and Robert Scigliano, *Technical Assistance in Vietnam: The Michigan State University Experience* (New York: Frederick A. Praeger, 1965), 4; Michigan State University *State News*, 25 April 1966.

18. Quoted in Dressel, *College to University*, 292.

19. Smuckler interview; Dressel, *College to University*, 279–95; Lucian W. Pye, "Foreign Aid and America's Involvement in the Developing World," in Anthony Lake, *The Vietnam Legacy: The War, American Society and the Future of American Foreign Policy* (New York: New York University Press, 1976), 378–80; Ralph Smuckler and Robert J. Berg with David F. Gordon, *New Challenges, New Opportunities: U.S. Cooperation for International Growth and Development in the 1990s* (East Lansing, Mich.: Center for Advanced Study of International Development, 1988).

20. Emerson, *Winners and Losers*, 302, 306; Department of Information Services, 1974, Wesley R. Fishel Papers, Michigan State University Archives and Historical Collections, East Lansing, Michigan.

21. Quoted in Emerson, *Winners and Losers*, 306.

22. *Cleveland Plain Dealer*, 14 November 1971.

23. Emerson, *Winners and Losers*, 284.

24. Graham Greene, *The Quiet American* (1955; reprint, New York: Penguin Books, 1977), 124, 17–20, 31, 41; *Cleveland Plain Dealer*, 14 November 1971.

25. Hannah, interview.

BIBLIOGRAPHY

PRIMARY SOURCES

Manuscript Collections

Fishel, Wesley Papers. Michigan State University Archives and Historical Collections, East Lansing, Michigan. (The current condition of the Wesley Fishel Papers differs from when I first examined them in 1992. At the time, they were being processed and in some cases neither a box nor folder number existed. The documents have since been catalogued and can be located with a little patience.)

Hannah, John A. Papers. Michigan State University Archives and Historical Collections, East Lansing, Michigan.

Jonas, Gilbert Papers. Michigan State University Archives and Historical Collections, East Lansing, Michigan.

Michigan State University Student Radicalism Collection. Michigan State University Special Collections, Michigan State University Library, East Lansing, Michigan.

Michigan State University Vietnam Project Papers. Michigan State University Archives and Historical Collections, East Lansing, Michigan.

Williams, Samuel L. Papers. U.S. Military History Institute Archives, Carlisle Barracks, Pennsylvania.

Interviews

Adams, Walter. Interview by author. East Lansing, Michigan, 10 August 1993.

Aschom, Don. Interview by author. East Lansing, Michigan, 24 July 1992.

Brandstatter, Arthur. Interview by author. East Lansing, Michigan, 17 July 1992.

Hannah, John. Interview by David Anderson. East Lansing, Michigan, 14 June 1985.

Hunter, John. Interview by author. East Lansing, Michigan, 22 July 1992.

Sheinbaum, Stanley. Interview by author. Santa Monica, California, 18 March 1993.

Smuckler, Ralph. Interview by author. Washington, D.C., 13 May 1993.

Taylor, Milton. Interview by author. Mt. Gretna, Pennsylvania, 11 May 1993.

Turner, Ralph. Interview by author. East Lansing, Michigan, 9 July 1992.

Wickert, Fred. Interview by author. East Lansing, Michigan, 20 July 1992.

Correspondence

Harvard College Library. Letter to author, 22 December 1993.

Hickey, Gerald C. Letter to author, 28 January 1993.

Shields, Paul. Letter to author, 5 April 1994.

Turner, Ralph. Letter to author, 16 December 1993.

Government Documents

Sheinbaum, Stanley K. " Statement by Stanley K. Sheinbaum to the Los Angeles City Council Confirmation Hearing Reappointment to the Police Commission," 3 April 1991.

U.S. Department of State. *Foreign Relations of the United States, 1946. Vol. 6, Eastern Europe; The Soviet Union.* Washington, D.C.: U.S. Government Printing Office, 1969.

———. *Foreign Relations of the United States, 1955–1957. Vol. 1, Vietnam.* Washington, D.C.: U.S. Government Printing Office, 1985.

———. *Foreign Relations of the United States, 1958–1960. Vol. 1, Vietnam.* Washington, D.C.: U.S. Government Printing Office, 1986.

———. *Indochina Files, 1955.* Washington, D.C.: U.S. Government Printing Office.

Newspapers

Michigan:

Ann Arbor News
Detroit Free Press

Detroit News
Michigan State University *State News*
Escanaba Daily Press
Grand Rapids Press
Lansing State Journal

United States:

Cleveland Plain Dealer
Milwaukee Journal
National Observer
New York Times
Portland Oregonian
St. Louis Post-Dispatch
San Francisco News-Call Bulletin
Saturday Evening Post
Southern Illinois University *Daily Egyptian*

SECONDARY SOURCES

Books

Adams, Walter. *The Test*. New York: MacMillan Company, 1971.

Adams, Walter, and John A. Garraty. *Is the World Our Campus?* East Lansing: Michigan State University Press, 1960.

Allen, Douglas, and Ngo Vinh Long. *Coming to Terms: Indochina, the United States, and the War*. Boulder, Colo.: Westview Press, 1991.

Allen, Luther, and Pham Ngoc An. *A Vietnamese District Chief in Action*. Saigon: Michigan State University Vietnam Advisory Group and the National Institute of Administration, 1961.

Ambrose, Stephen E. *Eisenhower*. 2 vols. New York: Simon and Schuster, 1983–84.

Ambrose, Stephen E. with Richard E. Immerman. *Ike's Spies: Eisenhower and the Espionage Establishment*. Garden City, N.Y.: Doubleday, 1981.

Anderson, David. *Trapped by Success: The Eisenhower Administration and Vietnam, 1953–1961*. New York: Columbia University Press, 1991.

Aronson, James. *The Press and the Cold War*. Indianapolis and New York: Bobbs-Merrill Company, 1970.

Beers, Howard W. *An American Experience in Indonesia: The University of Kentucky Affiliation with the Agricultural University at Bogor.* Lexington: University Press of Kentucky, 1971.

Bush, Vannevar. *Pieces of the Action.* New York: William Morrow and Company, 1970.

Buttinger, Joseph. *Vietnam: A Dragon Embattled.* 2 vols. New York: Praeger, 1967.

Colby, William, and Peter Forbath. *Honorable Men: My Life in the C.I.A.* New York: Simon and Schuster, 1978.

Colby, William, and James McCargar. *Lost Victory: A Firsthand Account of America's Sixteen-Year Involvement in Vietnam.* Chicago: Contemporary Books, 1989.

Conant, James B. *My Several Lives: Memoirs of a Social Inventor.* New York: Harper & Row, Publishers, 1970.

Cooney, John. *The American Pope: The Life and Times of Francis Cardinal Spellman.* New York: Times Books, 1984.

Critchfield, Richard. *The Long Charade: Political Subversion in the Vietnam War.* New York: Harcourt, Brace and World, 1968.

Dahm, Bernard. *History of Indonesia in the Twentieth Century.* Trans. P. S. Falla. London, New York, and Washington: Praeger Publishers, 1971.

Dang, Nghiem. *Vietnam: Politics and Public Administration.* Honolulu: East-West Center Press, 1966.

DeBenedetti, Charles, and Charles Chatfield (assisting author). *An American Ordeal: The Antiwar Movement of the Vietnam Era.* Syracuse, N.Y.: Syracuse University Press, 1990.

Diamond, Sigmund. *Compromised Campus: The Collaboration of Universities with the Intelligence Community, 1945–1955.* New York and Oxford: Oxford University Press, 1992.

Donoghue, John D. *My Thuan: A Study of a Delta Village in South Vietnam.* Saigon: Michigan State Vietnam Advisory Group, 1961.

Dressel, Paul L. *College to University: The Hannah Years at Michigan State, 1935–1969.* East Lansing: Michigan State University Publications, 1987.

du Berrier, Hilaire. *Background to Betrayal: The Tragedy of Vietnam.* Boston and Los Angeles: Western Islands Publishers, 1965.

Duncanson, Dennis J. *Government and Revolution in Vietnam.* New York and London: Oxford University Press, 1968.

Emerson, Gloria. *Winners and Losers: Battles, Retreats, Gains, Losses and Ruins from a Long War.* New York: Random House, 1976.

Encyclopedia Americana. Vol. 11. Danbury, Conn.: Grolier, 1992.

Fishel, Wesley. *The End of Extraterritoriality in China.* Berkeley: University of California Press, 1952.

——, ed. *Vietnam: Anatomy of a Conflict.* Itasca, Ill.: F.E. Peacock Publishers, 1968.

——, and Alfred H. Hausrath. *Language Problems of the US Army during Hostilities in Korea.* Chevy Chase, Md.: Johns Hopkins University Operations Research Office, 1958.

FitzGerald, Frances. *Fire in the Lake: The Vietnamese and the Americans in Vietnam.* New York: Random House, 1972.

Gaddis, John Lewis. *The Long Peace: Inquiries into the History of the Cold War.* New York: Oxford University Press, 1987.

Greene, Graham. *The Quiet American.* New York: Penguin Books, 1977.

Hannah, John A. *A Memoir.* East Lansing: Michigan State University Press, 1980.

Heineman, Kenneth J. *Campus Wars: The Peace Movement at American State Universities in the Vietnam Era.* New York and London: New York University Press, 1993.

Herring, George C. *America's Longest War: The United States and Vietnam, 1950–1975.* New York: John Wiley & Sons, Inc., 1979.

Herring, George C. *America's Longest War: The United States and Vietnam, 1950–1975.* 2d ed. New York: Knopf, 1986.

Herring, George C. *America's Longest War: The United States and Vietnam, 1950–1975.* 3d ed. New York: McGraw-Hill, 1996.

Hickey, Gerald C. *Free in the Forest: Ethnohistory of the Vietnamese Central Highlands, 1954-1976.* New Haven, Conn.: Yale University Press, 1982.

Hickey, Gerald C.. Preliminary Research Report on the High Plateau. Saigon: M.S.U.G., 1957.

——. *Sons of the Mountains: Ethnohistory of the Vietnamese Central Highlands to 1954.* New Haven, Conn.: Yale University Press, 1982.

——. *Kingdom in the Morning Mist: Mayréna in the Highlands of Vietnam.* Philadelphia: University of Pennsylvania Press, 1988.

——. *Shattered World: Adaptation and Survival among Vietnam's Highland Peoples during the Vietnam War.* Philadelphia: University of Pennsylvania Press, 1993.

——, and Bui Quang Da. *The Study of a Vietnamese Rural Community: Sociology.* Saigon: Michigan State University Vietnam Advisory Group, 1960.

Hinckle, Warren. *If You Have a Lemon, Make Lemonade: An Essential Memoir of a Lunatic Decade.* New York: G.P. Putnam's Sons, 1973.

Huntington, Samuel P. *Political Order in Changing Societies.* New Haven, Conn., and London: Yale University Press, 1968.

Kahin, George McT. *Intervention: How America Became Involved in Vietnam.* New York: Knopf, 1986.

Kennan, George. *Memoirs, 1925–1950.* Boston: Little, Brown and Company, 1967.

Kerr, Clark. *The Uses of the University, With " Postscript-1972."* Cambridge: Harvard University Press, 1972.

Klare, Michael T. *War Without End: American Planning for the Next Vietnams.* New York: Alfred A. Knopf, 1972.

LaFeber, Walter. *America, Russia, and the Cold War, 1945–1992.* 7th ed. New York: McGraw-Hill, 1993.

Lake, Anthony. *The Vietnam Legacy: The War, American Society and the Future of American Foreign Policy.* New York: New York University Press, 1976.

Lansdale, Edward Geary. *In the Midst of Wars: An American's Mission to Southeast Asia.* New York: Harper and Row Publishers, 1972.

le Carré, John. *The Honourable Schoolboy.* New York: Bantam Books, 1977.

Lens, Sidney. *The Military-Industrial Complex.* Philadelphia and Kansas City: Pilgrim Press and The National Catholic Reporter, 1970.

Levy, David W. *The Debate Over Vietnam.* Baltimore: Johns Hopkins University Press, 1991.

Lindholm, Richard, ed. *Viet-Nam: The First Five Years, An International Symposium.* East Lansing: Michigan State University Press, 1959.

Mackenzie, Angus. *Secrets: The CIA's War at Home.* Berkeley and Los Angeles, California: University of California Press, 1997.

McNamara, Robert S., with Brian VanDemark. *In Retrospect: The Tragedy and Lessons of Vietnam.* New York: Times Books, 1995.

Millikan, Max F., and W. W. Rostow. *A Proposal: Key to an Effective Foreign Policy.* New York: Harper and Brothers, 1957.

Montgomery, John D. *Aftermath: Tarnished Outcomes of American Foreign Policy.* Dover, Massachusetts and London: Auburn House Publishing Company, 1986.

New Encyclopaedia Britannica. Vol. 4. Chicago: Encyclopaedia Britannica, 1991.

Niehoff, Richard. *John A. Hannah: Versatile Administrator and Distinguished Public Servant.* Lanham, Md.: University Press of America, 1989.

Olson, Gregory A. *Mansfield and Vietnam: A Study in Rhetorical Adaptation*. East Lansing: Michigan State University Press, 1995.

Penders, C. L. M. *The Life and Times of Sukarno*. London: Sidgwick and Jackson, 1974.

Scigliano, Robert. *South Vietnam: Nation Under Stress*. Boston: Houghton Mifflin Company, 1963.

Scigliano, Robert, and Guy H. Fox. *Technical Assistance in Vietnam: The Michigan State University Experience*. New York: Praeger, 1965.

Sheehan, Neil. *A Bright Shining Lie: John Paul Vann and America in Vietnam*. New York: Random House, 1988.

Smuckler, Ralph H., and Robert J. Berg with David F. Gordon. *New Challenges, New Opportunities: U.S. Cooperation for International Growth and Development in the 1990s*. East Lansing: Michigan State University Center for Advanced Study of International Development, 1988.

So, Alvin Y. *Social Change and Development: Modernization, Dependency, and World-System Theories*. Newbury Park, London, and New Delhi: Sage Publications, 1990.

Spector, Ronald H. *The United States Army in Vietnam: Advice and Support: The Early Years, 1941–1960*. Washington, D.C.: GPO, 1983.

———. *Advice and Support: The Early Years of the U.S. Army in Vietnam, 1941–1960*. New York: Free Press, 1985.

Sperling, Cass Warner, and Cork Millner with Jack Warner. *Hollywood Be Thy Name: The Warner Brothers Story*. Rocklin, Calif.: Prima Publishing, 1994.

Tindall, George Brown. *America: A Narrative History*. Vol. 2. New York and London: W.W. Norton and Company, 1984.

Weidner, Edward W., ed. *Development Administration in Asia*. Durham, N.C.: Duke University Press, 1970.

Weiner, Myron, and Samuel P. Huntington, eds. *Understanding Political Development*. Boston: Little, Brown and Company, 1987.

Who's Who in America, 1954–1955. Vol. 28. Chicago: Marquis Who's Who, 1954.

Wiesner, Louis A. *Victims and Survivors: Displaced Persons and Other War Victims in Viet-Nam, 1954–1975*. Westport, Conn.: Greenwood Press, 1988.

Williams, Roger L. *The Origins of Federal Support for Higher Education: George W. Atherton and the Land-Grant College Movement*. University Park: Pennsylvania State University Press, 1991.

Wills, Garry. *Nixon Agonistes: The Crisis of the Self-Made Man*. Boston: Houghton Mifflin Company, 1970.

Woodruff, Lloyd W. My Thuan: Administrative and Financial Aspects of a Village in South Vietnam. Saigon: Michigan State University Vietnam Advisory Group, 1961.

Woodruff, Lloyd W., and Nguyen Ngoc Yen. The Study of a Vietnamese Rural Community: Administrative Activity. Vol. 1. Saigon: Michigan State University Vietnam Advisory Group, 1960.

Yergin, Daniel. Shattered Peace: The Origins of the Cold War. New York: Penguin Books, 1990.

Periodicals

Child, Frank. " Vietnam—The Eleventh Hour." New Republic 145 (December 1961): 14–16.

Connor, Walker. " Nation-Building or Nation Destroying?" World Politics 24 (April 1972): 319–47.

" A Costly Victory In Vietnam." Life 49 (November 1960): 30.

Fishel, Wesley. " Vietnam's Democratic One-Man Rule." The New Leader 42 (November 1959):10–13.

Hendry, James B. " American Aid in Vietnam: The View from a Village." Pacific Affairs 33 (December 1960):387–91.

Hinckle, Warren, Robert Scheer, and Sol Stern. "The University on the Make." Ramparts 4 (April 1966): 11–22.

Horowitz, Irving D. " Michigan State and the C.I.A.: A Dilemma for Social Science." Atomic Scientist 22 (September 1966): 27.

Jaffe, Adrian, and Milton C. Taylor. " A Crumbling Bastion: Flattery and Lies Won't Save Vietnam." New Republic 144 (June 1961): 17–20.

Kennan, George F. " The Sources of Soviet Conduct." Foreign Affairs 25 (July 1947): 566–82.

Kirk, Russell. " From the Academy." National Review (February 1968): 192.

———. " New Left v. National Security." National Review (January 1970): 18.

Klare, Michael. " The Military Research Network—America's Fourth Armed Service." North American Congress on Latin America (1970).

Michigan State College Catalog, 1955–56.

Michigan State University Catalog, 1960–61.

Nicolaus, Martin. " The Professor, the Policeman, and the Peasant." Viet-Report (February and March 1966).

Norton-Taylor, Duncan. " Megaversity's Struggle with Itself." Fortune (May 1967).

Rabe, Stephen G. " Eisenhower Revisionism: A Decade of Scholarship." *Diplomatic History* 17 (Winter 1993): 97–115.

Samuels, Gertrude. " Passage to Freedom in Viet Nam." *National Geographic Magazine* 167 (June 1955): 858–74.

Scheer, Robert. " Prince of the City." *L.A. Style* 8 (March 1993): 24–26.

———, and Warren Hinckle. " The Viet-Nam Lobby." *Ramparts* 4 (July 1965):16–24.

———. *How the United States Got Involved in Vietnam.* (Santa Barbara, Calif.: Center for the Study of Democratic Institutions, 1965).

Scigliano, Robert. " Political Parties in South Vietnam Under the Republic." *Pacific Affairs* 33 (December 1960): 327–46.

Sheinbaum, Stanley K. " Vietnam—A Study in Freedom." *Michigan State University Magazine* 1 (February 1956): 9–12.

Taylor, Milton C., and Adrian Jaffe. " The Professor-Diplomat: Ann Arbor and Cambridge Were Never Like This." *The New Republic* 146 (5 March 1962): 28–30.

" University Presidents, Exit Methuselah." *Time* (March 1969): 42.

Unsworth, Michael E. " War on Campus: Michigan State." *Vietnam* 8 (August 1995): 26–32.

" A Billion For Vietnam—For U.S., Trouble." *U.S. News and World Report* (November 1960): 84.

Waltman, Howard L. " Cross-Cultural Training in Public Administration." *Public Administration Review* 21 (summer 1961): 145.

Wickert, Frederic R. " An Adventure in Psychological Testing Abroad." *American Psychologist* 12 (February 1957): 86–88.

Dissertations and Theses

Blanchard, Carlene Marie Bagnall. " *Ramparts* Magazine: Social Change in the Sixties." Ph.D. diss., University of Michigan, 1969.

Morgan, Joseph G. " The Vietnam Lobby: The American Friends of Vietnam, 1955–1975." Ph.D. diss., Georgetown University, 1992.

Stasiowski, Susan Cecilia. " A History and Evaluation of *Ramparts* Magazine, 1962–1969." Master's thesis, San Jose State College, 1972.

INDEX

Adams, Walter: and Jaffe-Taylor publication, 120; and John Hannah, xiv, 5, 6; and Ngo Dinh Diem visit to Michigan State, xiii; and propriety of university involvement in foreign affairs, xiv, 119
Adkins, Elmer, 71, 72, 73, 117
Agency for International Development, the (AID), 132
Allubowicz, Henriette, 43
American Friends of Vietnam, the (AFVN), 10, 27, 129–31
Anderson, Marian, 81
Anti-Communist Denunciation Campaign, the, 66
antiwar movement, U.S., 124, 125, 129, 130, 131
Association for Administrative Studies, the, 45
Austin, Ruben, 107, 119

Bajaraka movement, the, 34
Bao Dai, 30, 64
Barrows, Leland, 78
Binh Xuyen, the, 12, 14, 15, 23, 64, 66, 70
Boudrias, Louis, 64, 67–68
Brandstatter, Arthur F., 12, 63, 64, 76, 79–80, 92
Brazil, U.S. technical assistance to, 7, 8

Brown, Gordon, 46
Bryan, Stanley E., 122
Bui Ngoc Tre, 25
Bui-Quang-Da, 44
Bui Van Luong, 23, 24, 26, 28, 29, 34, 36
Bui Van Tinh, 68
Bundy, McGeorge, 122
Buttinger, Joseph, 27, 129, 131
Buu Dich, 102–3, 105
Buu Nghi, 93, 94

Camp des Mares crime laboratory, 67, 70, 73-74
Cao Dai Sect, the, 14, 15
Cardinaux, Alfred L., 23, 35
Catholic Church, the: influence of in South Vietnamese government, 27; support of Ngo Dinh Diem, 27; and Vietnam refugee resettlement, 10, 21, 22, 26–27, 28
Catholic Relief Services (CRS), 26–27, 28
Center for International Studies, the (Michigan State University), 131, 144
Center for the Study of Democratic Institutions, the, 124
Central Identification Bureau, the, 70
Chamberlin, Everett A., 71
Chapin, Richard, 43

Cherne, Leo, 27, 129
Chiang Kai-shek, 2
Child, Frank C., 121
Churchill, Winston, 2
civil guard, the (Vietnam), 78–80, 121, 142
civil service, Vietnam: exams, 42; rigidity of, 98
Colby, William, 127
Cole, David C., 103–4
Colegrove, Albert M., 75
Collins, J. Lawton, 11, 14–15
Colombia, U.S. technical assistance to, 7
Colombo Powers Conference, the, 74
COMIGAL. See Commissariat for Refugees, the
Commissariat for Land Development, the, 34
Commissariat for Refugees, the (COMI-GAL), 22, 23, 24–25
Compton, Karl T., 4
Conant, James B., 4
Concerned Students for Academic Freedom and Responsibility, 132
containment policy, the, 2, 3
counterespionage training, Vietnam, 66, 67–68
Country Team, the, 78, 79, 80
Cunningham, Elsie, 103, 105

de Gaulle, Charles, 2
decentralization, 24, 25, 29
Denison, James H., 11–12, 126
Diem, Ngo Dinh. See Ngo Dinh Diem
Dorsey, John T., 46, 47, 49, 96–97
Douglas, William O., 10
du Berrier, Hilaire, 124
Dulles, Allen, 124
Dulles, John Foster, xi, 11, 21
Duncanson, Dennis J., 65
Durbrow, Elbridge, 78, 116
Dymond, Corey, 64, 71

Eastern Regional Organization for Public Administration, the (EROPA), 45
Ecole de Droit d'Administration, the, 42
Ecole des Hautes Etudes Indochinois, the, 42
Eisenhower, Dwight D., xi, xv, 1, 21
Ellsberg, Daniel, 133
Engle, Byron, 76

Fenton, John, 102
fingerprint classification systems, Vietnam, 70–72
Finkle, Jason, 106
Fishel, Wesley: and the American Friends of Vietnam, 10, 129, 130, 131; anti-communist stance of, 8; and antiwar movement, 130, 145; and the Binh Xuyen, 15; as ÒBogart professor,Ó 143; break with Ngo Dinh Diem, 121-22, 130, 142; Central Intelligence Agency connections of, 124, 127; and the civil guard, 78; and the Colombo Powers Conference, 74; correspondence with Ngo Dinh Diem, 9, 116, 118; death of, 133; editorials by, 118, 130; educational background of, 8, 9; and formation of the Michigan State University Group, xii, 2; friendship with Ngo Dinh Diem, xii, 8, 9, 10–11, 141; and Geneva Accords, 11; harassment by student activists, xiv, 116, 131–33, 144; military career of, 8–9, 13; and the Montagnards, 31; and National Institute of Administration curriculum, 49; and the participant program, 93, 106, 108; poor relations with Michigan State University Group staff, 80–81; and Ramparts exposé, xiv, 10, 116, 126, 128, 129, 131, 144–45; support of Vietnamese government's repressive tactics, 66; and the Vietnam Lobby, xii

Foreign Operations Administration, the (FOA), 12
Fox, Guy, 15, 16, 54, 56
Francis Cardinal Spellman, 10, 27
Franklin, Jerome D., 77
"Freedom Singers,Ó 131
Fulbright, J. William, 129

Gabis, Stanley, 104, 105, 107
Gardiner, Arthur Z., 76
Garraty, John A., 119
Geneva Accords, the, 11, 21
GI Bill, the, 5
Gittinger, Price, 31, 32
Greer, Thomas, 130

Hagelberg, Milton, 74
Hannah, John: academic background of, 5; anticommunist stance of, 4–5, 129, 133; and expansion of Michigan State University, xiv, 5–6, 143–44; and formation of the Michigan State University Group, 2; land-grant philosophy of, xiv, 1, 6; and Michigan State University Group - Central Intelligence Agency connection, 82, 133; Ngo Dinh Diem visit to Michigan State, xiii; and *Ramparts* exposé, 127, 128, 129, 131; and role of university in foreign affairs, xiv, 6; and termination of Michigan State University Group contract, 123; and the Agency for International Development, 7, 132, 133; and the Civil Rights Commission, 7; and the Medal of Freedom, 7; and the Michigan State University Institute of Foreign Studies, 6; support of nation building, 141, 143, 144; support of Ngo Dinh Diem, 35, 118
Hannah, Sarah. *See* Shaw, Sarah
Harnett, Joseph J., 26, 28

Hemmye, Jerome H., 74, 76, 77
Hendry, James B., 119, 120
Henry, Sir Edward Richard, 71
Henry fingerprint system, 70, 71
Hickey, Gerald C.: and Vietnam highlands research, 31–34
highlands, Vietnam: Michigan State University Group studies of, 30–34; Ngo Dinh Diem's policies toward, 30, 33, 34; under French control, 30
Hinckle, Warren, xiii, 126, 129
Hoa Hao Sect, the, 14
Hoyt, Howard: and the Michigan State University Group police administration division 64, 67, 68, 75, 77; and National Institute of Administration curriculum, 49; and the participant program observation tours, 99; and Wesley Fishel, 80
Humphrey, Hubert, 130
Hunter, John M., 50–51, 122, 128
Hutchins, Robert Maynard, 124
Huynh Van Dao, 98

In-Service Training Newsletter, the, 54
Indochina, colonial history of, 2
Institute of Foreign Studies, the (Michigan State University), 6
International Control Commission, the (ICC), 15
International Cooperation Administration, the (ICA), xii, 47, 64, 75–76, 95, 103
International Rescue Committee, the (IRC), 26, 27, 129

Jaffe, Adrian, 120, 122, 127
Johnson, Lyndon B., 126

Keating, Edward, 128
Kennan, George, 2

Kennedy, John F., 10, 115, 123
Kennedy, Joseph P., 10
Killingsworth, Charles C., 12, 92
Kirkpatrick, Lyman, 82
Komatsu, Koyashi, 9
Krim, Arthur, 130

Ladejinsky, Wolf, 11, 32, 33, 116
Land Development Project, the (1957),
    34
"Land Grant Man," 131
Lansdale, Edward, 10, 11, 22, 124
Le Cang Dam, 99, 100
Le Pichon, Jean, 29
Long, Norton, 93

MacAlister, Robert J., 35
Madame Nhu, 116, 122
Magsaysay, Ram—n, 12, 92
Mansfield, Mike, 10, 11, 93, 118, 143
Marlow, Joseph S., 77
McNamara, Robert S., 143
Mesta, Perle, 16
Michener, James A., 16
Michigan State University Group, the
    (MSUG): and Camp des Mares crime
    laboratory, 67, 70, 73–74; and the
    Central Identification Bureau, 70;
    chain of command of, 13; and the civil
    guard, 78–80, 82, 121, 142; and the
    Colombo Powers Conference, 74–75,
    77; conflict within over role in foreign
    affairs, 117, 118–19; conflicts with the
    Catholic Church, 22, 28, 29; conflicts
    with the Military Assistance Advisory
    Group, 63–64, 78, 79; conflicts with
    the National Institute of
    Administration staff, 43, 44, 51, 52,
    56–57; conflicts with Ngo Dinh Diem,
    22, 31, 63, 64, 79, 80, 119, 121; con-
    flicts with the United States

Operations Mission, 63–64, 75, 76–77;
    connection to the Central Intelligence
    Agency, 64, 66–67, 81, 82–83, 116,
    123, 126–27; counterespionage train-
    ing division, 66, 67–68; criticism of
    Ngo Dinh Diem within, 115; establish-
    ment of, xii, 1–2, 11–13, 141; Field
    Administration Division of, 23–24;
    first days in Vietnam, 15–16; goals of,
    xii, 4; and the in-service training pro-
    gram, 53–54, 55; and modernization of
    Vietnamese fingerprint operations,
    70–72; and the National Identity Card
    program, 70, 72, 73; and the National
    Institute of Administration, 41, 42–57;
    and the National Police Academy, 68;
    orientation programs of, 14; and the
    participant program, 91–108; pedagog-
    ical differences with the National
    Institute of Administration, 43, 44, 48,
    51, 56–57; police administration divi-
    sion, xii, 66–67, 68–78, 83–84; police
    communications project of, 74–75, 76,
    77; problems in effectiveness of,
    13–14, 41, 50–51, 65; public adminis-
    tration studies of, 44–45; Ramparts
    exposé of, xiii, 81–83, 116, 123, 126;
    and refugee resettlement, 21, 22,
    23–26, 29, 35–36; and reorganization
    of the Vietnamese Bureau of
    Investigation, 66–68, 69–74; and
    Saigon traffic control project, 77–78;
    staff from outside Michigan State
    University, 14, 81; studies of
    Vietnamese highlands, 30–34; termi-
    nation of contract of, xiii, 47, 55–56,
    80, 82, 115, 120, 121
Military Assistance Advisory Group, the
    (MAAG), 63–64, 78, 79, 80
Mode, Walter, 23, 54
modernization school, the, 3

Montagnards, the: dislike of Ngo Dinh Diem's government, 32, 34; displacement of by Catholic refugees, 28, 30–31, 34; land tenure system of, 31–32; nationalist movement among, 34; parallels with nineteenth-century American Indians, 30–31; ties to Communist guerrillas, 32, 34–35

Montgomery, John D., 44–45, 49, 52

Morrill Land-Grant College Act, the, 6

Morris, Delyte W., 132

Morse, Wayne, 125, 129

Muelder, Milton E., 82

Muir, James I., 79

Musolf, Lloyd D., 54, 76, 104–5, 106, 118

nation building: university involvement in, xii, 4, 7, 141; development of, xii, 3, 141; importance of public administration in, 42; reasons for failure of, xiv–xv, 3–4, 41, 84, 141–43

National Catholic Welfare Conference, the (NCWC), 26

National Identity Card (NIC) program, 70, 72–73

National Institute of Administration, the (NIA): conflicts with MSUG staff, 51, 52, 56–57; construction of new campus and library, 46–47; curriculum of, 48, 49–50; entrance requirements of, 42; establishment of, 42; faculty of, 48, 50–51, 56; faculty publications, 45–46; graduate employment statistics, 56; in-service training program, 52, 53, 54–55; lack of Vietnamese resources at, 44–46; library at, 43–44; night school at, 53; and the participant program, 48–49, 52, 91, 100–8; pedagogical differences with the Michigan State University Group, 43, 44, 48, 51, 56–57

National Police Academy, the, 68–69

National School of Administration, the, 42

Nghiem Dang, 45, 49, 101, 102, 104

Ngo Dinh Diem: anticommunist stance of, 8, 9, 10; appointment as prime minister, 10; assassination of, 115, 123; bias toward Catholic population, 22, 27–28; and the Binh Xuyen, 12, 14, 15, 64; Buddhist political threat to, 29–30; Catholic political support for, 22, 28; and the civil guard, 78, 79, 121; concentration of power in family of, xiii, 122; conflicts with the Michigan State University Group, 31, 63–64, 79, 80, 119, 121; correspondence with Wesley Fishel, 9, 118; coup attempt on, 115, 116–17; educational background of, 9; and the French, 9; friendship with Wesley Fishel, xii, 8, 9, 10–11, 141; and the in-service training program, 53, 54; lack of Vietnamese support for, 29–30, 115, 142; as Michigan State University Southeast Asian consultant, 10; and the Montagnards, 30, 33, 34; and National Institute of Administration, 42, 44, 47, 48, 50, 53, 56; not constrained by Geneva Accords, 21; obsession with security, 44, 47, 64; as obstacle to nation building, 141–42; and the participant program, 52; and the Presidential Lectures, 54; recruitment by Vietminh, 9; and refugee resettlement, 22; repressive tactics of, 66, 68; and termination of Michigan State University Group contract, xiii, 47, 55–56, 80, 82, 115, 120, 121; United States press coverage of, 118, 120–21; and Vietnamese fingerprint operations, 71; visit to Michigan State University, xi–xii, xiii, 1

Ngo Dinh Khoi, murder of, 9
Ngo Dinh Nhu, 116, 122
Ngo Dinh Thuc, 27
Nguyen Dinh Thuan, 77, 104
Nguyen Duy Xuan, 46, 51, 52, 103–4, 106, 107
Nguyen Huu Bang, 96
Nguyen Ngoc Tho, 127
Nguyen Quoc Lan, 92
Nguyen Thuan, 98
Nguyen Van Dai, 96
Nguyen Van Hay, 99, 100
Nguyen Van Huong, 99
Nicol, Joseph, 73–74
Nolting, Frederick, 47, 127

Office of Strategic Services, the (OSS), 67

Pacific Affairs, 119–20
Paper, the, 131
Parisian fingerprint system, 70
participant program, the: difficulties with, 91, 93–94, 95, 96–97, 98–99, 104–5, 106, 108; doctoral project within, 101–7; fieldwork within, 94, 95, 96; first group to Michigan State, 92–93, 94; high-level observation tours, 99–100; host countries of, 91, 92; in the Philippines, 92; purposes of, 91, 108; selection of candidates for, 98, 99; staff increases in, 96–97
"Passage to Freedom," 21
Pentagon Papers, the, 133
Pham Xuan Chieu, 71
Pottecher fingerprint system, 70
Potter, Charles E., 93
Presidential Lectures, the, 54
Progress, 54

Quang Duc, 123

Radford, Arthur, 15
Ramparts, xiii, 81, 115, 126
refugees: Buddhist, 21, 28, 29–30; Catholic, 21, 22, 27–28, 29; communities of, 26; numbers to North Vietnam, 21; numbers to South Vietnam, 15, 21; relocation of, 21, 26; resettlement of, 21, 22–23, 24–26
Rogers, Richard, 64
Roosevelt, Franklin D., 2
Rostow, Walt Whitman, 3
Rundlett Affair, the, 75
Rundlett, Lyman M., 74–75, 76
Ryan, Jack, 64, 69–70, 73, 78, 80, 83
Ryukyu Islands, U.S. technical assistance to, 7–8

Scheer, Robert, 83, 124, 128
Scigliano, Robert, 119, 120
Shaw, Robert Sydney, 5
Shaw, Sarah, 5
Sheinbaum, Stanley K.: and the antiwar movement, 124, 125; and John Hannah, 6; and the participant program, 93–94, 97, 105, 108; political career of, 125–26, 133; and Ramparts exposé, 123, 125, 128, 129
Shelby Gilbert, 64, 100
Shields, Paul, 65
Simek, Emil, 76
Sloane, Charles, 64
Smith, Chitra, 131
Smuckler, Ralph: and the civil guard, 78; and Hotel Majestic anticommunist riot, 15; and Michigan State University Group - Central Intelligence Agency connection, 66, 82–83; and MSUG Field Administration Division, 23; and

National Institute of Administration 43, 49; and the participant program, 103, 104; and propriety of university involvement in foreign affairs, 118; and termination of Michigan State University Group police responsibilities, 81

Snyder, Wayne W., 23–24

Strecher, Victor, 97, 98, 117

Students for a Democratic Society, the (SDS), 131

Stump, Felix B., 79

sureté, the. *See* Vietnamese Bureau of Investigation

Taggart, Glen, 81

Tang Thi Ty, 43, 92

Taylor, Milton C., 120, 122, 127, 128, 133

Technical Cooperation Administration, the (TCA), 7

Ton-That-Thien, 92–93

traffic control project, Saigon, 77–78

Trager, Frank, 131

Tran Ngoc Phat, 105–7

Tran Phuoc Thanh, 93

Tran Thi Kim Sa, 43

Tran Van Chuong, 93

Tran-Van-Kien, 49

Truman Doctrine, the, 2

Truman, Harry S., 2

Truong Ngoc Giau, 49, 92

Turkey, U.S. technical assistance to, 7

Turner, Ralph: and Camp des Mares crime laboratory, 73, 74; and the civil guard, 80; and coup attempt on Ngo Dinh Diem, 117; and the National Identity Card program, 72; and police communications project, 75, 76; and Vietnamese fingerprint operations, 71, 72; and Vietnamese use of repressive police tactics, 68

Ugly American, The, 128

United States Operations Mission, the (USOM): and building of new NIA facility, 46–47; conflicts with the Michigan State University Group, 63–64, 75, 76–77; and the participant program, 52, 91, 94–95, 97, 101; public safety department of, 73, 74, 76–77, 80; and refugee resettlement, 23,25

University of Ryukyus, the, 7–8

Vietminh, the, 115

Vietnam Lobby, the, xii, 10, 27

Vietnam Perspectives, 130, 131

Vietnam project, the. *See* Michigan State University Group, the (MSUG)

Vietnamese Bureau of Investigation, the (VBI): personal relations with Michigan State University Group, 69–70; as political control agents, 65–66; reorganization of, 66–68, 69–74; repressive methods of, 66, 84; responsibilities of, 65

Vu Quoc Thong, 45, 47–48, 102

Waltman, Howard L., 97, 98, 100, 105, 108

Walton, Frank, 76, 80

Warner, Betty, 125

Weidner, Edward, 11–12, 13

Weinberg, Sidney, 130

Weisinger, Herbert, xiii

Weisl, Edwin, Sr., 130

Wickert, Frederic R., 15–16, 23, 28, 31–32, 50, 68–69, 128

Williams, G. Mennen, xi

Williams, Royce, 64, 74, 128

Williams, Samuel, 78–79

Wilson, Charles E., 141